DIFFERENT STROKES

DIFFERENT
STROKES

Serena, Venus,
and the Unfinished
Black Tennis Revolution

CECIL HARRIS

University of Nebraska Press | Lincoln

Library of Congress Cataloging-in-
Publication Data
Names: Harris, Cecil, 1960– author.
Title: Different strokes: Serena, Venus, and
the unfinished Black tennis revolution /
Cecil Harris.
Description: Lincoln: University of Nebraska
Press, 2020. | Includes bibliographical refer-
ences and index.
Identifiers: LCCN 2019032959
ISBN 9781496214652 (hardback)
ISBN 9781496221476 (epub)
ISBN 9781496221483 (mobi)
ISBN 9781496221490 (pdf)
Subjects: LCSH: African American tennis
players—Biography. | African American
women tennis players—Biography. | Tennis—
Social aspects—United States. | Tennis—
United States—History.
Classification: LCC GV994.A1 H365 2020 |
DDC 796.342092/2 [B]—dc23
LC record available at https://lccn.loc.gov
/2019032959

Set in Lyon Text by Laura Ebbeka.
Designed by L. Auten.

CONTENTS

DIFFERENT
STROKES

Introduction

I wouldn't be playing tennis for a living if it
wasn't for Venus and Serena.

SACHIA VICKERY

On August 31, 2018, a humid Friday evening in New York City, more
than twenty-three thousand people filled Arthur Ashe Stadium—the
world's largest tennis venue—to watch a third-round match at the
United States Open.

The match pitted two sisters who have carried the banner for
American tennis over the past three decades. That Venus Williams,
a two-time U.S. Open champion, and her younger sister, Serena, a
six-time U.S. Open champion, are black women in a sport that was
closed to blacks at the highest level for generations has made their
tennis achievements that much more remarkable.

Consider this: No American man has won a major tennis title since
Andy Roddick won the U.S. Open in 2003. But Venus and Serena have
combined to win thirty major titles in singles in their careers—twenty-
three for Serena, seven for Venus—and fourteen more as a doubles
team.

The sisters' meeting at the 2018 U.S. Open would be their thirtieth
as professionals. It is a matchup that Serena has dominated since

2002, the year she supplanted Venus as the world's No. 1 player. In the twenty-nine previous "sister acts," Serena had won seventeen, Venus twelve. The vast majority of their matchups had occurred in finals, including each of tennis's four Grand Slam tournaments—the Australian Open, held each January; the French Open, which runs from late May to early June; Wimbledon, which is contested in July; and the U.S. Open, which runs from late August until early September.

It is never just another match when Venus and Serena face each other because the Williams sisters have done more than anyone else to revolutionize their sport. They made their major tennis debuts in the 1990s and brought a previously unseen level of power, speed, and athleticism to the sport while essentially telling their opponents to adapt or get out of the way. Merely by their appearance on court, the brown-skinned sisters have shown other young people of color that tennis could also belong to them.

"When I saw Venus and Serena playing tennis as black girls, with those braids in their hair and those beads in their braids, it made me want to play too, because they looked just like me," said Sachia Vickery, a player from Hollywood, Florida, who debuted as a pro in 2009 and who ended 2018 with $965,838 in career prize money. "I wouldn't be playing tennis for a living if it wasn't for Venus and Serena, and I think a lot of other players would say the same thing."

When Venus made her U.S. Open debut as a seventeen-year-old in 1997, she advanced all the way to the final, having survived a racially charged semifinal match against a Romanian player named Irina Spirlea. In the title match played the very next day, an emotionally spent Venus lost in straight sets to Martina Hingis of Switzerland, then the world's No. 1 player.

Two years later Serena, in her second U.S. Open, won six matches to reach the final against Hingis, still the world's No. 1 player. Serena, only seventeen, got revenge for the family in a straight-set victory while also serving notice that the winds of change had come to tennis. The Williams sisters' era had begun, and it is still not over.

In every major tournament, thirty-two women and thirty-two men are seeded players. Those players get a more favorable draw in the early rounds based on the success they have had in previous tournaments. Venus and Serena were both seeded at the 2018 U.S. Open, albeit far lower than usual. Venus was seeded sixteenth, Serena seventeenth. For players who had been ranked No. 1 in the world, that's quite a drop.

The U.S. Open seeded Venus sixteenth because she had not won a title in 2018 after reaching the final in three of the five biggest tournaments in women's tennis the year before—the Australian Open, where she lost to Serena; Wimbledon, where she fell to Garbiñe Muguruza of Spain; and the Women's Tennis Association (WTA) Finals in Singapore, where she lost to Caroline Wozniacki of Denmark.

Serena was seeded seventeenth because, until the end of the 2018 season, the WTA did not know what to do with a player who missed tournaments because of pregnancy and childbirth. When a player does not compete for an extended period, her ranking plummets. It does not matter if the player missed time because of an injury, a drug suspension, or childbirth. Hence, Serena's extraordinary accomplishment of winning the 2017 Australian Open while pregnant ended up costing her a ton of rankings points (because she was unable to defend her Australian title in 2018). She gave birth to a daughter, Alexis Olympia, on September 1, 2017, while the U.S. Open took place, and she did not return to tournament play until March 2018.

After the 2018 season, the WTA revised its rules to protect the rankings of new mothers who return to the pro tour. The WTA now guarantees that returning players won't have to face seeded opponents in the early rounds of tournaments, which used to lead to early-round defeats and a tougher road for returning players trying to recover their previously high rankings. Before the rule change, players who had been in the world top ten, including Serena Williams and Victoria Azarenka of Belarus, saw their rankings fall out of the top two hundred.

Serena's lengthy absence made her return to the pro tour the biggest story in tennis in 2018. Fans wondered, "How will she look?" "How will she perform?" "Will she still possess the same competitive fire that made her a champion?"

As the most celebrated black tennis player ever, Serena had a chance to make history at the 2018 U.S. Open: another major title would give her twenty-four, tying the all-time record set by Australia's Margaret Court, a star in the 1960s and 1970s.

Although Serena and Court played in different eras, Serena is widely considered the better player. Eleven of Court's titles came at the Australian Open, including seven in a row from 1960 to 1966. Many tennis stars did not make the long round trip to Australia when it was summer Down Under and winter in North America and Europe, so Court often played against less formidable competition. Serena has played her entire career during the "Open Era," which began in 1968 and made tennis a truly professional sport with total prize money and winner's shares for the players instead of under-the-table payments only for certain stars. Court won thirteen of her twenty-four major titles before the Open Era.

When Serena captured the 2017 Australian Open for her twenty-third major title, she passed Germany's Steffi Graf for the most major championships in the Open Era. Serena's three decades of greatness have made her a fan favorite, particularly at the U.S. Open, where the predominantly white crowds used to respond with a certain indifference during matches involving her or Venus. It is not that the Williams sisters have changed over the years, but rather the way that tennis fans perceive them has changed. Venus and Serena are world champions, made in America, and America's tennis fortunes since the 1990s would have been virtually nonexistent without them.

The Williams sisters' legacy includes other black female players whom they have inspired to become champions, including Sloane Stephens, the 2017 U.S. Open titleholder, who was once told by a tennis academy director in Florida that she lacked the skills to become successful—in major college tennis. The legacy also includes Naomi Osaka, an effervescent player of Haitian and Japanese descent who has patterned her power-hitting game after Serena's and is now a major champion herself.

In perhaps the clearest sign of the improved status and greater cultural impact of blacks in tennis, Serena appeared, naked and pregnant, on the cover of the August 2017 issue of *Vanity Fair*. Yes, a magazine hardly noted for putting brown-skinned people on its cover honored the world's greatest female tennis player. Photographed by the famed Annie Leibovitz and interviewed by acclaimed author Buzz Bissinger, Serena was referred to on the cover by her first name only.

Serena. Beyoncé. Madonna. No last name necessary.

Serena, the first athlete to make *Forbes* magazine's list of the richest self-made women, ended 2018 with $88.2 million in career prize money. Her net worth as of June 2019 stood at $225 million. She has earned more than $100 million through endorsements for such companies as Nike, Gatorade, Wilson Sporting Goods, JP Morgan Chase, Audemars Piguet watches, Beats by Dre electronics, AccorHotels, the Lincoln Motor Company, Tempur-Pedic mattresses, Intel technology company, Wheaties cereal, and Berlei sports bras. She had invested in more than thirty start-up businesses before the April 2019 launch of Serena Ventures, which focuses on companies founded by women and nonwhites. Why? That's where the need is greatest. In 2018, for example, just 2.3 percent of total venture capital invested in the United States went to start-ups founded by women, according to *Forbes*.

Venus, a tennis icon herself with seven major singles titles, ended 2018 with career tennis earnings of $40.9 million, second all-time among female tennis players behind Serena. Venus is also making her mark in the business world. Her clothing line, EleVen, expanded in June 2019 from tennis wear to include clothes for women who play golf. "I knew EleVen needed to speak to female golfers," said Venus, whose items are sold on NBC Universal's Shop with Golf website. "Our line has always been about empowering women to be their best selves and this applies whether you're on the court or on the course."

Venus, whose net worth is $95 million, receives endorsement income from Nike, Ralph Lauren, Electronic Arts, Wilson Sporting Goods, and Systane Eye Drops, a product Venus needs to cope with Sjögren's syndrome, a debilitating autoimmune disease with which she was diagnosed in 2011. Prior to the diagnosis, Venus went through several years of losing to players who were not on her skill level, as well as bouts of fatigue and joint pain. "If you have cold symptoms, but you don't have a cold, then see your doctor," Venus has said, because it could be a tell-tale sign of Sjögren's syndrome. There is no cure for the disease, and it can take as long as six years to diagnose. However, through medication and a mostly vegan diet, Venus has shown that a world-class athlete can still compete at a high level with Sjögren's syndrome—although Venus is not as dominant a player as she used to be. She has not won a major championship since Wimbledon 2008. But the biggest reason for Venus's inability to dominate women's tennis has been the dominance of her younger sister.

There is no more recognizable female athlete in the world than Serena; few male athletes are more recognizable. Serena, thirty-eight, and Venus, thirty-nine, are athletic superstars as well as cultural icons and fashion trendsetters. Because of them, young people who otherwise would not have given tennis a serious look are picking up rackets and diligently practicing their strokes.

Not only are Serena and Venus champions, but they also have staying power. It has been twenty-two years since the aforementioned Irina Spirlea deliberately bumped Venus in their U.S. Open semifinal match as the players walked toward their chairs during a changeover. Venus had neither said nor done anything to provoke the bump. But it happened anyway. Millions of television viewers saw Spirlea look toward her friends' box and laugh about the premeditated act. After losing the match, Spirlea ranted to the media about how unimpressed she was by a seventeen-year-old she referred to as "the fucking Venus Williams." That Spirlea has become a mere footnote in tennis history seems entirely appropriate.

It has been eighteen years since Serena was booed throughout a championship match against Belgium's Kim Clijsters in Indian Wells, California. This happened because at least one other player, along with some tennis fans and some journalists, became convinced without a shred of evidence that the outcome of a scheduled semifinal match between Venus and Serena would be determined by their father, Richard Williams. The conspiracy theorists believed that Richard had decided it was Serena's turn to win to improve her professional ranking. Following a loss to Venus in the quarterfinals, Russian tour pro Elena Dementieva was asked by a reporter to predict the outcome of the Venus-Serena semifinal. "I don't know what Richard thinks about it," she said. "I think he will decide who is going to win." Dementieva later insisted that she had been joking, but the die had been cast.

On the day of the title match between Serena and Clijsters, Venus and Richard Williams entered the stadium to take their seats—less than an hour's drive from their former home in the Compton section of Southern California—and they were roundly booed. Richard Williams wrote in his autobiography that someone in the crowd that day subjected him to racial slurs: "A white man in the front row yelled out, 'N——, if this was back in '65, I'd skin your black ass alive.' I looked him straight in the eye and said, 'Why don't you act like it's '65?' I actually made a move in his direction, but he scampered away when another man told him, 'Leave those n——s alone, and just boo the hell out of them.'"

Some in the tennis world consider Richard Williams's account apocryphal. Occasionally, he is given to exaggeration and hyperbole. But there is no question that the crowd booed Serena that day and cheered her errors. Nevertheless, Serena won the championship match. The pain of that experience lingered, however. Neither Serena nor Venus played again at Indian Wells until 2015. The sisters ended their boycott of the event after discussions with tournament officials.

Tennis has not always been welcoming to the only family in the sport's history to produce a pair of legends—two players who have achieved the world No. 1 ranking in singles, become indomitable as a doubles team, and each won Olympic gold medals in singles and doubles.

Serena has become the face and formidable clenched fist of women's tennis while setting a standard for competitiveness and on-court brilliance that will likely never be matched.

Venus was the first in the family to become world No. 1. She has yet to regain that title largely because Serena keeps getting in the way. In 2002 and 2003, Serena held all four major titles simultaneously—an achievement she dubbed "the Serena Slam"—and she defeated Venus in all four of the title matches.

Two generations of sports fans have grown up seeing the Williams sisters as the gold standard in American tennis. To be an avid fan of American tennis is to enter into a female-led relationship—more specifically, a relationship led by women of color. The meritocracy of a tennis court prevents those who are racially insensitive from questioning the talent, commitment, competitive drive, and intelligence of black athletes who rise above all to become the best at their craft.

The Williams sisters' longevity is the most underrated aspect of their success. As Serena and Venus remain among the elite, former rivals such as Hingis, Clijsters, Jennifer Capriati, Lindsay Davenport, Justine Henin, and Amelie Mauresmo have long since retired. Another factor in the sisters' success: they have always had a life outside of tennis. Venus has established careers in interior design and fashion design. Serena has made her mark in fashion design and acting. Both are involved in many philanthropic and humanitarian endeavors. Serena, for example, has supplied funds to help build schools for underserved youth in Kenya, Uganda, Senegal, Zimbabwe, and Jamaica. She has also made it clear to each country that she wants girls to receive a quality education rather than an indoctrination that imposes upon them a second-class status. The absence of tennis myopia has enabled both Serena and Venus to keep their athletic careers in proper perspective.

The success of the Williams sisters has brought bigger purses to tennis—including equal prize money for women at the Grand Slam events—and higher television ratings. The men's and women's champions at the 2018 U.S. Open each received a record payday of $3.8 million. The women's final, in which Serena played, was televised in the United States by ESPN and drew an audience that surpassed the viewership of the men's final by more than one million people.

According to Jerry Caraccioli at CBS, in 2001, the year CBS made the U.S. Open women's final a prime-time event, the title match between Venus and Serena outdrew a Saturday night college football game on ABC between nationally ranked schools Notre Dame and Nebraska, 6.8 to 4.8 in ratings points and 13 percent to 9 percent in ratings share.

The days of tennis as a country-club sport for the aristocracy have long passed. As have the days when blacks faced long odds just to be invited to play in the U.S. Nationals (the forerunner of the U.S. Open), Wimbledon, the French Nationals, or the Australian Nationals. Tennis fans today are quite familiar with seeing the Williams sisters and other players of color competing for major championships.

The list of black players making an impact in professional tennis today includes but is not limited to American women Stephens, Vickery, Madison Keys, Asia Muhammad, Taylor Townsend, and Victoria Duval, along with Naomi Osaka of Japan, Heather Watson of England, and Francoise Abanda of Canada, and American men Donald Young, Michael Mmoh, Chris Eubanks, Evan King, Nicholas Monroe, and Frances Tiafoe, along with Jo-Wilfried Tsonga of France, Gael Monfils of France, Darian King of Barbados, Dustin Brown of Germany, Felix Auger-Aliassime of Canada, and Jay Clarke of England. Also, the last two girls to enter the U.S. Open junior singles event ranked world No. 1—Whitney Osuigwe in 2017 and Coco Gauff in 2018—are African Americans inspired by the Williams sisters.

"I respect both of them a lot, for everything they've done in tennis and for tennis," said Osuigwe, the 2017 French Open junior champion who competed in the main draw at the 2018 U.S. Open and 2019 Australian Open as a sixteen-year-old professional. "Venus and Serena are definitely players I look up to." Osuigwe, a Bradenton, Florida, native, has a younger sister, Victoria, who aspires to play professionally. Both were taught by their Nigerian-born father, Desmond Osuigwe, who coaches at the IMG Academy.

Despite the worldwide impact of blacks in the sport, it is not as if the tennis revolution is over and blacks have won.

The next time you watch tennis, take a close look at the umpire, the person sitting in the high chair at courtside. Also, look at the tournament referee and the tournament director, the people who actually run the tournament. In those seats of power and influence, blacks are still woefully underrepresented. And look at those who coach the players and represent their financial interests. Few are black. And the media members covering the sport? Again, few are black.

The unparalleled athletic and financial success of the Williams sisters—particularly Serena, a multimillionaire athlete who married

Alexis Ohanian, the wealthy cofounder of the website Reddit—has overshadowed a slow road to progress for blacks on the business side of tennis. The sport is a $5.57-billion-a-year industry, according to the Tennis Industry Association.

Whites who dominate the business side of tennis likely would insist that the only color they see is green, as in the color of money. But should that response excuse Nike for giving blonde Russian Maria Sharapova an endorsement deal worth $10 million more than Serena's after Sharapova upset Serena in the 2004 Wimbledon final? Sharapova is still considered by marketers to be more bankable than Serena, even though Sharapova was suspended for eighteen months (bridging 2016 and 2017) for failing a drug test and Serena has defeated her every time they have met on a tennis court since 2004. Serena, who refers to herself sarcastically as "the most drug-tested tennis player in history," has never failed a drug test.

Althea Gibson would love to have had the problem of not receiving as much endorsement money as an inferior competitor. Gibson, the first black player (male or female) to win a major tennis title, excelled when tennis was an amateur sport. In her first Wimbledon title match in 1957, she defeated Darlene Hard, a part-time tennis player and full-time waitress. Gibson won the French Nationals in 1956 along with consecutive Wimbledon and U.S. Nationals singles titles in 1957 and 1958, and was ranked world No. 1. Yet, as a champion far ahead of her time, she barely made a dime.

Arthur Ashe, the black champion, social activist, and humanitarian after whom the U.S. Open's marquee stadium is named, fared better. His three major singles titles—1968 U.S. Open, 1970 Australian Open, and 1975 Wimbledon—occurred during the Open Era. However, his strong and resolute voice would be stilled in 1993 under tragic circumstances.

When the year 2018 ended, so did the tenure of Katrina Adams, the first African American to serve as president and chair of the United States Tennis Association, the sport's national governing body. A former tour pro and doubles champion, Adams served two terms. In her first term, she also held the title of chief executive officer, but, strangely, she was told by the USTA board of directors to relinquish that title in exchange for a second term as president and chair.

The American Tennis Association, the country's oldest black-led sports organization, celebrated its one-hundredth anniversary in 2017. Both Gibson and Ashe were nurtured and developed in the ATA. Black umpires, tournament directors, and tournament referees—all sorely underrepresented at pro events—could theoretically also be developed in the ATA. However, no such program is in place. Blacks in tennis have long viewed the USTA and its predecessor, the United States Lawn Tennis Association, as an impediment to their progress in the sport. Gifted black players who excelled before Gibson's emergence in 1950 were never given a chance to compete against the best white players in the U.S. Nationals.

Lawsuits that alleged discrimination based on race, gender, and age were filed against the USTA a decade ago by two black umpires. As a result the career of one of those umpires ended, and the other umpire's career has not fully recovered. However, in another result from the lawsuit, the New York State attorney general determined that the USTA needed to take steps to eradicate discrimination in its organization. The biggest step involved the hiring of an officer in charge of diversity and inclusion. But that officer, a black former umpire once called "one of the best in the business" by the USTA, eventually was forced out of both jobs. He then filed a lawsuit against the USTA for racial discrimination.

The USTA describes itself as "the recognized leader in promoting and developing the sport's growth on every level in the United States, from local communities to the highest level of the professional game." But when it comes to tangible signs of progress by American players on tennis courts in the first two decades of the twenty-first century, Serena and Venus are still Exhibits 1 and 1A—even though the sisters did not come up through the traditional tennis system. The Williams family largely shunned junior tennis and all the cronyism, favoritism, and stage-door parenting that comes with it. Each Williams sister turned professional at the age of fourteen, and each was homeschooled by her mother, Oracene Price, while building her credentials in the sport. Rather than follow the usual path created by the USTA, the Williams family charted its own, and the results have been phenomenal. It is why Serena and Venus, now well into their thirties, could turn a third-round match at the 2018 U.S. Open into a highly anticipated spectacle.

1 | Serena

After God, I owe everything to her.

SERENA WILLIAMS

A sound that Serena Williams had not always heard in New York City—thunderous applause—greeted her as she took the court at Arthur Ashe Stadium for a third-round match against her older sister, Venus, at the 2018 U.S. Open. Serena waved to the adoring crowd as she emerged from one end of the stadium and walked into a spotlight that followed her to a courtside chair. Hard-driving music blared on the public address system in a scene befitting the entrance of a boxing champion or the designated "good guy" in World Wrestling Entertainment.

On the night before the first birthday of her daughter, Alexis Olympia, Serena was back on stage for an eagerly awaited match. Someday, tennis will have to carry on without Serena, who entered the match one month shy of her thirty-seventh birthday. Already, she has far exceeded the career span of a typical player, and defeated death on at least two occasions. She has conquered every foe, friendly or otherwise, in her profession. But for now, neither Serena nor tennis is prepared to let go of the other.

Cheers and cries of support for Serena continued long after she had reached her chair and opened her bassinet-sized tennis bag to remove the plastic wrapping from a Wilson racket that would be her tool for battle against her sister. Here was Serena, a six-time U.S. Open champion, attempting to reach a second major final the year after a complicated childbirth. In *Being Serena*, a five-part series that appeared on HBO in May 2018, she chronicled that health scare, as well as her journey to athletic supremacy. For Serena, strength and resilience are not limited to a tennis court.

Venus also received a hearty ovation when the stentorian-voiced stadium announcer called her name, but not as hearty as Serena's. Fans yelled their support for Venus, the elder sister by fifteen months, but not as passionately as Serena's fans. The "sister act," as Venus-Serena matches have become known, sometimes leads to awkward decision-making. For whom should you root? And why?

In the early years of the sister act, the matches tended to lack drama because of the striking similarities in their playing styles. Both possess an abundance of power, speed, and athleticism. From their years of practicing together, on roughhewn public courts in Compton and beautifully maintained courts in Palm Beach, Florida, the sisters knew each other's games so well that there were no secrets. It seemed impossible for one sister to surprise the other with a kick serve, a chipped return, a forehand slice, a drop volley, a two-hander crosscourt, or any other weapon in the family arsenal. Other than their different examples of physical beauty—Venus has a lean, lithe, traditional model-type physique, and Serena has a fuller-figured, muscular, superheroine physique—there was little contrast between them. Even Serena's more expressive personality is muted when big sis is across the net. Each sister's clear disdain for having to defeat the other and the always-subdued celebration by the winner have made the Serena-Venus matches more historic than enthralling.

However, these two athletic and cultural icons have smashed stereotypes as well as opponents on their way to becoming global stars. Their exploits filled African Americans with pride and significantly expanded the ranks of black tennis fans worldwide. However, it took longer for the sisters to feel the embrace of many white tennis fans.

In the 2002 U.S. Open semifinals, for example, Venus was the No. 2 seed and the defending champion. Serena, the No. 1 seed, was the previous year's runner-up. Fans should have been thrilled to have two American players heavily favored to win their semifinal matches at America's Grand Slam event. Yet the crowd that day clearly rooted for Venus's opponent, No. 10 seed Amelie Mauresmo of France, and for Serena's American opponent, No. 4 seed Lindsay Davenport. In Venus's semifinal, she served for the match at 5-4 in the third set. When she lost the first three points to give Mauresmo triple break point, the crowd cheered wildly. Nevertheless, Venus showed her mental toughness and won the match, 6-3, 5-7, 6-4. In Serena's semifinal, her unforced errors and double faults were often cheered by a crowd that responded to Davenport's unforced errors with collective groans. Still, Serena drew upon her mental strength and prevailed, 6-3, 7-5. Afterward, Oracene Price, the mother of the Williams sisters, told the *New York Times* that she believed the crowd reaction had racial overtones.

"I've been thinking about it and I think that's it," she told *Times* columnist William C. Rhoden. "I guess women can't have power, no matter what race it is. That's a problem in America. It's ridiculous."

Had the traditional (that is, white) spectators that day been injected with truth serum, their response would likely have been, "We don't want to see Venus and Serena in another major final." Not only had the sisters faced each other in the 2001 U.S. Open final won by Venus, but they had also met in the 2002 French Open final and the 2002 Wimbledon final, both won by Serena. Perhaps the fans simply did not know for whom to root. But given the history of racial segregation in tennis and the unsubstantiated charges by some players and media members that the Williams sisters' father was acting as some sort of Svengali by deciding which daughter would win in their matchups, it is far more likely that traditional tennis fans were acutely aware that Venus Ebony Starr Williams and Serena Jemeka Williams were taking over women's tennis, and those fans simply were not ready for it.

Venus and Serena saw no reason to wait. They simply went ahead and rewrote the tennis record book while revolutionizing the women's game into something faster, quicker, more athletic, and harder-hitting than anything seen before. Eventually, enough of the traditional fans came around. They had no choice, really. The Williams sisters have accomplished so much for so long that they now command the sort of respect and reverence reserved for legends.

Serena, in particular, has reached previously unscaled heights in tennis. On two occasions, she has held all four major titles simultaneously. She first accomplished this rare feat when she won the French Open, Wimbledon, and U.S. Open in 2002 and the Australian Open in 2003. She did it again when she captured the U.S. Open in 2014 followed by the Australian Open, French Open, and Wimbledon in 2015. However, neither achievement was a Grand Slam. According to tennis tradition, a Grand Slam is achieved if a player wins all four major titles in the same calendar year.

Only five players in history have won the Grand Slam:

Don Budge, 1938
Maureen Connolly, 1953
Rod Laver, 1962 and 1969
Margaret Court, 1970
Steffi Graf, 1988

Serena had a golden opportunity to become the sixth member of that club in 2015. She needed the U.S. Open crown to become the first Grand Slam winner in twenty-seven years. When Serena, the No. 1 seed, defeated Venus, seeded No. 23, in a quarterfinal match, 6-2, 1-6, 6-3, most observers assumed that she had cleared her biggest hurdle. But nobody told Roberta Vinci of Italy, then thirty-two years old and ranked world No. 1 in doubles. The unseeded Vinci, embracing her underdog status, played the finest singles match of her life. Serena won the first set easily, but got more nervous as the match went on, while Vinci played free and easy throughout. The result was the biggest upset in tennis history: Serena lost the semifinal match, 2-6, 6-4, 6-4. "I don't want to talk about how disappointing this is for me," Serena told reporters afterward, the pain clearly etched on her face. If any-thing, the pressure of being on the precipice of tennis history while competing against an opponent who had absolutely nothing to lose proved too great. (Vinci came back down to earth in the U.S. Open final, losing in straight sets to her countrywoman Flavia Pennetta.)

Today, the Williams sisters are elder stateswomen in a young per-son's sport. While neither may win a Grand Slam, both have achieved tennis immortality. It is easier nowadays for fans to decide whom to root for in a Serena-versus-Venus matchup, and the reasons don't necessarily have to do with tennis. Fans who preferred Venus in their most recent U.S. Open matchup hoped that a victory would propel her to a first major title since Wimbledon 2008. In so many matches, including the 2017 Australian Open final, Serena has been the only player standing between Venus and a major championship. But on those occasions, Serena has proven more unscalable than Mount Everest.

Fans who chose Serena may have done so for the same reason boxing fans chose Muhammad Ali and basketball fans swooned over Michael Jordan's tongue-wagging genius on the court: they knew they were watching brilliance, the likes of which they may never see again. Other Serena devotees were simply thrilled to see her back on court after a complicated pregnancy and childbirth that included blood clotting in her lungs, a sometimes nonreceptive hospital staff, and a lengthy recovery. After that harrowing experience, Serena created the Twitter hashtag #ThisMama as a forum for her and other mothers to share experiences and vital information on issues of pregnancy, childbirth, child-rearing, and women's health. Serena is passionate about the need for the medical establishment to provide better care for expectant mothers. A quartet of 2020 Democratic presidential candidates—U.S. senators Kirsten Gillibrand of New York, Kamala Harris of California, Elizabeth Warren of Massachusetts, and Amy Klobuchar of Minnesota—has taken up the cause:

"We lose hundreds of women to pregnancy- and childbirth-related complications in the U.S. every year, more than in any other developed country in the world," Senator Gillibrand wrote in reference to the MOMS Act, which the senators hope will become law. "In this modern age of incredible medical advancements, mothers are dying from preventable and treatable complications like hemorrhage, preeclampsia, or sepsis. For each mother who dies, another seventy nearly do. And the terrible truth is that black mothers are three to four times more likely to die from pregnancy- and childbirth-related complications than white women."

The most gifted female tennis player in history nearly became one of those black women. Serena's willingness to use her celebrity status to bring media attention to issues of importance has endeared her to millions around the world. Not only did she survive a perilous pregnancy and childbirth in 2017, but she also survived a pulmonary embolism—blood clots in the heart—after a pair of foot operations in 2011. She has openly discussed both episodes to raise public awareness, which has increased the number of her supporters, whether they are passionate about tennis or not.

Venus has raised public consciousness about her battle with Sjögren's syndrome, a chronic autoimmune disease that went undiagnosed until 2011. More than four million people have the disease. Symptoms include dry eyes, dry mouth, joint pain, and fatigue. Those last two symptoms in particular can be anathema to a world-class athlete. The disease occurs when white blood cells attack moisture-producing glands, making it difficult for a person to perform any task. Even sitting for a prolonged period can be painful. For several years, Venus did not know why she would tire so much from match to match, or even from set to set. But after she began losing matches to players who should not have been beating her, she needed to find answers. Once she received the diagnosis, she altered her diet dramatically to help decrease inflammation in her body and counteract the energy-sapping symptoms of the disease.

"I became a raw vegan," she said. "I do a lot of juicing, a lot of wheatgrass shots." Yet old habits can die hard. Sometimes she will eat something that is neither raw nor vegan; hence, she refers to herself as a "chegan." Yet in 2017, Venus showed that her energy level was high enough to produce great tennis. She handled the rigors of the two-week Grand Slam events, reaching the finals of the Australian

Open and Wimbledon, as well as the semifinals of the U.S. Open. She ended 2017 with more prize money for the season than any other player on the Women's Tennis Association tour: $5,468,741. Although she is the clear underdog whenever she faces Serena now, she will likely remain the toughest opponent Serena has ever faced.

Those who are among the most rabid and knowledgeable tennis fans root for Serena because her A game is like no other in women's tennis history. Her serve has long been women's tennis's most dominant weapon, the one shot for which no opponent over three decades has found a consistently effective response. Since her ball toss is so consistent, opponents cannot read where she is going to hit the ball. What a luxury it has been for Serena over the years to use her serve to fight off break points or win games without extended rallies, thus giving her more energy to attack her opponent's serve. Why more coaches of female players do not emphasize the importance of the serve, using Serena's incomparable serve as an example, is a mystery. Serena's forehand is considered solid but not spectacular, and her two-fisted backhand tends to lead to most of her unforced errors. However, the sheer power of her groundstrokes and her ability to go from defense to offense in a single stroke are without peer. Furthermore, the speed and purposefulness with which she covers the court has raised her unique brand of tennis to an art.

Female champions of decades past such as Hall of Famers Gabriela Sabatini of Argentina and Monica Seles, an American immigrant born in Yugoslavia, brought loud sighs and grunts to the tennis court. But Serena has taken the sport's soundtrack a few octaves higher. Fans have had to get used to Serena's full-throated screams and self-encouraging shouts of "come on!" She doesn't just feed off a tennis crowd. The crowd also feeds off her. Often, her screams and shouts are accompanied by clenched fists—from the player and her supporters. Serena's on-court intensity and competitive fire are unmatched. As much as she loves to win, she hates to lose even more. There is nothing genteel about the sound of a Serena match, and her fans would not have it any other way. She not only appears proud of her work, but she also sounds proud. Her style of play may not be every tennis fan's four o'clock cup of tea.

Her occasional racket-smashing and verbal outbursts may be over the top for some, but Serena is undeniably and unabashedly human. To watch her perform in person is to also see clearly that her fans are as empathic and proud as the champion herself.

Serena transcended tennis long ago and entered the realm of the cultural icon. Therefore, it was not surprising to see her, accompanied by her husband, Alexis Ohanian, at the May 19, 2018, royal wedding of England's Prince Harry and America's Meghan Markle. Serena and Meghan, now Duchess of Sussex, have been friends for more than a decade, back to the days when Meghan opened suitcases on the television game show *Deal or No Deal*. It was also not surprising when Serena served as one of the hosts of the 2019 Metropolitan Museum Gala, the annual Super Bowl for fashionistas, in New York City. Or that she opened a pop-up shop to promote and sell her own line of women's fashions during the 2018 Art Basel showcase in Miami. Serena herself is known to pop up at any time on the Home Shopping Network to market her clothes for women of all sizes, because she personifies the truism that beauty comes in all shapes and sizes.

If any female athlete other than Serena were to appear in a Beyoncé video, people would do a double take. But when Serena appeared on screen alongside Beyoncé, the image just fit. Serena is part of that cultural galaxy. When a celebrity graces a magazine cover, it is expected—such images are the lifeblood of those publications. Still, a Serena magazine cover tends to stand out—whether she is seen naked and pregnant in *Vanity Fair*, or with a black-stockinged leg seductively dangling from a throne in *Sports Illustrated*, or as #ThisMama with then four-month-old Alexis Olympia in *Vogue*, or lauded as the Woman of the Year in *Gentlemen's Quarterly*, or baring her enviably solid abdominal muscles in *Time*. The *Time* cover included a quote that may have aptly summarized who she is: "Nothing about me right now is perfect, but I'm perfectly Serena."

Serena's third-round match at the 2018 U.S. Open was her third in prime time during the tournament's opening week; she would play two more evening matches during the second week. That was by design.

The United States Tennis Association knows that a Serena match attracts not only the rabid fans but also the casual ones, along with enough of the merely curious to make it an event.

For Serena, a seventh title at the U.S. Open would break the all-time record she shares with Hall of Famer Chris Evert. Another distinction Serena hoped to achieve at the Open dealt with fashion: she could become the first player in tennis history to win a major title in a tutu. Serena collaborated with fashion designer Virgil Abloh—the first-ever black menswear designer at Louis Vuitton—to create ballet-inspired, Nike-branded tennis outfits to wear at the Open. Called "The Queen Collection," the wardrobe featured tutu-like skirts made of tulle and asymmetrical silhouettes inspired by Serena's love of dance. The outfits came in several colors, and Serena chose to wear basic black for her match against Venus.

Although Serena had decided on the ballet-inspired attire weeks ahead of the U.S. Open, her decidedly feminine choice of a tutu served as a backhanded smash to Bernard Giudicelli, the head of the French tennis federation, who announced the week before the U.S. Open a new dress code for his 2019 French Open, which began in late May. The new dress code would ban certain outfits, including Serena's fashion choice for the 2018 French Open, a skintight black catsuit inspired, she said, by *Black Panther*, a film that won three Academy Awards in 2019. Serena, who reached the fourth round in Paris before withdrawing with an abdominal injury, said she felt like "a superhero" while wearing the catsuit on the red clay courts. Unfortunately, Giudicelli, unwittingly cast himself as Lex Luthor by declaring the outfit too risqué. "It will no longer be accepted," he told *Tennis* magazine. "One must respect the game. I think sometimes we've gone too far."

Giudicelli's comments suggest that he found Serena's catsuit disrespectful. He has yet to explain why. Was the catsuit "disrespectful" because a strong woman chose it? If anything, Serena should be credited for looking beyond traditional tennis dresses, often created by men, and asserting the right to express her personality through her wardrobe in a way that was not at all salacious.

Besides, it was strange for Giudicelli to accuse anyone of disrespecting tennis. In September 2017, he was convicted of defamation for falsely accusing former French player Gilles Moretton of being involved in a French Open ticket-selling scandal. Giudicelli was ordered to pay a fine of 10,000 euros ($11,600) to Moretton, plus 5,000 euros ($5,800) in damages, and 2,500 euros ($2,900) to Moretton's attorney.

Serena proved long ago to be more fashion-forward than her sport. You never know what she's going to wear from one year to the next, or from one tournament to the next, and that is part of her appeal. Pictures of Serena in 2002, when she held all four major titles at once, show her as a blonde. That was followed by a return to her black-hair roots and the unveiling of her on-court tennis "boots," which were actually black ankle coverings that she removed before the match. At the 2006 U.S. Open, she decided that purple would be her primary color in Asian-accented dresses. At the 2015 U.S. Open, the blonde hair was back and blown out along with an assortment of curve-hugging dresses.

While talking with reporters in New York City about the French Open's new dress code, Serena took the high road and attempted to skirt the controversy. She had spoken with Giudicelli by phone, she said, and indicated that there may be room for negotiation. "He's been really amazing, so easy to talk to," she said. "I'm sure we would come to an understanding and everything will be okay."

The WTA never had a problem with Serena's catsuit. After the 2018 season, the women's tour officially approved the outfit as suitable for tennis. However, the WTA's decision does not pertain to the four Grand Slam events, which can establish their own dress code. Given Serena's penchant for making a fashion statement once and then moving on to the next expression, she probably would not wear the catsuit again in Paris anyway.

Still, many took to social media to denounce the French federation's ruling as sexist. Among the famous names asserting that position were *Harry Potter* author J. K. Rowling, actress-director Elizabeth Banks, and television producer Shonda Rhimes. Others viewed the ruling as insensitive because Serena, who has a history of blood clots, had said publicly that the catsuit helped to improve her circulation during matches. The French Open was the first Grand Slam event she played in after her return to competitive tennis in March 2018. Asked at the U.S. Open why she no longer wore the catsuit, she said her health had improved since the spring and she no longer needed it. "I wear tights that keep everything going with my blood," she said, "to make sure I'm staying pretty healthy out there."

Every July at Wimbledon, players must wear white as the dominant color. But even a white catsuit would not pass muster at Wimbledon. In 1985 Anne White, a white player from West Virginia, wore a skin-tight outfit in her first-round match. Wimbledon promptly banned the catsuit after the match.

Since Giudicelli has declined requests to fully explain himself, he has not commented on whether race played any role in the decision. Perhaps an irrational need by some men to control what women wear was the guiding principle. "We still have some people like the president of my federation that live in another time and can still do these kinds of comments," said French tennis pro Alize Cornet, indirectly comparing Giudicelli to a caveman. "They are totally for me shocking and, I mean, I'm just saying what I think. He's the president of the French federation and he doesn't have to do that."

This was not the first time that French men in charge of a popular annual event have made a fashion-related decision that prompted charges of sexism. In 2015 the Cannes Film Festival declared that women attending red-carpet events must wear high heels instead of flats. The Tour de France cycling event also continues to display women in tight-fitting outfits on the podium alongside the male winner of that day's stage, with the women serving as nothing more than eye candy.

When it comes to fashion, each Williams sister takes the lead in designing what she wears on court. Venus debuted a new collection of her EleVen clothing line at the 2018 U.S. Open. Moving as far away from traditional tennis whites as her sister, Venus took the court in a neon-hued outfit featuring a printed skirt in pink and purple. "I wanted this collection to feel like something you've never seen before," Venus said, referring to the bold colors and graffiti-style design. Several women on the pro tour have worn Venus's EleVen outfits, including 2004 U.S. Open champion Svetlana Kuznetsova of Russia, whom Venus defeated in the first round. For her match against Serena, Venus wore a multicolored sleeveless dress with thin straps and deep pink wrapping just above the waist along with a visor of the same multicolored design as her dress. There were "V" logos on the dress and one "V" on the front of the visor. Each sister appeared to have her fashion game and tennis game up to par. In their only previous on-court meeting in 2018, Venus won in straight sets at Indian Wells. That was Serena's first tournament after a fourteen-month maternity leave. The rematch would be demonstrably different.

The latest meeting of the most successful siblings in sports history had fans yearning for something special. They got it from one side of the net. In a commanding performance, Serena routed Venus, 6-1, 6-2, and sent notice that her A game remains the most imposing sight in women's tennis.

"Absolutely, this was my best match since I came back," said Serena, who took an 18-12 lead in the sister act, including nine wins in the past eleven.

"She played so well, I barely got to touch any balls," Venus said. "After every shot I hit well, she hit a better shot."

Venus looked severely overmatched, which at times seemed to pain Serena.

"She's the only reason I'm still here," Serena said. "After God, I owe everything to her."

Once Serena survived a mild scare in the second game of the match, the night was hers. She called for a trainer during the first changeover because she rolled her right ankle while pursuing a shot in that second game. Immediately after the ankle was retaped, Serena broke serve for a 3-1 lead.

A forehand passing shot in the sixth game produced another service break for Serena, who then put an exclamation point on the first set with an ace.

With the stadium roof closed, Serena had optimal conditions to unleash her power game. She kept the pressure on with a third consecutive service break to start the second set. Since Venus rarely troubled Serena's serve on this night, the match essentially ended after Serena broke Venus at love for a 4–1 lead.

The official end came on a forehand winner into the open court after a punishing first serve. When Serena and Venus hugged at the net, the crowd rose to its feet seemingly in appreciation of what the sisters represent, athletically and culturally.

Here is a testament to their longevity in a physically demanding sport: Frances Tiafoe, a promising African-American on the men's tour, was born January 20, 1998—the day before Venus beat Serena in straight sets in their first-ever meeting as professionals, in the second round of the Australian Open.

"It almost doesn't matter who wins—just them being on the court together for the thirtieth time is unbelievable," Tiafoe said. "If I could be half the athlete they are and have half the career they've had, that would be insane."

Almost as insanely amazing as the story of two African-American sisters from humble beginnings who became global superstars while transforming a sport whose grandest tournaments were once closed to members of their race.

When Venus and Serena became dominant at the dawn of the twenty-first century, they sent an unmistakable message to their on-court rivals: get stronger and fitter, or step aside. Thanks to the Williams sisters, women's tennis is played at a higher level of athleticism than ever before.

While racking up major titles, Serena and Venus have inspired a wave of female players of color, including 2017 U.S. Open finalists Sloane Stephens and Madison Keys, and then a second wave led by two top-ranked juniors from Florida: Whitney Osuigwe and Coco Gauff.

As for why Venus, the No. 16 seed, and Serena, the No. 17 seed, met so early at the 2018 Open, the USTA seeded Serena higher than her No. 26 world ranking. She had been world No. 1 before her maternity leave. In the blind draw that determines who plays whom at the Open, the sisters ended up in the same quarter of the 128-player field.

That proved to be a most unfortunate draw for Venus who, for the first time since 2014, played in all four Grand Slam events without getting past the third round in any. On this particular night, she again came in second to a sibling who is the best her sport has ever seen.

2 | Venus

> If one woman could win that much money,
> I wanted two daughters to play that game.
>
> RICHARD WILLIAMS

Writers and photographers crammed into the U.S. Open's main interview room inside Arthur Ashe Stadium to hear what Serena and Venus had to say about Serena's 6–1, 6–2 romp—the most lopsided match the sisters had ever played against each other. Despite Venus's obvious disappointment, she surely would not duck the interview because she's too classy for such behavior, and because there would be a financial penalty for doing so. Skipping a postmatch interview at a major tournament could mean a deduction of $10,000 to $15,000 from their earnings at that event. So, even if a player would rather be anywhere else in the world, even in a dentist's chair, it is better to endure five to nine minutes of questions from the media than to sacrifice money.

As is customary in tennis, the losing player enters the interview room first. The interview is usually brief, closer to five minutes, because the pain from a defeat, particularly at a Grand Slam event, is sharp and tends to linger. The USTA supplies a moderator for the news conference so the athlete is not bombarded with shouted questions, as a politician might be at a public appearance. There is a certain decorum to the postmatch interview at a tennis tournament, as well as a tacit but undeniable pecking order among the questioners. Reporters from the larger media outlets—the *New York Times*, the *Washington Post*, the *Times of London*, and most television networks—are more likely to be called upon to ask questions. Given the brevity of the group interview, the questions should pertain to the match just played or the tournament. Sometimes, however, the questioning can veer into bizarre territory. For instance, a reporter asked Haitian-Japanese player Naomi Osaka, "What's your favorite hot beverage and favorite cold beverage?" Just knowing that Osaka's answer to both questions was green tea may well be worth the cost of this book.

Venus did not feel like saying much after being routed by her sister, but her professionalism shone through. She answered questions in a low tone, a voice of resignation. Never before in her twenty-five-year pro career had she won only three games in a marquee match.

QUESTION: Will you just completely put this match in the back of your mind?

VENUS: Yeah, I'm going to rest. I mean, she played so well. I never got to really even touch any balls. When your opponent plays like that, it's not really anything to be upset about. She just played much better than—the only thing I maybe could have done was put more first serves in. Even then, she returned the first serve really well. Any shot that I hit great, she hit a greater shot. Not a lot I can do.

QUESTION: John McEnroe said that what you and your sister have done is the best sports story in history. What is your sense of what kind of impact the two of you have had?

VENUS: That's obviously a great compliment. I don't know that—like I said, we don't sit around and reflect. That's not how you get out here and win these matches, by reflecting and looking back. You work hard, look forward. As soon as you beat one person, there's another one standing in front of you. At the moment, our main focus is winning these matches. Perhaps when all is said and done, there will be a time to reflect. We're in too deep right now.

The time has not come for Venus or Serena to reminisce about their numerous tennis achievements, not when there are so many challengers to face, so many goals to set and pursue. Venus, who ended 2017 ranked No. 5 in the world, made major changes to her camp after a disappointing 2018 season, which ended with her ranked No. 38. She fired coach David Witt, who had been part of her camp (first as a hitting partner, then as a coach) since 2007. Witt became the full-time coach after Richard Williams, who is seventy-six years old, opted to spend far less time on the road. Witt, who lives in Jacksonville, Florida, called the firing "a total surprise." He said he was preparing for Venus's first tournament of 2019 in Auckland, New Zealand, when she called to deliver the news. "When it happened, both of us were emotional about it," he said. "After, you sit there and go, 'Man, after eleven years, it's over after a two-minute phone call. Wow.' Part of you sits there and says that, and the other part says that it's a business decision, which I totally understand, and I respect her decision. I don't even need to know why." Venus also dismissed her hitting partner, Jermaine Jenkins of Atlanta—the brother of Serena's hitting partner, Jamere Jenkins. (In 2019 Jermaine Jenkins became the coach of Naomi Osaka.)

Serena, having beaten Venus so thoroughly in their third-round encounter, had little to celebrate. The postmatch hug at the net seemed to bring Serena the most relief of the evening. Although Serena and Venus have faced each other thirty times as professionals, the victor cannot truly enjoy defeating someone for whom she has such deep love and respect.

QUESTION: How much different is it playing against each other now versus when you were kids?

SERENA: It's totally different now. I feel like we want it so bad now. I mean, we wanted it really bad when we were younger, but we had a lot more years in our future. We definitely want to continue to play, but it's not like we're eighteen and nineteen anymore.

QUESTION: When you're dominating an opponent the way you did tonight, you look across the net, you see it's your sister, how do you realize I've got to get this done, out of the way, against somebody you care so much about?

SERENA: It's just about focusing on each point. It's not necessarily Venus, and it is my sibling, but it's one of the greatest players of all time. She's by far the greatest player I've ever played against.

Venus is also the richest player Serena has ever faced. In a quarter century on the professional tennis tour, Venus has accumulated $40.9 million in prize money, including her $156,000 share from the 2018 U.S. Open. Yes, Venus made $156,000 for losing in the third round. No wonder their father once had a crazy tennis dream.

On a Sunday afternoon in 1977, Richard Williams watched on television as Virginia Ruzici of Romania received an oversized check for $40,000 for winning the now-defunct Eckerd Open in Palm Harbor, Florida. The image compelled him to set an insanely ambitious goal: produce a pair of daughters who would change the tennis world. "I found myself fantasizing about my as-yet unborn daughters playing tennis," he wrote in his autobiography. "If one woman could win that much money, I wanted *two* daughters to play that game. Double the winnings!"

Venus entered the world on June 17, 1980. Serena arrived on September 26, 1981. Once the girls were old enough to run without falling, Richard Williams and his wife, Oracene Price, set in motion his plan to create two tennis champions. It is a blueprint that other parents of color have tried to follow for their offspring, including the parents of Mari and Naomi Osaka of Japan. Although Naomi Osaka has a U.S. Open title and an Australian Open title on her resume, no other offspring are likely to approach the level of success attained by Venus and Serena.

Richard Williams, a self-made businessman, dipped into funds from various companies he operated, including building maintenance, cement supply, and security, to buy tennis books and videos to teach himself and his wife what they needed to know to teach their daughters. Williams bought used tennis balls and used rackets of various sizes that the girls could use as they grew. He also took tennis lessons from a neighborhood player in Compton, a "Mr. Oliver" who insisted on being paid in whiskey. According to Williams, "Mr. Oliver" died before either Venus or Serena began to make indelible impressions on the tennis scene.

Both parents proved to be excellent teachers. Before long, the tennis establishment had become aware of the two fast, quick, smart, strong, athletic, hard-hitting, attractive, and polite brown-skinned sisters who played tennis with beads in their braided hair. Endorsement contracts with athletic sponsors Wilson, Nike, and Puma enabled the family to leave hardscrabble Compton for placid Palm Beach. The girls soon attended a tennis academy in Boca Raton, Florida, run by a highly regarded coach named Rick Macci.

"When Venus and Serena signed their first big sports contracts, deals worth upward of $50 million, I made them sit at the same table as the agents and the lawyers through every negotiation until they understood every clause in every contract," Williams wrote. "I could buy my daughters whatever they needed, so it wasn't hard to turn down all the initial sponsorship deals we were offered, or to tell the USTA we weren't going to play more than one or two of their tournaments a year. Or that staying in school was more important than the USTA's need for new stars."

Venus and Serena were homeschooled by their mother, a nurse by trade. Rather than lament missing out on high school memories, Venus and Serena said their lives were enhanced by learning at home and becoming a closer-knit family. (Oracene Price had three daughters, Yetunde, Isha, and Lyndrea, before marrying Richard Williams.) Whenever Venus or Serena needed someone with whom to study, play board games, watch television, go shopping, or practice tennis, the other sister was always there. Indeed, having a gifted sister as a hitting partner and friendly competitor undoubtedly accelerated both girls' learning and development. The sisters played few junior tennis tournaments, not only because they had each other, but also to shield them from the kind of racial animosity that would surface later in their professional careers.

Nerves had a hold on Venus when she made her pro debut on Halloween night in 1994 at the Bank of the West Classic at the Oakland Coliseum. The fourteen-year-old prodigy left her tennis dress draped over the television set in the hotel room. No matter. She defeated Shaun Stafford, the No. 58 player in the world. In her next match, she led by a set and a service break against the No. 1 seed and future Hall of Famer Arantxa Sánchez Vicario of Spain before losing in three sets. Those who had thought all the talk about Venus was mere hyperbole had to think again. Venus was the real deal. Fans clamored to see more. But rather than throw Venus to the tennis wolves, her parents patiently charted her path to stardom.

At six feet, one inch, Venus possessed enviable tennis gifts—a long and lithe body, a crackling serve, a potent return of serve, a swinging forehand volley that robbed an opponent of time and space during a rally, a punishing two-fisted backhand, deft volleys, a high tennis IQ, speed, quickness, court coverage, and the mental toughness to shake off an error and play the next point with laser-like concentration. Her father did not mind coming across as the P. T. Barnum of tennis, so he did not hesitate to tell reporters how successful his "ghetto Cinderella," as he called Venus, would become. The media soon learned that he was not carnival barking, he was prophesizing. Venus had the goods. In her U.S. Open debut in 1997, she showed resilience and determination to match her athleticism.

Venus's semifinal match against feisty Romanian Irina Spirlea, the No. 11 seed, featured "the Bump Heard 'Round the Tennis World." As the players walked to their respective chairs during a changeover, Spirlea walked directly into Venus in a clear attempt to intimidate. They collided as a capacity crowd of twenty-three thousand at the newly christened Arthur Ashe Stadium gasped. Neither player said a word to the other. Venus looked startled and continued on to her chair. But when Spirlea got to her chair, CBS television cameras caught her laughing and smiling at people in her friends' box at courtside. "A reporter informed me that while I was reading my notes, Irina was smirking and laughing and gesturing to her coach and friends in the stands," Venus would say later.

If Spirlea's body bump had been done to try to convince Venus that a seventeen-year-old black girl had no business in the U.S. Open semifinals, and no business in the white-dominated world of tennis, then she failed miserably. Venus, ranked No. 66 at the time, summoned enough physical and mental strength to fight off two match points and take down Spirlea, 7-6 (7-5), 4-6, 7-6 (9-7). The players' postmatch handshake at the net looked colder than a meat locker. But seconds later, Venus, the first African American female to qualify for a U.S. Open final since Althea Gibson won the 1958 U.S. Nationals, was all smiles on the stadium court. As for Spirlea, she tried to explain to reporters why she had walked into Venus despite eyeing her the whole time. "I'm not going to move," Spirlea said with defiance. "I mean, she's never trying to turn or whatever. She thinks she's the fucking Venus Williams." Richard Williams said afterward that Spirlea's racism led to the collision. He called the Romanian "an ugly white turkey." Venus took the high road in her postmatch comments, saying, "I thought we both weren't looking. No one said, 'Excuse me.'"

Having won a contentious semifinal on a Friday afternoon, Venus had precious little time to rest. Bowing to the preference of CBS, the U.S. Open's main television rightsholder in those days, the USTA had the women and men play their semifinal and final matches on consecutive days (Friday and Saturday for the women, Saturday and Sunday for the men). The other three Grand Slam events gave the finalists a day off before the championship match. But not the U.S. Open, at least not then. (Since ESPN became the main U.S. Open rightsholder in 2009, there has been a day off before every championship match.) In the 1997 final Venus took the court barely twenty-four hours after the biggest victory of her life, and she looked absolutely spent. World No. 1 Martina Hingis of Switzerland routed her, 6-1, 6-1. Yet Venus had shown her mettle throughout the U.S. Open fortnight and had given Serena a firsthand look at how a talented black teenager can navigate treacherous waters and find her way to shore—smiling all the way and accumulating previously unseen riches and gleaming hardware of gold and silver.

In 2018 Venus actually faced her biggest challenge off the court. After defeating Elise Mertens of Belgium in a first-round match at Wimbledon, she walked into an interview room much like the one at the U.S. Open and heard from reporters who were not so interested that day in the quality of her tennis. They asked about a remark from a police official in Venus's hometown of Palm Beach Gardens, Florida, who had accused her of "violating the right of way" of another driver in a crash on June 9, 2017, that resulted in the death of a passenger in the other vehicle.

Given that an investigation of the crash had not even occurred, the police statement seemed demonstrably unfair. It would also be proven completely false. The investigation cleared Venus, who had driven her Toyota Sequoia that day for approximately ten minutes, the time necessary to cover the distance between her home and Serena's. Yet the police official's unsubstantiated statement had cast Venus in the worst possible light on the first day of the biggest tournament in tennis. Media and fans watching Wimbledon could now quote an inaccurate public statement that Venus had caused the death of a seventy-eight-year-old man.

Anyone involved in an auto accident that results in death, regardless of who is at fault, would be shaken by the experience. It would be impossible to forget. Now imagine being a continent away and trying to concentrate on winning a tennis tournament while your good name is being dragged through the mud back home. For Venus, the emotional turmoil became too much. When a reporter asked her about the fatal crash and the police official's statement, Venus attempted to respond and began choking back tears. The Wimbledon moderator asked if Venus needed time to compose herself. She did not respond immediately. A few seconds later, she said through tears, "Maybe I should go." She left the room. Although she returned about five minutes later to take tennis questions, video of Venus leaving the interview room in tears is all that most people remember. A year after her joyful and surprising run to the Wimbledon final, Venus had become ensnared in a controversy that essentially doomed her chances of success at Wimbledon 2018. She lost to Kiki Bertens of the Netherlands 8–6 in the third set of their third-round match.

The other driver filed a wrongful death civil suit against Venus. Venus's legal team released a transcript of her deposition in the case. It revealed that Venus denied using her iPhone at the time of the crash. Attorneys for the other driver asked a judge to force Venus to relinquish her iPhone to prove that she had not been using it. But Venus's attorneys successfully argued that her phone and text records had already proven she had not been using the phone at the time and that the request was an invasion of her privacy and an attempt by the other side to gain "unlimited access to anything and everything on her phone to satisfy a wild goose chase."

According to the final police report, Venus entered the intersection of Northlake Boulevard and Ballenisles Drive on a green light, but the light turned red while Venus stopped to try to avoid hitting a Nissan Altima making a left turn in front of her. The other vehicle T-boned Venus's vehicle, and a passenger in the other vehicle died. "I did not see my light turn yellow or red in the intersection," Venus said in her deposition. Her legal team argued that the other driver operated "carelessly and recklessly" and failed to stop before entering the intersection.

Both sides reached an out-of-court settlement in November 2018, with Venus paying an unspecified amount to the other driver, according to the website TMZ. But the pain lingers. "I'm very sad about everything that's happened in this accident," Venus said.

Richard Williams raised more than a few eyebrows when he told reporters at the turn of the twenty-first century that Serena would become a superior player to then world No. 1 Venus. "Serena understands angles better," he said. "And she's meaner." He has been proven correct about his daughters' place in the tennis pantheon. Serena has won more than three times as many major titles as Venus: 23–7. Serena leads in head-to-head matchups 18–12, including an 11–5 edge at Grand Slam events. In all championship matches, Serena has the advantage, 9–3.

The athletes with which Serena is most closely associated nowadays are not other female tennis players. She associates with the icons. In an ESPN interview during Serena's 2018 U.S. Open quarterfinal match, Academy Award–winning filmmaker Spike Lee said from his courtside seat that watching Serena at work fills him with the same combination of wonderment and awe he got from watching Michael Jordan and Muhammad Ali in their prime years. The shoe fits. Serena shares the same rarefied air as Jordan, Ali, Jack Nicklaus, Tiger Woods, Wayne Gretzky, LeBron James, Pele—those who have acquired the acronym GOAT: Greatest of All Time.

As with any iconic athlete, Serena loves a challenge. Here is the challenge she faced in her quarterfinal match against Karolina Pliskova of the Czech Republic: a 2–4 deficit in the first set and the possibility of going down by a second service break against a player who had defeated her at the 2016 U.S. Open.

"I just thought that I wasn't playing my best tennis. I was thinking, you know, I can play better," Serena said. She responded with eight games of awesomeness—covering every inch of her court, pounding winners, slamming aces, applying relentless pressure, defying her thirty-six years, winning every single game.

After that eight-game run, she owned the first set and a commanding lead in the second in an eventual 6–4, 6–3 victory—her fourteenth consecutive triumph in the quarterfinals of a major tournament. The win was also her first against a top ten player since her return to competitive tennis in March.

Serena gave a raucous crowd at Ashe Stadium exactly what it came to see: an American idol living up to her reputation. She ended with more winners (thirty-five) than unforced errors (thirty), hit thirteen aces, and won 71 percent of her first-serve points.

Pliskova, the No. 8 seed, trailed 4–2 in the second set before earning four break points that would have put the set back on serve.

Another challenge for Serena. Another forceful response. She held serve thanks in large part to a brilliant running forehand passing shot down the line. "One thing I've really worked on was my moving because it was a little suspect right after my return [to tennis]," she said. "I know that I'm fast when I want to be. I can get any ball that I want to."

Only the legends can talk that way without hesitation, for they know they have the athletic gifts to back it up. Now only a match against a crafty player from Latvia stood between Serena and another U.S. Open final.

Even with the Ashe Stadium roof closed to keep spectators dry on the evening of September 7, Serena reigned. In her semifinal, she transformed herself into a locomotive, winning twelve of the final thirteen games, and blowing past Anastasija Sevastova of Latvia, 6–3, 6–0.

"This is just the beginning of my return," Serena said. "I'm still on the way up. You don't reach your best a couple months in." After she smacked a forehand winner on match point, a deliriously partisan crowd rose to salute a tennis royal who would pursue two more pieces of history in the championship match:

One, a victory would be her twenty-fourth title at a Grand Slam event, tying Margaret Court's all-time record.

Two, a victory would also bring her a seventh U.S. Open crown—nineteen years after her first—breaking the record she shares with Chris Evert.

"I'm just going to keep trying," said Serena, who lost to Angelique Kerber in the 2018 Wimbledon final. "If it doesn't happen, I'll keep trying for the next one."

Sevastova, the No. 19 seed, came into the match with momentum, having upset defending champion Sloane Stephens in the quarterfinals. Sevastova plays a mature game with an impressive array of slices and spins that had confounded opponents at the Open.

Serena eventually made her look ordinary.

Surprisingly, Serena struggled to control her forehand and lost the first two games. The sluggish start was reminiscent of her quarterfinal match against Pliskova when Serena dropped four of the first six games. She then found a higher gear and left Pliskova in the dust.

This time, Serena strung together five consecutive games to take a 5–2 lead for command of the first set and, eventually, the match.

Serena served the Latvian a bagel in a second set that lasted twenty-seven minutes. Throughout the match, Serena relied on the most underrated aspect of her tennis supremacy—intelligence—to overwhelm a difficult opponent.

Sevastova favors the slice, which keeps the ball low and forces an opponent to hit up to clear the net. Had Serena tried to play from the baseline consistently, Sevastova could have used the strategic advantage to pull off an upset. Instead, Serena came forward early and often, turning the tables on Sevastova, taking away her opponent's time and space and winning twenty-four of twenty-eight points at the net.

"I know how to play at the net," Serena said. "I have great volleys, or else I wouldn't have won fourteen Grand Slam doubles titles. I know how to do it. It's just the fact of turning it on and actually doing it."

Coming into the match, Sevastova had broken her opponent's serve twenty-eight times, more than any other woman at the 2018 Open. But Serena ruled the court on this night, earning five service breaks to one for Sevastova.

With rain forecast for Saturday, the roof at Ashe would likely be closed again and a capacity crowd would gather to roar for Serena in a championship match that could look more like a coronation.

Both the men's and women's champions of the 2018 U.S. Open received a record-high $3.8 million. Pay equity did not always exist during tennis's Open Era. Today, it is the norm at every Grand Slam event, but it took nearly forty years of female activism to bring equal pay to Wimbledon. Many players, past and present, can take a well-deserved bow for contributing to that cause, among them Hall of Famer Billie Jean King. (The official name of the U.S. Open's home is the USTA Billie Jean King National Tennis Center.) However, the woman most responsible for upending patriarchy a decade ago and bringing equal pay to Wimbledon was Venus.

The tennis record book may show that Venus has conquered Wimbledon five times—in 2000, 2001, 2005, 2007, and 2008. However, her most impactful victory at the All England Lawn Tennis and Croquet Club, where Wimbledon is staged each July, occurred in 2007, the culmination of a three-year battle to achieve the sensible goal of having female professionals be paid the same as male professionals.

Wimbledon had been the last holdout among the four majors. The U.S. Open became the first to offer equal prize money in 1973, when the male and female champions each received $25,000 from a total prize purse of $227,200. Eventually, the Australian Open and the French Open followed suit. But Wimbledon resisted—because it could. Each Grand Slam event can set its own rules. That's why players must wear white at Wimbledon. The All England Club says so. No other major tournament has a whites-only dress code. Wimbledon, the oldest major with the grandest tradition and the most persnickety customs, began in 1877—for men. Women were not allowed to play there until 1884. Hence, it was disturbing to women players in 2005, but not shocking, that a full thirty-two years after the U.S. Open offered pay equity, Wimbledon still had not.

The argument from the All England Club went like this: The men play best-of-five-set matches at the Grand Slam events while the women play best-of-three, so the men have to work longer for the money. Thus, men should be paid more. But women's tennis, certainly by 2005, had proven itself to be as big a draw as the men's game. Indeed, the emergence of Venus and Serena as preeminent champions made the sisters as much of a drawing card as any of the leading men.

Yet Wimbledon refused to budge, and the members of the WTA seethed. Their collective anger then morphed into a plan. Each year, the Grand Slam committee, which consists of representatives from each of the four majors, along with the heads of the WTA (women's) and ATP (men's) tours, meets at Wimbledon on the second Friday of the event, the day before the women's final. Prior to the committee meeting, Steve Simon, the CEO of the WTA, convened a gathering of the ten highest-ranked female players, including Venus and Serena. Simon had sought volunteers to attend the committee meeting with him. No player had ever attended before. Venus and Serena were among those who said yes. Then the tournament began and, as is always the case, unexpected things happened. Serena lost to fellow American Jill Craybas in a third-round shocker. Other players, focusing more on their singles and doubles matches, seemed to forget all about the Grand Slam committee meeting. But not Venus. Not even after her emotional victory against defending champion Maria Sharapova in the semifinals—the day before the meeting. The WTA hierarchy would have understood if Venus had asked out of the meeting to rest for the championship match against Californian Lindsay Davenport, with whom she had an intense tennis rivalry. "There was a lot on my mind, but I wanted to be there," Venus said. She attended the meeting.

In a room full of men with decision-making power in tennis, Venus was not sure of what she would say. She decided to follow her head and her heart. "I had no script," she said. "I told everyone in the room, 'Close your eyes. No peeking. Now, I would like you to imagine being a young girl growing up with dreams and aspirations—dreams of being an athlete, a scientist, an artist, president of the United States. And then, one day, somebody tells you that you can't be that, you can't reach the same level as a boy who has worked as hard as you, done as well as you. You're told that there's a limit. There's a limit to what you can achieve because of your gender.'"

Venus could not be sure if she had moved enough men in the room to convince the Wimbledon officials to accept pay equity. During her presentation, the men could well have been visualizing a poker convention because, afterward, they refused to show their hands. Still, she felt good about her presentation. "When your eyes are closed, you do have to visualize what the person is talking about," she said. "You lose that sense of sight that you rely on so much. People had to really look inside themselves and say, 'Is this what we want to keep doing?'"

According to Simon, some members of the committee had questions about the pay equity issue, but nothing was resolved that day. Venus, meanwhile, played an epic final against Davenport, fighting off a match point in the third set with a sparkling two-handed backhand down the line. A capacity crowd of fifteen thousand on Centre Court eschewed its characteristic restraint and roared after the sensational rallies and spectacular shot-making from both women. At 7-7, Venus broke serve and then held her own for a dramatic victory, 4–6, 7–6 (7–4), 9–7.

As entertaining as Venus versus Serena can be, the most memorable and exciting matches involving a Williams sister often come against someone outside the family—Sharapova, Davenport, Martina Hingis, Jennifer Capriati, Kim Clijsters, Victoria Azarenka, Petra Kvitova—because of the contrast in styles. Also, because of the emotional freedom that competing against someone else affords Venus or Serena—neither has to console her sister at the end. Venus's battle against Davenport lasted two hours, forty-five minutes, the longest women's final in Wimbledon history. It should also be regarded as the finest. "I had bad knees," Venus said. "But when I won, I fell to my knees. I don't know why I did that. I've never done it again. My knees didn't break, so I said, 'Thank God.'"

After watching such a sensational display of women's tennis on the sport's grandest stage, the patriarchs at Wimbledon surely would get off their high horses and endorse pay equity. Wouldn't they? Whoa. Wimbledon always announces its prize-money decision in February for a tournament played in July. Because it can. The verdict: no pay equity in 2006, but instead a modest increase would be made to the women's prize purse. Men would continue to be paid more across the board, but the female champion would make "only" 30,000 pounds less than the male champion. That is equivalent to $39,000. The difference in pay would be so modest now as to seem spiteful. The patriarchs seemed to be asking, "Who do these women think they are?" "Why aren't they satisfied just to be playing at Wimbledon?" Perhaps the men genuinely believed that they were offering a fair increase. But it was not comparable to what the U.S. Open, Australian Open, and French Open were already offering: equality.

"Okay, I'm ready to fight some more," Venus told her WTA colleagues, sounding somewhat like Sally Field's factory worker and activist in *Norma Rae*. "What are we going to do next?"

With Venus as the anchorwoman, the WTA went public with its demand for pay equity before Wimbledon 2007. The WTA secured the backing of female politicians in the United Kingdom such as Tessa

Jowell, the secretary of state for culture, media, and sport, and Patricia Hewitt, the trade and industry secretary. After Venus watched a video by the United Nations Educational, Scientific, and Cultural Organization (UNESCO) that showed women in a Middle Eastern country playing soccer inside high walls so as not to offend the patriarchy with such a blatant display of athleticism, she and her tennis sistren met with UNESCO and agreed to promote their mutual struggles for equality in pay and opportunity.

Venus then wrote an editorial that appeared in the *Times of London* on June 26, 2006, one that effectively put the Wimbledon patriarchs on the defensive: "It is a shame that the greatest tournament in tennis, which should be a positive symbol for the sport, has been tarnished," Venus wrote. "How can it be that Wimbledon finds itself on the wrong side of history?"

Venus reminded readers that although men played longer matches at Wimbledon, women already received equal billing at the tournament and, thus, added at least the same value to the tournament as men. Once Venus's editorial appeared, the issue of pay equity became a hot topic in the United Kingdom—in workplaces, homes, neighborhoods, even in Parliament. Janet Anderson, a Member of Parliament, wore a bright red jacket to the weekly Prime Minister's Questions, the better to be noticed by the speaker who selected those who could question British leader Tony Blair. When Anderson asked Blair about the need for pay equity at Wimbledon, Blair endorsed the idea.

Having the prime minister's support abruptly and irrevocably changed the scoreboard: game, set, and match—WTA. The All England Club announced it would award equal prize money to women at Wimbledon beginning in 2007. It has been the policy ever since. With Venus tapping into her power and using her voice to amplify and persuade, women in sports achieved a major victory. It is a part of her legacy now—her sixth triumph at Wimbledon.

3 | Early Black Tennis

She was really angry that she
couldn't play in the big leagues.

ROBERT RYLAND

It is impossible to imagine tennis without Venus and Serena Williams.
What if those who follow the most prestigious tournaments in the
sport had never seen the awe-inspiring power, speed, and athleticism that the sisters display on court? What if tennis at its highest
level of public interest and media attention had never included the
fierce determination, grace, and creativity that Serena and Venus have
personified across three decades of competition? As hard as one tries
to imagine tennis without them, it is an unrealistic vision, for their
greatness has become so indelibly linked to the sport that it cannot
be erased or obscured.

For all their laudatory achievements as singles players, Serena and
Venus also combined to win fourteen major championships in doubles:

Wimbledon (6)—2000, 2002, 2008, 2009, 2012, 2016
Australian Open (4)—2001, 2003, 2009, 2010
U.S. Open (2)—1999, 2009
French Open (2)—1999, 2010

The Williams sisters' fourteen major titles are the second-most by any doubles team. The record of twenty-one is held by Hall of Famers Martina Navratilova and Pam Shriver.

The Williams sisters won Olympic gold medals as a duo in 2000, 2008, and 2012, and they also represented the USA in the 2016 Olympics. They formed a successful doubles team for the USA in the Fed Cup competition of nations in 1999, 2003, 2007, 2012, 2013, 2015, and 2018. (Although Navratilova and Shriver are both U.S. citizens, they never played as an Olympics duo representing the United States. Navratilova, born in the former Czechoslovakia, became a U.S. citizen in 1981. Shriver, a Maryland native, teamed with African American Zina Garrison of Houston to win an Olympic doubles gold medal in 1988.)

The tennis record book is virtually overrun with entries that attest to the prowess, consistency, and longevity of the Williams sisters. But imagine if Venus and Serena had been two sisters from Washington DC, possessing the same enviable athletic gifts in the 1930s and 1940s, long before the debut of Open Era tennis in 1968, and before the white gatekeepers allowed the racial integration of major tennis with Althea Gibson's debut at the U.S. Nationals in 1950. If such racial barriers had been erected to block Venus and Serena, then the Williams sisters would be as unfamiliar to tennis fans today as the Peters sisters, Margaret and Roumania.

Margaret and Roumania Peters were such formidable talents in singles play that they were known on their unique tennis circuit as "Pete" and "Re-pete." As a doubles team, they were virtually unbeatable. Many years later, when the sisters were in their eighties, the Women's Tennis Association honored them at a Fed Cup event in Washington DC. A fine gesture, indeed. But too little, too late. The Peters sisters never competed at Wimbledon or at Roland Garros in Paris, the site of the French Nationals, or at the West Side Tennis Club in New York City, the site of the U.S. Nationals. Racism prevented that. The Peters sisters competed in cities and towns where blacks were welcomed as part of the American Tennis Association. It would be easy to say that the ATA was to white-run tennis what the Negro Leagues were to Major League Baseball. It would also be inaccurate. Unlike the Negro Leagues, the ATA is still here.

The ATA was founded by professional men who endured discrimination and still became successful in medicine, law, education, religion, and business. The ATA staged its first championship in Druid Hill Park in Baltimore in August 1917, and today it is the oldest black-run sports league in America.

The players in ATA tournaments were amateurs, as were the stars of the major white-run tournaments. But there were no under-the-table payments to ATA champions that could keep the top players afloat financially while they competed as amateurs. Given the oppressive racial segregation of the time, no companies or entrepreneurs arranged lucrative exhibition matches for ATA champions that would allow them to travel from coast to coast as star attractions. Both of the Peters sisters, now deceased, worked full time as educators.

Whatever dreams of tennis immortality the Peters sisters may have had were dashed by racism. All competitive athletes, particularly those who have achieved success, want to match skills against the best in their specialty. Just as Negro League legend Josh Gibson may have died of a broken heart because the slugging catcher never got to compete in Major League Baseball, each of the ATA champions undoubtedly experienced a deep emotional void that could have only been filled through competition in the major tennis tournaments while in their athletic prime. Tennis fans also were seriously shortchanged for not having seen *all* the best players in the world competing in the most prestigious events until a semblance of racial equity occurred in the 1950s.

Ora Washington, a highly versatile black athlete who also starred in basketball, won eight ATA singles titles (1929–35, 1937). She partnered with various other players to win twelve doubles crowns between 1925 and 1936. Standing nearly six feet tall, she was an intimidating force on the court. Sadly, she also became embittered about being denied a chance to perform on the sport's biggest stages. "Ora was really angry about never getting a chance to play against the best white women," said Robert Ryland, a former ATA champion who in the 1950s became the first black tennis professional as part of a men's touring league that included Hall of Famers Pancho Gonzalez, Bobby Riggs, and Tony Trabert. "She would hear about the white women winning at Wimbledon and the U.S. Nationals, and those other [major] tournaments, and she'd be saying, 'I could beat them.' She had to work as a domestic, and she was really angry that she couldn't play in the big leagues."

Tennis fans in France got to know Suzanne Lenglen during the 1920s and 1930s. She won the French Nationals twice after the event was opened to athletes from other countries in 1925. Today, the French Open women's championship trophy is named for her. But most tennis fans know nothing about Ora Washington.

Tennis fans in Australia adored their countrywoman Daphne Akhurst, who won the Australian Nationals five times, including three in succession from 1928 to 1930. Memories of her live on because the Australian Open women's champion receives the Daphne Akhurst Cup. But Ora Washington has been largely forgotten.

Alas, Washington has plenty of company among unsung black tennis pioneers and early champions. Edgar Brown, for instance, was one of the first players to use topspin—hitting the top of a tennis ball to create a higher and trickier bounce. He won four ATA championships in the 1920s. Tally Holmes also won four ATA men's titles between 1917 and 1924 and drew raves for his smooth strokes and fierce backhand. Ted Thompson, a two-time ATA champ, had a formidable forehand slice. Dr. Reginald Weir, noted for his on-court grace and quickness, captured ATA titles in 1931, 1932, 1933, 1937, and 1942. When the doors of racial segregation were finally pried open, Weir became the first black man to play in the United States Lawn Tennis Association (USLTA) national indoor championships in 1948. He lost in the second round to Trabert.

Knowledgeable tennis fans have heard the names of Helen Wills Moody, Alice Marble, and Helen Jacobs, and those fans may be well-versed in the exploits of those white champions from the first half of the twentieth century. Wills Moody, for instance, won nineteen major singles titles. Only Margaret Court, Serena Williams, and Steffi Graf have won more. But it is highly unlikely that those same fans have heard of Isadore Channels, Lulu Ballard, and Flora Lomax, each of whom captured four ATA singles titles prior to 1950. There is, of course, no guarantee that the aforementioned black players would have defeated their better-known white counterparts in major tournaments. But there is also no guarantee that they would not have. The tragedy for the black champions is that they were never given the opportunity to try.

Only the foolhardiest would argue that the history of major tennis would not have been altered, perhaps substantially, had the black champions of the ATA been allowed to compete in the world's biggest tournaments prior to 1950. One need only look at how black participation enhanced other sports after the major leagues ceased segregation.

The tenor and style of Major League Baseball has been forever altered since Jackie Robinson's debut with the Brooklyn Dodgers in 1947. The game became quicker, faster, and more athletic. Blacks also brought more raw power to the game. The 714 home runs by Babe Ruth, the pinnacle of baseball power for generations, has been surpassed by two black players—Hank Aaron (755) and Barry Bonds (762). Even those who would argue that Bonds benefited from performance-enhancing drugs can make no such accusation against Aaron.

Look at how football at the professional and collegiate levels changed significantly after that sport's resistance to black talent lessened. Woody Strode and Kenny Washington in 1946 became the first blacks in thirteen years to play in the National Football League. It did not take long for each white owner of an NFL franchise to understand that he could neither win a championship nor adequately compete without black players on the roster. The black presence at football's most pivotal position—quarterback—has produced the most dramatic changes. Considered the thinking man's position, quarterback is also the foremost leadership position on the field. Hence, racial stereotypes used to prompt white coaches to move blacks to other positions even if those players were blessed with the skill set, leadership qualities, and intelligence to play quarterback. But the glass ceiling that once kept black quarterbacks from achieving stardom was shattered after players such as Warren Moon of the University of Washington, Turner Gill of the University of Nebraska, and Condredge Holloway of the

University of Tennessee began to excel in major conferences; and after Andre Ware of the University of Houston and Charlie Ward of Florida State University won the Heisman Trophy, awarded annually to college football's best player; and other black quarterbacks including Doug Williams, Randall Cunningham, Michael Vick, and Cam Newton (also a Heisman Trophy winner) excelled as professionals.

As for basketball, does one even recognize what the game looked like before Nat "Sweetwater" Clifton, Charles "Tarzan" Cooper, and Earl Lloyd debuted as the first blacks in the National Basketball Association in 1950? A game once played by men who could barely touch the rim is now played above the rim—on the NBA level and the collegiate level. The iconic Wilt Chamberlain—the only man to score one hundred points in an NBA game—once wrote that white team owners colluded to have no more than two black players on any team. Why? The owners foresaw what has since become reality: black talent, personified by (but hardly limited to) Chamberlain, Bill Russell, Oscar Robertson, Elgin Baylor, Kareem Abdul-Jabbar, Magic Johnson, Michael Jordan, and LeBron James has taken over the game.

In tennis, particularly women's tennis, Serena and Venus have forever altered the landscape since their debuts in the mid-1990s. In the heyday of the ATA, opponents who entered a singles tournament that featured Roumania and Margaret Peters often had to pick their poison. The sisters routinely played before large and enthusiastic crowds at the Twentieth Street courts in the Georgetown section of Washington. Gene Kelly, the famed actor and dancer, once stopped by to watch the Peters sisters while stationed at a nearby naval base during World War II. When it came to facing the Peters sisters in doubles, the other teams essentially competed for second place. The same has largely held true for opponents of Serena and Venus in WTA events, with the most obvious difference being the media coverage that has allowed fans around the world to see and read about the exploits of the Williams sisters.

In its earliest years, the ATA circuit included areas with large black populations such as New York City, Washington, Baltimore, and Philadelphia. It also included historically black colleges and universities

(HBCUs), which highlighted the importance of higher education for the tournament participants as well as the spectators. The list of HBCUs included Wilberforce University—the oldest private black university in America—in Wilberforce, Ohio, which was once a destination on Harriet Tubman's underground railroad; Central State University in Wilberforce, Ohio; Hampton Institute in Hampton, Virginia; South Carolina State University in Orangeburg; Lincoln University in Lincoln, Pennsylvania; and Tuskegee Institute, founded by human rights icon Booker T. Washington, in Tuskegee, Alabama.

The original ATA mission statement expressed three objectives:

give black tennis players venues where they could play and socialize;

hold an annual tournament; and

promote the game among blacks and other groups.

Arthur Ashe and Althea Gibson, both inductees in the International Tennis Hall of Fame, cultivated their skills in the ATA. A pair of future pros from Houston, Zina Garrison, a 1990 Wimbledon finalist, and Lori McNeil, won their first championships in the ATA. To this day, the ATA remains aware of its unique role as an amateur league that allows talented tennis players to be encouraged, nurtured, and developed. Headquartered in Largo, Maryland, the ATA has always welcomed players of all backgrounds.

In its early years, the ATA sought to become part of the USLTA—a request that the white-run association summarily rejected. Undeterred, the ATA continued to provide its members with places to play the game they loved, as well as a much-needed salve from the emotional, physical, and physiological effects of daily life.

During the era of government-mandated segregation, ATA events gave black-run businesses immediate access to consumers. Black newspapers and other media devoted extensive coverage to the matches and social events connected to the annual tournament. "Most people used to play and have their vacations at the ATA championships," former ATA president Wilbert Davis said. The tournament included fashion shows, dinners, luncheons, and formal dances along with the tennis.

By 1942, a quarter century after the inaugural ATA championships, there were 145 ATA-affiliated tennis clubs in the United States with a total membership of more than one thousand.

"The ATA was amazing," said Kim Sands of Miami, the 1976 ATA champion who later played on the WTA tour. "Before I went to the tournament, I didn't realize how many people of color were playing tennis. Just to be in that environment really emphasized to you that you were not alone. I never saw so many beautiful shades of black—black people, brown people, yellow people, red people like me. And it was all very traditional. Most of the people wore tennis whites. When I won the ATA title, that let me know I was ready for Chrissie [Evert] and Billie Jean [King] on the next level."

But it has taken quite some time for the USTA, and its predecessor the USLTA, to prove itself ready for black talent. Despite the appointment of Katrina Adams as the USTA's first black president and chair in 2015, America's governing body for tennis could still be more inclusive and diverse. That particular problem is as old as the institution itself. The official minutes from a February 1922 meeting of the USLTA committee in New York reveals the casual disregard with which the association handled a request by Howard University, a historically black institution in Washington DC, to join the USLTA. Officials and representatives from USLTA regional chapters attended the meeting, which was chaired by USLTA president Julian Y. Myrick:

JULIAN Y. MYRICK: We have a request from Howard University for membership in the USLTA.

R. N. WILLIAMS: I move that they be asked to join the American Tennis Association.

STEWART: We had this thing come up in Chicago. A colored club with very good courts applied for membership in the Western association. The application was received and we sent somebody out to look over the grounds and situation, and it seemed to be in what we term the "Negro belt." We asked one of their members to appear. We told him we would take it up and report to him later. *We decided in view of the fact that that they would be*

*able to enter any tournament in the country that their application
should be turned down* [author's emphasis]. They had a perfect
right to enter the Public Park Tennis Association. We cancelled
the two tickets they bought to go to our annual banquet.

JULIAN Y. MYRICK: Why not do as Mr. Williams suggested?
Tell them they probably should have written to the American
Lawn Tennis Association [*sic*].

ABNER Y. LEECH: Could we possibly refer it to the membership
committee and let an indefinite period pass?

P. B. WILLIAMS: So far as the American Tennis Association is
concerned, the secretary of that organization came into the
office and he asked me what the attitude of this Association
would be if they applied for membership. I told him I would
never make application. I said Southern clubs would "see red"
on that. I told him there would be no chance in the world of a
club of Negroes getting membership in the Association.

STEWART: I move that their application be refused. Carried.

The person taking the minutes at this meeting added a note that a
letter should be sent to each of the USLTA's regional sections stating
that this was now the established policy regarding any black organization seeking admittance to the USLTA.

The importance of preserving the history of black tennis and sharing
that knowledge with others has never been lost on Dr. Dale Caldwell, a
New Jersey–based educator and a former USTA board member. More
than a decade ago, Caldwell wrote to Tony Trabert, a 1970 inductee
of the International Tennis Hall of Fame, about staging an exhibit on
black tennis at the ITHF. The result was *Breaking Barriers*, a traveling museum of black tennis history curated by Caldwell and Arthur
Carrington, a former ATA champion and ATP tour pro who runs a
tennis academy in Massachusetts. With an assist from Gary Coger,
the director of the ITHF museum, *Breaking Barriers* debuted at the
2007 U.S. Open and has been viewed by tens of thousands since then.

Although the exhibit highlights the noteworthy careers of Althea Gibson and Arthur Ashe, *Breaking Barriers* is also an homage to black stars who were denied the opportunity to compete in major tennis. The list includes, but is not limited to, the Peters sisters, Weir, Holmes, Channels, and Washington. Visitors to the exhibit also will learn of accomplished black players and the larger contributions they made to society. For instance, Lucy Diggs Slowe, one of the original sixteen founders of the Alpha Kappa Alpha sorority—the first sorority founded by black women—won the inaugural ATA women's title in 1917. Eugene Kinckle Jones, who played in ATA events, was among the seven founders of the Alpha Phi Alpha fraternity at Cornell University in 1906, and he later became the executive director of the National Urban League.

In *Breaking Barriers*, tennis fans learn about exhibition matches featuring black stars and prominent white players during an era of segregated tennis. One such exhibition occurred on July 29, 1940. Don Budge—who in 1938 became the first player to win the Grand Slam—played Jimmie McDaniel, the reigning ATA champion from Xavier University of New Orleans, in a match that drew an overflow crowd of more than two thousand to the Cosmopolitan Tennis Club in Harlem. Hundreds more without a bleacher seat watched the match from apartment windows and trees. Wilson Sporting Goods, whose products Budge endorsed, sponsored the clay-court match. McDaniel, a hardcourt specialist, lost 6–1, 6–2.

In a mixed doubles exhibition at the Cosmopolitan Tennis Club on August 19, 1944, Alice Marble, the No. 1 player in the world, partnered with Private First Class Robert Ryland of Walterboro (South Carolina) air base to face Mary Hardwick of England and Reginald Weir. "I was the No. 1 seed in the ATA then, and the army thought it would be good publicity to send me to New York for the match," Ryland said. "It was two black men and two white women, but we were in Harlem, so the army didn't worry about anyone getting upset. We couldn't have done that in the South, though."

In November 2007 Dale Caldwell founded the Black Tennis Hall of Fame (BTHF). Its executive director is Bob Davis, a former ATA player who runs the Panda Foundation, which provides tennis scholarships to promising youngsters. The BTHF is a nonprofit, privately funded venture that does not have a physical building. Instead, it has a website (blacktennishistory.com) that, in Caldwell's words, "celebrates tennis players and contributors who have broken through barriers of race and honors those who use tennis to help young people break through barriers of poverty." Davis and Caldwell consult with a nominating committee to induct members in three categories. The first two categories, players and contributors, are the same used by the International Tennis Hall of Fame. The third BTHF category, pioneers, refers to those with "an outstanding record of success on the tennis court or who made a significant contribution to tennis during segregation or prior to the passage of civil rights legislation in the U.S. in 1964," Caldwell said.

The BTHF also pays tribute to players who performed with distinction after the Open Era began in 1968—players who will never be as well known as the Williams sisters, but who helped pave the way. The list includes, but is not limited to, former world top ten players Zina Garrison, Lori McNeil, and Chanda Rubin, a judge's daughter from Louisiana who teamed with Spain's Arantxa Sánchez Vicario to win the 1996 Australian Open doubles title; Leslie Allen, who was ranked No. 17 in the world in 1981; Ann Koger, one of the first black players on the WTA tour; Rodney Harmon, a former NCAA doubles champion at the University of Tennessee who in 2008 became the first African American to coach the U.S. Olympic men's team; Martin Blackman, a two-time NCAA champion at Stanford University who heads the USTA player development program; and Bryan Shelton, who achieved world rankings of No. 55 in singles and No. 56 in doubles in the 1990s. Shelton and McNeil reached the French Open mixed doubles final in 1992.

Also included among the BTHF inductees is a white woman, Angela Buxton. A British native and the daughter of Russian Jews, Buxton partnered with Althea Gibson to win major doubles titles at the 1955 French Nationals and at Wimbledon in 1956. Buxton, who faced anti-Semitism, and Gibson, who faced racism, became lifelong friends after meeting at a tournament in India in 1955. Gibson used to stay in Buxton's home in Manchester during Wimbledon. In 1995, when an ailing and despondent Gibson contemplated suicide, Buxton helped raise more than $1 million for the tennis great, which, in Buxton's words, "gave Althea another eight years of life."

Another white member of the BTHF is Nick Bollettieri, an International Tennis Hall of Famer who started his own hugely successful tennis academy in Bradenton, Florida, in 1978. (It is now the IMG Academy.) Bollettieri partnered with Arthur Ashe to found the Ashe-Bollettieri Cities Program in 1988 to, in Ashe's words, "gain and hold the attention of young people in the inner cities and other poor environments so that we could teach them about matters more important than tennis."

The BTHF logo features Gibson, Ashe, and a tennis-loving physician who coached both of them, Dr. Robert Walter Johnson. The International Tennis Hall of Fame inducted Gibson in 1971, Ashe in 1985, and Johnson, posthumously, in 2009. Johnson acquired three colorful nicknames: "the Godfather of Black Tennis," "Dr. J," and "Whirlwind." He earned the third moniker because of his speed and ability to evade tacklers while playing football at Lincoln University in the 1920s. He later coached football, baseball, and basketball. He became a tennis fan while studying at Meharry Medical School in Tennessee. He opened his own clinic in Lynchburg, Virginia, at a time when blacks were not permitted to practice at white hospitals.

Using his own money and resources, Johnson started the ATA Junior Development Program, which he ran for twenty years until his death in 1972. Each summer, he invited as many as twelve black teenagers and preteens to his home for on-court tennis instruction and lessons in developing discipline. He believed that the USLTA would eventually curb its racism and open its doors to blacks, and when it happened, he wanted to have players at the ready.

"When we trained them, we were not interested in just changing their grips; we intended to improve their game from a minor-league status to a major-league status," Johnson once said. "In the minors, a pitcher tries to throw a strike over the plate to reach the big leagues. A pitcher in the big leagues must throw for the corners. So, our job was to teach the players how to serve for the corners and the lines instead of down the middle of the court."

However, any youngster expecting a summer vacation at Dr. J's got a quick dose of reality. He had his juniors do chores in exchange for their room and board. "It was a strict regimen," said Juan Farrow, a former ATA champion who later played on the pro tour. "We were up at six in the morning. We hit about a thousand balls a day from a ball machine. He would come out and sit and yell and scream." More than one hundred of Johnson's pupils earned college scholarships. Others eventually became successful pros, including Leslie Allen, a six-footer who won ATA championships before playing at the University of Southern California.

"When my mom sent me to Dr. J's, I knew I was going to a place of tradition, and when Dr. J spoke, we listened to him like he was the king," she said. "You knew that everyone had your best interests at heart, and you never felt threatened because someone was better than you. What I liked most about his approach is that he made it simple for you to understand what you had to do to get better. And a lot of it wasn't about stroke production."

"You had to do what Dr. Johnson told you to do," added Willis Thomas Sr., a former ATA treasurer. "He'd send you home in a minute if you didn't measure up to what he wanted."

Gibson not only measured up, but also became his star pupil. He offered her coaching and counsel after watching her lose in an ATA final largely because of her inexperience. He sold Gibson on the notion that he could help make her a champion, and he delivered. Further, he convinced Gibson that he could teach the former truant a refinement that would benefit her in any walk of life, whether major tennis ever accepted black players or not. She lived with the family of Dr. Hubert Eaton, another black physician, in Wilmington, North Carolina, during the school year, and attended Johnson's program in the summer.

Arthur Ashe began playing tennis in the 1950s in his hometown of Richmond, Virginia. At age seven, he hit regularly with Ronald

Charity, a Virginia Union University star who also played in the ATA. Charity brought him to Lynchburg, Virginia, to meet Johnson. The doctor convinced Arthur's father, no particular fan of tennis, to let the boy spend a summer in the junior development program. There, Arthur refined his strokes, learned court etiquette and the nuances of the game, and practiced with older boys, whom he usually outplayed.

It did not take long for Dr. J to identify Arthur as "the one," the player who could ascend higher in tennis than any black male before him. Through persistence, Dr. J eventually convinced the region's USLTA officials to allow Arthur to compete against the best white players in the area. To prepare, Dr. J often had Arthur serve five hundred balls before breakfast and another five hundred afterward. Showing no favoritism, he also had Arthur pick up trash and smooth the backyard clay court just like the other juniors. "Don't be as strong or as tough as those white boys," Dr. J told him. "Be stronger. Be tougher."

Johnson taught his juniors to always concede a point to an opponent on a close call. He hammered away at this demand until it became almost second nature. He did this with an eye toward the inevitable integration of white-run tennis tournaments in the region. He believed that if his players showed how well mannered they were, then they would be invited back to compete in those tournaments year after year.

Once those tennis events became integrated, Arthur emerged as the dominant male junior in the region, winning titles for boys' twelve-and-under in 1955, sixteen-and-under (as a fourteen-year-old) in 1957, and the same title again in 1958. Yet his on-court success hardly quelled the racial hostility he faced off the court. After Arthur won the championship as the only black participant in a tournament in Charlottesville, Virginia, the boys went to a local movie theater to unwind. The box office manager refused to let Arthur inside.

Fortunately, Dr. J taught Arthur not to internalize the racist actions of others. They may treat you as a second-class citizen, Dr. J told his charges, but always know that you are not. Those who attended Dr. J's junior development program said his teachings prepared them to handle daily challenges from people bent on treating them with disrespect. Black people who were hungry and eager to prove themselves, whether in an integrated society or in their own communities, always made for Dr. J's best pupils.

Thirty-seven years after his death, Johnson was inducted into the International Tennis Hall of Fame. His grandson, Lange Johnson, delivered the acceptance speech. He was introduced by Ashe's widow, Jeanne, whose remarks at the ceremony drew parallels between Ashe and his former mentor:

"Dr. Johnson channeled his athletic ability and competitiveness into tennis. Arthur Ashe Jr. used the sport of tennis as a platform to move important issues forward that he cared so deeply about. Dr. Johnson, during the age of segregation, played host to the only tennis court and venue in Virginia where all races could play. In 1968, when Arthur Ashe won the first U.S. Open, a year later he founded the National Junior Tennis League, as a way to bring tennis to people across the country, regardless of color or race. Dr. Johnson used his influence, personal funds, and determination to fight for equal rights and to advance the sport in a way that would make the world proud. Now, to those of us who did not personally know Dr. Johnson, doesn't this sound familiar? Is there any question as to how Dr. Johnson had an impact on Arthur Ashe's life?"

A selfless act by a member of Ashe's own family also had a profound effect on his life. It is a story with which the masses are still largely unfamiliar.

4 | Arthur Ashe

> It is so inspiring to see the name Arthur Ashe
> on the world's biggest tennis stadium.

SKYLAR MORTON

At the 2018 U.S. Open, three significant milestones were celebrated:

It was the fortieth year since the event moved from the quaint West Side Tennis Club in Forest Hills, which major tennis had outgrown, to the USTA Billie Jean King National Tennis Center in the inelegantly named Flushing Meadows section of New York City.

It was the fiftieth year of Open tennis, when the sport became truly professional with players eligible to receive prize money instead of only star players receiving hush-hush payments to compete at events.

Fifty years had passed since Arthur Ashe put himself on the sports map by slamming twenty-six aces to defeat South Africa's Tom Okker and win the first U.S. Open men's title. Ashe also won the 1968 U.S. Amateur championship, making him the only man to capture both titles in the same year.

Ashe, a man who elevated tennis by his presence, was remembered at the 2018 U.S. Open in black-and-white photos strategically placed throughout the National Tennis Center. Images included a bespectacled Ashe on court looking "pipe-cleaner skinny," as his widow, Jeanne, once said jokingly; Ashe in discussion with the singer, actor, and fellow activist Harry Belafonte, with whom he founded Artists and Athletes Against Apartheid; Ashe in a solitary moment of contemplation; and Ashe encircled by more than a dozen reporters (all white and male) during a postmatch interview. Portions of a documentary, *Ashe '68*, also debuted at the tournament, giving fans unique 360-degree views of Ashe's U.S. Open triumph.

Because Ashe was still an amateur in 1968, he could not accept the $14,000 first prize. All he received from the U.S. Open was $20 for daily expenses. However, an anonymous donor sent him one hundred shares of General Motors stock, which at the time sold for $84 a share.

On becoming the first Open champion, Ashe, a police officer's son from Richmond, Virginia, wrote in his first autobiography, *Off the Court*, "The award ceremony that day will always hold a special place in my heart. My father came onto the court with me, and it felt wonderful to share that moment with him."

From 1968 until his retirement from tennis in 1979 because of a heart condition, Ashe played with an uncommon grace while debunking racist mythology about the ability and comportment of black athletes in a sport from which they had long been barred at the highest level. He understood that he had to not only excel in competition, but also display exemplary behavior. It was a heavy load.

"Sure, I get fed up being the nice guy," he told an interviewer in 1985. "But back in the '60s, if you were black and the first one, you simply had to behave yourself. I couldn't have gotten away with coming on like [boxing legend Muhammad] Ali—it wouldn't have been tolerated. I genuinely believe that if [tennis legend John] McEnroe were black, he wouldn't be allowed to do some of the things he does."

Ashe became the first black man to win the U.S. Nationals indoor title in 1960 and again in 1961, as well as the 1960 U.S. Nationals interscholastic title. Although his face and his game became familiar to predominantly white tennis audiences, he initially felt merely tolerated, not welcomed, in a segregated environment. "I played in clubs where the only blacks were waiters, gardeners, and busboys," he said. "The game had a history and tradition I was expected to assimilate, but much of that history and many of those traditions were hostile to me."

In 1966 one tennis event in which Ashe wanted to play had to be moved from the Dallas Country Club, first because the club did not want to invite him and then because the club, after agreeing to invite him, refused to admit black spectators. The tournament was moved to Samuell Grand Tennis Center in a public park and Ashe ended up winning both the singles and doubles titles.

Ashe's prodigious talent became his ticket out of segregated Richmond, a city he simply outgrew. He became an avid traveler, a connoisseur of cultures, a true citizen of the world. The journey included his enshrinement in the International Tennis Hall of Fame in Newport, Rhode Island, in 1985. "It was always interesting being in my position," he said in his acceptance speech. "I never wanted to be in another sport or not be in the minority. I always thought the system was wrong, not that it was me that was wrong."

Ashe was not the first black player to achieve greatness in major tennis. Althea Gibson won Wimbledon and the U.S. Nationals (the forerunner of the U.S. Open) two times each, and won the French Nationals title, all in the 1950s. But Ashe's three major championships, including the 1970 Australian Open and Wimbledon 1975, are better remembered than Gibson's, not only because they occurred during the Open Era, but also because they occurred in the television age. As many American families were buying their first color television sets, Ashe became one of the sports stars whose image came into their living rooms fairly regularly. He became known as "the black tennis champion." The first U.S. Open was televised nationally by CBS, and it has been an annual summer staple on national television ever since.

Americans got to know and admire Ashe, an eloquent gentleman with a potent serve-and-volley game, a degree in business administration from UCLA, and a stint as an Army lieutenant. The world learned that Ashe possessed a high intellect, compassion, and sensitivity, and he drew upon those qualities to raise public consciousness about the important issues of his time, such as racism in America and human rights abuses around the world.

Yet we may not have been afforded the opportunity to learn as much as we did from Ashe were it not for the sacrifice of his brother.

Johnnie Ashe, five years younger, excelled in academics and sports in segregated Richmond. Rather than concentrate on tennis, as Arthur had, Johnnie earned high school letters in football, basketball, baseball, track, and tennis. After Arthur left Richmond for St. Louis, where he could play tennis on indoor courts and compete in enough white-run tournaments to qualify for a major college tennis scholarship—opportunities that Richmond would not allow a black boy—Johnnie stayed home and became one of the first black students at John Marshall High School. In 1965 Johnnie joined the Marines at the age of seventeen. That same year, Arthur led UCLA to a national championship and won the NCAA singles title. In 1966 he became an Army data processing instructor in West Point, New York.

With the Vietnam War raging, Arthur could have been called into combat. Athletic prowess would not necessarily have exempted him. Johnnie was in Vietnam; friends of his had been killed in combat. Blood brothers serving in the same combat zone were rare, but not without precedent. Johnnie wanted to do whatever possible to keep Arthur away from war. "Arthur was always different," Johnnie said. "I realized that at an early age." For that reason, Johnnie told the Marines that he wanted another tour of duty in Vietnam. His stated reason: he wanted to become an officer. When Arthur found out, he told his brother he was almost sure that the military would not send him into combat. But Johnnie wanted to make absolutely sure. He returned to Vietnam and survived the bloodiest year of the conflict, 1968, when almost seventeen thousand American soldiers and twenty-eight thousand South Vietnamese soldiers were killed.

Arthur went on to have a superb professional tennis career, winning fifty-one titles, appearing in ninety-six finals, achieving a career-best world ranking of No. 2 in 1976, and earning $1,584,109 in prize money. Johnnie spent twenty years in the Marines, rising to the rank of captain. On September 3, 2018, the USTA honored Johnnie Ashe's sacrifice in a ceremony inside the largest tennis venue in the world: Arthur Ashe Stadium.

Just as the U.S. Open had outgrown Forest Hills two decades earlier, America's Grand Slam needed a bigger, more modern home base in the 1990s. Louis Armstrong Stadium, named after the legendary trumpeter, bandleader, and singer who had lived in the nearby St. Albans section until his death in 1971, existed as a music venue before the tennis center was built around it. Armstrong Stadium had eighteen thousand seats, but the USTA wanted a stadium that would accommodate more fans and provide enough luxury suites for the well heeled. Since the tennis center exists on land owned by New York City, the city council had to approve the construction of a new main court that would open in 1997.

But what should the USTA call this new twenty-three-thousand-seat stadium, constructed at a cost of $254 million? Some members of the board argued in favor of calling it USTA Stadium in the hope of eventually landing a lucrative naming-rights deal. (Nearly adjacent to the tennis center is Citi Field, the home of baseball's New York Mets, which opened in 2009. Citigroup agreed to pay the Mets $20 million a year for twenty years for the naming rights.) However, the USTA opted for class over cash. Harry Mannion, then the USTA president, announced that the new stadium would be named after the 1968 U.S. Open champion "because Arthur Ashe was the finest human being the sport has ever known."

Naming its marquee stadium after a humanitarian who also played a mean game of tennis may be the single greatest thing the USTA has ever done. Ashe's legacy includes the founding of the Association of Tennis Professionals (the men's tour); the National Junior Tennis League (NJTL), which is now run by the USTA and uses tennis as a gateway to educational opportunities through more than 350 local programs that serve 230,000 inner-city youngsters; the Safe Passage Foundation, a nonprofit organization modeled after the NJTL that provides academic scholarships for youngsters; and the Arthur Ashe Foundation for the Defeat of AIDS.

"It's so inspiring to see the name Arthur Ashe on the world's biggest tennis stadium—because of who he was and everything he did for the sport and the world," said Skylar Morton, a female WTA pro who played at UCLA and the University of Virginia. Decades earlier, segregation prevented native son Ashe from ever hoping to play college tennis for Virginia.

Morton, twenty-four, spoke at the Citi Open in Washington DC, a hardcourt tournament held every August that would not exist if not for Ashe. In 1963 he became the first black player to represent the United States in the Davis Cup, an annual competition among nations dating to 1900. Captained by Donald Dell, Team USA featured Ashe, Charles Pasarell, Dennis Ralston, Stan Smith, Clark Graebner, and Bob Lutz. The United States routed Australia 4–1 in the final, which began a streak of five consecutive Davis Cup titles. A decade later, Dell, a Washington attorney and Ashe's agent, lamented that there was no pro tennis tournament in the DC area. Dell learned that there were sponsors interested in providing financial backing, but only if Ashe played. Ashe agreed under one condition: the tournament would have to be in a residential community, not at a country club, so fans in the predominantly black DC area would feel comfortable attending. The tournament has had various corporate names since its inception in 1969, but it has always been staged in Rock Creek Park, the home of the Washington Tennis and Education Foundation. The WTEF's program director is Willis Thomas Jr., who was Ashe's friend and doubles partner when they were teenagers in the ATA.

Ashe could be self-effacing when discussing his tennis skills. He was not the best player of his era, but he was consistently among the best until he retired at the age of thirty-six. His most prolific year was 1970, when he won eleven of fourteen finals, including the Australian

Open title. In 1975 he won nine of fourteen title matches, including the crown jewel, Wimbledon.

"I was not a great athlete," Ashe once wrote, "but I was fast, had quick hands, good eye-hand coordination, and repertoire and attitude together at a time when the pro game was mushrooming with prize money and commercial endorsements."

Cliff Drysdale, a South African who lost to Ashe in the 1968 U.S. Open quarterfinals, has a much more favorable view of Ashe the player. "In my dictionary he was a great player—he could probe until he found an opponent's weakness and then attack it," said Drysdale, now an ESPN tennis commentator, who was 2-8 in career matches against Ashe. "He would not compare with a [Pete] Sampras, an [Andre] Agassi, a [Rod] Laver, because he never won that many Grand Slam titles and that's usually a barometer for greatness."

Ashe never played against fellow Hall of Famers Sampras and Agassi, but here is how he fared against the top players of his era:

Ashe vs. Jimmy Connors: 1-6
Ashe vs. Rod Laver: 3-19
Ashe vs. John Newcombe: 4-10
Ashe vs. Ken Rosewall: 6-14
Ashe vs. Bjorn Borg: 8-9
Ashe vs. Guillermo Vilas: 5-5
Ashe vs. Ilie Nastase: 6-5
Ashe vs. Stan Smith: 11-6
Ashe vs. Roy Emerson: 14-2
Ashe vs. Tom Okker: 17-8

The lone victory against Connors, in the 1975 Wimbledon final, was exquisite. Transforming Centre Court into a chessboard, Ashe devised a superior strategy that featured heavy doses of spins and slices, known by the players as "junk," along with well-conceived serves and volleys that kept Connors, the world's No. 1 player, off balance. Many in attendance that day expected to see Connors steamroll to another major title. Instead, they witnessed a historic first—a black man won Wimbledon.

"I remember being scared to death that Arthur was going to be terribly embarrassed," said Hall of Fame journalist Bud Collins, who handled the match commentary for NBC. "We almost didn't want the match to happen because Connors was going to beat him one, one, and love [6-1, 6-1, 6-0]. We were glad for Arthur that he got to the final, but we didn't even want to watch."

Perhaps in Connors's mind, there were three million reasons to try to humiliate Ashe on Centre Court. In his capacity as president of the Association of Tennis Professionals, Ashe had publicly criticized Connors for not joining the players' union. Connors filed a lawsuit for $3 million, alleging slander and libel.

Collins, the dean of tennis journalists until his death in 2016, actually did see scores of 6-1, 6-1 in the first two sets. But, stunningly, Ashe won both of those sets. Rather than attempt to slug with Connors, Ashe hit forehand slices with underspin to Connors's two-fisted backhand. Connors was forced to stretch on his backhand wing to return shots, which diminished his power and control. Whenever a Connors backhand reply fell short, Ashe pounced on it and smacked a winning volley. Sometimes, Ashe chipped the ball to lure Connors to the net and then lobbed over him. Ashe effectively kept balls in the center of the court, forcing Connors to create his own angles. Ashe served solidly and never fell into a predictable pattern. For two sets, he gave a master class on how to declaw a tennis beast.

In the second set, after a fourth consecutive service break, Ashe led 6-1, 3-0. This prompted one stunned British fan to yell, "Come on, Connors!" An exasperated Connors replied, "I'm trying, for Christ's sake!"

Although Connors rallied to take the third set, 7-5, and seized a 3-0 lead in the fourth set, Ashe looked serene. He closed his eyes while in his chair during changeovers, visualizing success, before returning to the court to bring those images to life. He always seemed to personify coolness under pressure. Never in his career was that more evident than in the 1975 Wimbledon final.

Even after the match's momentum had swung in Connors's direction, Ashe refused to alter his strategy. He would not be lured into a slugfest. "I had to decide whether to continue as is or blast back," he wrote. "I decided to continue feeding him more junk, force him to the net and lob. When I broke serve at 3-1, he became a bit more tentative, which reinforced my belief that I was doing the right thing. He was human. Perhaps the pressure was getting to him."

Many spectators must have wondered if the pressure would finally get to Ashe with the score 5-4 and tennis's most prestigious title on his racket. Once again, he did not deviate from his routine during the changeover. Eyes closed in his moment of zen, he visualized himself winning one more game. Then, up from his chair, he paid no heed to the crowd's applause. He walked briskly to the service line. Ready for business.

Ashe hits a service winner: 15-love.

Connors strokes a forehand crosscourt winner: 15 all.

One of the few spirited rallies in the match ends with Connors dumping a forehand into the net: 30-15.

Ashe delivers another service winner: 40-15. Championship point.

A serve sliced to Connors's backhand pulls him off the court. The weak return floats over the net and toward Ashe like a beach ball. Ashe comes forward and smashes a volley into a wide-open court.

Game, set, match, championship: 6-1, 6-1, 5-7, 6-4.

"Arthur was so cool; just the way he looked in the chair, you knew he was going to come out and finish it like a champion," said Robert Ryland, a two-time ATA champion.

Rather than fling his racket into the air in triumph, or sink to his knees in a prayerful pose, Ashe punctuated his grandest tennis victory with a gesture that evoked memories of John Carlos and Tommie Smith, African American athletes for social justice, on the medal podium after the 200-meter dash at the 1968 Summer Olympics in Mexico City.

"Before I walked to the net to shake hands with Jimmy, I turned to the special friends' box and held up my right fist to Donald Dell," Ashe wrote. "It would be the only time in my career that I would feel such an urge."

Ashe had also beaten the litigation out of Connors, who dropped the lawsuit, joined the ATP, and, eventually, played in the Davis Cup for the United States.

Two years earlier, Ashe lost a best-of-five-set final to Connors in straight sets at the South African Open in Johannesburg. In a bold and controversial act, Ashe had secured a visa to visit South Africa, which in 1973 was a country tarnished by apartheid—government-mandated racial segregation in which a black majority was subjugated by a white minority. The power of celebrity undoubtedly helped Ashe in his quest to visit South Africa, but he also received much-needed help from Dell, his attorney; Andrew Young, a dear friend who in 1972 became Georgia's first black congressman since Reconstruction; and Robert Kelleher, a federal judge in Los Angeles who was once Ashe's Davis Cup captain. But why did Ashe want to go?

"I feel I have some credibility in talking about South Africa," he wrote. "I was brought up under a similar situation, having lived in the segregated South. I have more feeling being black, intuitively, than some northerner who may have a false feeling of integration."

Ashe said he firmly believed that his trip to South Africa "could play a significant role as far as raising the level of awareness within the white community, both in South Africa and the United States." He set four conditions for his trip, all of which were accepted by the apartheid regime:

there would be no segregated audiences at the tennis tournament in Johannesburg;
he would be recognized by white South Africa as a black man, not by the "honorary white" designation that the apartheid regime usually gave to nonwhite visitors;
he would not have to stay in a segregated area; and
he could go wherever he wanted and do whatever he pleased.

Although many in the United States and South Africa believed Ashe had been used by the apartheid regime, he wanted to raise public consciousness about the everyday horrors experienced under apartheid by black people, and, to a lesser degree, mixed-race people. A few notable American journalists, such as Collins and Frank Deford of *Sports Illustrated*, accompanied Ashe to shine more light on South Africa's atrocities. As a founding member of Artists and Athletes Against Apartheid, Ashe sought to convince athletes and entertainers to stop accepting lucrative payments to perform in South Africa and normalize its racism. He believed that his own accounts of what he would see and hear would be instrumental in dissuading others.

"I asked Arthur what South Africa was like because I considered going there for a tournament," said Kim Sands, a former WTA pro from Miami whom Ashe mentored. "He told me being in South Africa was like stuffing yourself with twenty pancakes and then having to eat twenty more. It just made you totally sick inside." Sands decided not to go.

Ashe made several more trips to South Africa. When he returned home, his spirit was buoyed by letters of resistance that he received from many friends and acquaintances he had made there. The common theme of those missives: change is coming; apartheid is on its last legs. Artists and Athletes Against Apartheid and other groups continued to keep the issue in the public eye, and activists around the world organized protests that branded South Africa as a pariah and gradually convinced many major companies and American colleges to divest their financial holdings from the country. With so many people pushing hard in the same direction, apartheid finally fell and disintegrated. In 1990 Nelson Mandela, the leader of the African National Congress, was released from prison after twenty-seven years of confinement. When Mandela visited America later that year, he and Ashe finally met face-to-face in New York City. They shared a warm embrace at City College of New York in Harlem after Mandela appeared at a town hall event moderated by ABC News anchorman Ted Koppel. In 1992 South Africa returned to the Olympic Games for the first time since 1960. And in 1994 Mandela was voted president in the country's first-ever election for people of all races.

In 1971 Ashe traveled with Stan Smith on a goodwill tour to various African countries, including Cameroon. Ashe played tennis with a group of Cameroonian boys who loved the sport. One boy stepped onto a makeshift court and, as Ashe said, "hit the ball with a wooden paddle with talent and conviction." Ashe went to a phone and immediately called his friend, Phillippe Chatrier, the president of the French Tennis Federation. "Phillippe," Ashe said, "there is a young boy here who you need to see." The boy's name was Yannick Noah. Through the tutelage of the French federation, as well as the boy's own considerable athletic gifts and work ethic, Noah became a tennis superstar. His 1983 French Open championship made him the second black man in history to win a major title, after Ashe. There has not been another one since.

A popular misconception grew out of Noah's tennis achievements. Because he succeeded Ashe as a major champion, as a Davis Cup winner (for France in 1991), and as an International Tennis Hall of Famer (Class of 2005), many viewed him as Ashe's protégé. Although they were close friends, and Noah certainly benefited from Ashe's advice and encouragement at tournaments, they did not have a player-coach relationship or a de facto father-son relationship. "What they didn't realize was that I wasn't helping Yannick that much," Ashe said. "Yannick Noah is not my protégé. I didn't teach him a single stroke."

Ashe said this in response to criticism he had heard from various African American tennis pros who believed he had not done enough to advance their careers. The list of players included Juan Farrow, Horace Reid, Luis Glass, and Arthur Carrington. According to Sydney Llewellyn, who coached Carrington in the 1970s: "[Ashe] only gave a handout here and there. Ashe never sincerely helped any of those kids." Farrow, the last promising ATA junior to be coached by International Tennis Hall of Famer Dr. Robert Walter Johnson, criticized Ashe for not playing doubles with him at pro events. Farrow believed that playing with Ashe would have enhanced his public profile and attracted sponsors. "Arthur wanted to make sure that he was the only one [to succeed]," Farrow said.

Other black tennis pros viewed Ashe in a much more favorable light.

"Arthur was a great coach and always supportive," said Sands, the former women's head coach at the University of Miami. "I came to tennis late, while I was playing basketball in high school. Arthur taught me how to play. He taught me how to serve. Today, I teach the serve exactly the way he taught me: point your arm toward the net post on your toss; don't vary the direction of your toss so your opponent won't know where you're going to hit it. He taught me so many technical things about the game, and he was always so positive."

Rodney Harmon, a former tour pro from Ashe's hometown of Richmond, added, "Arthur was not the kind of person who would publicize what he was doing to help other black players. That was not his way. He did what he thought was right in a quiet, thoughtful way. Some black players he helped financially, but he did it without wanting any publicity. You know the saying, 'Where good news travels, bad news travels faster?' It's so easy for people who didn't go as far in tennis as they think they should have to say that Arthur didn't help other blacks. But I can tell you as a black man myself and as a former player that Arthur was very helpful to me. With Arthur, I would say that if he saw you helping yourself along, he would help you. If he thought you were not helping yourself, he would not help you. That's what I saw."

On a trip to France during the 1980s, Ashe met Sekou Bangoura, an avid tennis fan from the West African nation of Guinea. "Arthur Ashe is the reason my dad moved to America," said Sekou Bangoura Jr., a twenty-seven-year-old player on the men's pro tour. "Because of Arthur Ashe, my dad became a tennis coach. I was born into the sport. I started playing when I was three. I have a special connection to Arthur. He mentored my dad and encouraged him to attend school in America. So, my dad moved to Bradenton, Florida, where I was born. He met and married my mom, who is from Alabama. I'm a professional tennis player today because of my dad and Arthur Ashe. I know the Ashe family pretty well, and that means a lot to me." Today, Sekou's father, a coach with more than thirty years of experience, runs the Sekou Bangoura International Tennis Academy in Sarasota, Florida.

Ashe knew that no matter how much he did in the black community, critics would accuse him of not doing enough. "They want you to be great as well as spend all your free time in the black community, and you can't do both," he wrote. "You can't be No. 1 on a tennis court and spend all your time in the black community. Muhammad Ali didn't do it. Martin Luther King didn't do it. No one's done it. It can't be done."

MaliVai Washington faced similar pressures, especially after he became a Wimbledon finalist in 1996 and a player ranked No. 11 in the world. It can be difficult to find the right balance between engaging with newly minted friends and supporters and not becoming distracted by them.

"As a great athlete, so much of what you have to do goes into your craft; anything else that you may have to do can become a distraction," Washington said. "When you have distractions, your level of athletic performance falls, understandably. But that didn't seem to be the case with Arthur."

The issue remains a sensitive one for black professional athletes. The black community celebrates their achievements; indeed, many seem to live vicariously through those achievements. Fans yearn to interact with their favorite athletes, particularly in this age of social media. But how much is too much? Those who lent a helping hand on an athlete's way up the ladder may want to see more of them once they reach the pinnacle. However, that is not always possible because success often comes with newfound demands on an athlete's time.

A case in point involves the strained relations that existed for several years between Ashe and the family of Johnson, because Ashe did not attend his former mentor's funeral. Johnson died on June 28, 1971, of a malignant brain tumor at the age of seventy-two. Althea Gibson, a struggling pro golfer at the time, attended the funeral. Ashe remained at Wimbledon, where he had already lost in the third round of singles to Marty Riessen, but was still in contention in doubles with partner Dennis Ralston. Ashe used to say that he never felt comfortable at funerals. He did not attend his mother's funeral when he was six years old. The Johnson family chafed at that excuse. But the families eventually reconciled. When Johnson was inducted posthumously into the Hall of Fame in 2009, Jeanne Ashe honored the family's request by introducing Johnson's grandson, Lange, who delivered the acceptance speech at the ceremony.

For Ashe, devoting time and energy to important social causes seemed to provide a spiritual sustenance and a sense of community that he needed away from the tennis court. It also enabled him to engage with members of the public who also shared a high level of social consciousness.

Ashe was a staunch supporter of the United Negro College Fund, a philanthropic organization established in 1944 to provide scholarships for black students and scholarship funds for historically black colleges and universities. Many are familiar with the UNCF's slogan: "A mind is a terrible thing to waste." At a UNCF benefit at Madison Square Garden on October 14, 1976, Ashe met the woman he would marry. Jeanne Moutoussamy, a strikingly beautiful woman of black and East Indian origin, was an NBC staff photographer assigned to shoot the event. "Jeanne captivated me," he wrote. "In looks, she was easily a '10,' but she did something else to me. She was a photographer and graphic artist who was bright, articulate, sensitive. Even with all my traveling in late 1976, to Europe and Australia, I knew I wanted to marry Jeanne."

They married on February 20, 1977, with Andrew Young, then the U.S. ambassador to the United Nations, serving as the officiant. Prior to Ashe's marriage, a newspaper reporter wrote, "Ashe travels to 20 countries yearly and owns no homes, cars, furniture or other trappings." However, his annual income grew considerably as a handsome, well-mannered, black star in the rapidly expanding world of professional tennis:

1970—$140,000
1971—$350,000
1972—$500,000 plus

Ashe landed endorsement deals with AMF Head rackets, Bufferin, Volvo, and Benefit cereal. He and Jeanne and their daughter, Camera, born in 1986, made their home in Mount Kisco, New York. He also served as the head tennis pro at the Doral Resort and Country Club in Miami.

As a humanitarian, social activist, philanthropist, broadcaster, author of an acclaimed three-volume series on African American athletes, *A Hard Road to Glory*, and tennis Hall of Famer, Ashe casts a giant shadow. A memorial statue of Ashe—with a tennis racket in one hand and books in the other as a group of children literally look up to him—stands on Monument Avenue in his hometown of Richmond, where only statues of confederate generals had stood. On June 22, 2019, a 2.4-mile street in Richmond formerly known as Route 161 was renamed Arthur Ashe Boulevard. Because of Ashe's on-court triumphs, any African American male player who shows any promise is invariably questioned by fans and media as to whether he may be "the next Arthur Ashe." James Blake, who rose to No. 4 in the world without winning a major title, heard those questions. As did such solid professionals as MaliVai Washington, Bryan Shelton, and Rodney Harmon. Washington remains the last African American male to reach a major final, losing in the 1996 Wimbledon final to hard-serving Richard Krajicek of the Netherlands. Washington said he heard plenty of "next Ashe" questions, but he did not consider them a burden.

"I never looked at them that way at all," Washington said from Jacksonville, Florida, where he founded an eponymous youth foundation and owns a real estate company. "I was honored to be compared to Arthur. I wish I had had half the tennis career that he had. What's even more significant to me was the success he was able to have on the tour in the era he was able to have it. For many of those years, black people were not necessarily welcomed on tennis courts in a lot of places. For him to be dealing with that in the 1960s was a burden in itself. For him to succeed in spite of that was admirable. But what I liked about Arthur wasn't necessarily his tennis accomplishments, but how he viewed his role—as a citizen, as a professional tennis player, as a humanitarian—and how he used his celebrity for the greater good. That is not something many athletes and nonathletes feel comfortable doing. [Basketball star] LeBron James is one who does it today, but there aren't many."

At a hastily arranged news conference on April 8, 1992, the world learned the shocking news that Ashe had contracted the virus that causes AIDS (Acquired Immune Deficiency Syndrome). Ashe called the news conference to get out in front of a story that *USA Today* was about to break. He wanted the public to find out this information on his terms. Through a transfusion of tainted blood in June 1981 (he also underwent a transfusion in December 1979), Ashe had contracted the virus. He tested positive for AIDS in September 1988 after undergoing brain surgery. At the time, only family members and a few close friends, including Cliff Drysdale, had known. "We were at a tournament together, preparing to broadcast a match for ABC," Drysdale said. "Arthur said, 'There's something I've got to tell you.' I said, 'Oh, geez, Arthur, don't tell me you're having heart problems again.' Then he told me about his condition. I was mortified. It was just awful."

Ashe had been blindsided by a phone call from a longtime friend, Doug Smith, a respected sports journalist and author. Ashe and Smith, African Americans from Virginia, used to compete against each other in ATA junior tournaments. Smith called seeking confirmation about a tip he had received about Ashe's condition. Ashe confirmed the news for Smith, but asked to speak with Smith's editor before the story ran. Ashe then tried to persuade *USA Today* sports editor Gene Policinski to respect his privacy and not run the story. He did not want the public to see him differently or treat him differently, or pity him, because he had AIDS. After Policinski told him that the story would be published, Ashe became an activist for yet another vital cause. In his final year, he founded the Arthur Ashe Foundation for the Defeat of AIDS. The AAFDA raised more than $5 million by the end of 1993, which was allocated for AIDS awareness and education as well as organizations devoted to AIDS research, clinical trials, and patient support. An August 1992 AAFDA fund-raiser at the National Tennis Center on the weekend before the U.S. Open has become Arthur Ashe Kids' Day, an annual event that continues to raise public awareness about AIDS while celebrating the life of a man devoted to education, activism, and social justice.

On September 9, 1992, Ashe was arrested outside the White House, protesting alongside such groups as the NAACP, the United States Commission on Human Rights, and TransAfrica in support of Haitians seeking asylum in the United States. The U.S. government had shown a stark difference in the way it treated light-skinned Cubans fleeing their island, then ruled by Fidel Castro, compared to brown-skinned Haitians yearning to escape violence on their island. Such injustice Ashe could not abide. On the day of his arrest, he wore a T-shirt that read HAITIANS LOCKED OUT BECAUSE THEY'RE BLACK. The word HAITIANS was superimposed onto an American map. Throughout his life, Ashe never stopped trying to make America live up to its creed: "liberty and justice for all." He did his utmost to try to make the world a better place and convince us that we should follow his lead.

Ashe died on February 6, 1993. The official cause of death was pneumonia. He was only forty-nine years old. An exemplary life ended far too soon. However, it must have provided some comfort to Ashe's family that his prodigious accomplishments were both recognized and celebrated during his lifetime, and he remains an iconic figure in American history. Sadly, the same cannot be said for the first black major tennis champion, Althea Gibson. Ashe once said of her, "As good as she was, she was the only great U.S. champion I know who had financial problems. If she were white, there's no question she would have been helped."

5 | Althea Gibson

> I was playing with a black player who
> the audience didn't really want to see.
>
> ANGELA BUXTON

On September 1, the middle Saturday of the 2018 U.S. Open, Katrina Adams, the first black president and chair of the U.S. Tennis Association, held a news conference at the National Tennis Center to announce a commemoration long overdue.

"My board of directors agreed to allow us to erect a monument of some sort to Althea Gibson to commemorate her greatness," said Adams, who had used her powers of persuasion to convince the board. "In our sport, she was the one who really broke the color barrier. She is the Jackie Robinson of tennis."

Gibson stepped onto a tennis court on August 28, 1950, at the West Side Tennis Club in Queens and ended major tennis's exclusion of black talent. The historic act occurred three and a half years after Robinson's debut at first base for the Brooklyn Dodgers ended Major League Baseball's exclusion of blacks. Gibson became a trailblazer for black tennis players more than a decade before Arthur Ashe. However, Ashe—eloquent, engaging, and well-mannered—became far better known to tennis fans and media and far more respected in the tennis community. It is, regrettably, a byproduct of a patriarchal society that a man is often revered for accomplishments that a woman had done first. But the disparate treatment by the tennis establishment of trailblazers Gibson and Ashe has gone, well, beyond the pale. It is not that Gibson did anything particularly offensive before, during, or after her Hall of Fame career. The problem has been that the tennis community has never truly appreciated Gibson for who she was and what she accomplished. Fortunately, Adams has ensured that Gibson will receive a modicum of the recognition she is due, albeit posthumously.

"She's very important to our society, in our sport," Adams said, "particularly back in the '50s, to be able to pave the road and provide pathways for [black players such as] Arthur Ashe, Zina Garrison, Lori McNeil, Chanda Rubin, Venus, and Serena, myself and others to be where we are today."

Joining Adams for the announcement were Eric Goulder, the sculptor commissioned to create a statue of Gibson, scheduled to be unveiled in August 2019, and Ben Doller, a board member of the USTA Foundation and the chairman of Sotheby's. Headquartered in New York, Sotheby's is among the world's largest brokers of fine and decorative art, jewelry, real estate, and collectibles. Doller compiled a list of potential sculptors for the project, and the USTA board, guided by his informed artistic eye, chose Goulder.

"Eric is one of the best figurative and modernist sculptors out there," Doller said. "One has to be careful when you're talking figurative, so that it doesn't look almost sort of machine-made, but that it really is art."

The USTA needed to get this one right. A bronze sculpture commemorating Ashe that now stands outside the National Tennis Center's No. 1 court has been panned by many for resembling a naked sumo wrestler. After all her years of public neglect, Gibson did not need a statue that would draw comparisons to the one created in tribute to comedienne Lucille Ball by her hometown of Jamestown, New York—a statue that literally frightened children and prompted a do-over because it had become known as "Scary Lucy."

The Gibson commemorative consists of more than a statue. There is also an interactive element, allowing visitors to watch footage of Gibson in action and hear from the woman herself. Visitors will notice Gibson's usual preferred choice of tennis attire—a shirt, vest, and shorts with a belt, rather than a dress or a skirt. They will also notice her clear and throaty voice, much like that of a jazz singer, a line of work in which she dabbled after her tennis career. They may also notice her aggressive serve-and-volley style of play. She was a net rusher who pressured her opponents. She preferred to finish points herself rather than wait for someone else's error. Despite playing in an era when the server had to keep one foot on the court at all times, she possessed a powerful and versatile serve. When she wanted, she could put enough spin on her serve to yank an opponent off court, leaving plenty of open space to win the point with a finishing volley. At five feet, eleven inches tall and 145 pounds, Gibson's size and style of play were quite rare in women's tennis in the 1950s. Today her playing style, but not her height, would still be rare. Her impact on tennis actually extended far beyond how she looked and what she wore. How she performed after tennis's gatekeepers finally allowed her inside the sport's biggest venues truly distinguished her. Perhaps the finest all-around female athlete of her generation, Gibson starred in tennis and basketball at Florida A&M University. She also became the first black player on the Ladies Professional Golf Association tour in 1963—at the age of thirty-seven.

Can a statue capture all that? Goulder, who promised to put his own spin on the piece, said the project "got me thinking of how I could approach a sculpture of a sporting figure in a new way instead of just a figurine, and also make something that doesn't just memorialize her, but also tells more of her story."

The only sign at the 2018 U.S. Open that Gibson ever existed was a plaque near the tennis center's south entrance, in a section called the Court of Champions. There, a gold-plated Gibson plaque with a black-and-white photo of her on court accompanied by a biographical paragraph rests alongside nearly two dozen plaques of other greats including Ashe, Billie Jean King, Rod Laver, Martina Navratilova,

Chris Evert, John McEnroe, Andre Agassi, and Steffi Graf. At some point during the next decade, plaques commemorating Serena and Venus undoubtedly will appear in the Court of Champions as well.

But if you entered the 2018 U.S. Open through a different gate and never ventured near the south entrance, then you would not have seen Gibson at all. That in itself was a shame considering that Gibson grew up in the Harlem section of Manhattan, less than a ten-mile drive from the National Tennis Center. When she debuted at the U.S. Nationals in 1950, she traveled to Forest Hills on the New York City subway from a Harlem brownstone she shared during the tournament's fortnight with her friend Rhoda Smith, against whom she competed in the black-led American Tennis Association. The easy angle of "local girl makes good" has been lost on the USTA. There is no court named for Gibson at the U.S. Open. Nor is there a trophy named for her that could be presented to the winner in singles, doubles, mixed doubles, or the junior competition.

In 2007 the U.S. Open devoted its opening night to Gibson, who had died four years earlier. Aretha Franklin, the legendary "Queen of Soul," performed, and Venus and Serena, tennis legends in the making, were the headliners in the singles matches. Of course, both Williams sisters won. However, the USTA did not inform Gibson's surviving relatives in Montclair, New Jersey, barely an hour's drive from the tennis center, about Althea Gibson Night. They had to learn about the event from a local sports journalist. A plaque with ALTHEA in block letters was displayed at both ends of the court while Aretha sang and Venus and Serena played. But the plaque was removed after opening night, and it has not been seen at the tournament again.

Finally, however, a Gibson statue exists on the grounds, sculpted in clay and cast in bronze and some elements of stone. It would be fitting if the Gibson memorial becomes a destination point at the tennis center, a place for selfies and self-education as well as reflection about an unsung star.

Gibson was born into poverty on August 25, 1927, on a cotton plantation in Silver, South Carolina. When she was three, her parents,

Daniel and Annie, moved the family to New York City in search of a better life. The Gibsons and their five children—Althea and sisters Millie, Annie, and Lillian, and her brother, Daniel Jr.—relocated to Harlem, known then as the mecca of black America. Because of racial segregation, Harlem was home to the elite, the middle class, and the poor. The Gibsons were in the last group. Daniel Gibson Sr. struggled to find work to support his large family, but eventually landed a job as a garage attendant on the night shift. The family lived in a third-floor apartment on 135 West 143rd Street, between Sixth and Seventh Avenues. The local Police Athletic League designated Althea's block as a play street during the summer, which closed the street to vehicular traffic and gave neighborhood kids a chance to frolic in an area where grass fields did not exist. Actually, Althea did not need a designated time and place to play. She found places to play on her own, especially when she was supposed to be in school. She became a truant. Instead of reading, writing, and arithmetic, she fancied pool halls, bowling alleys, and jazz clubs. She also didn't back down from a fight, particularly in defense of a sibling. "Nobody dared pick on us when we were kids," Daniel Gibson Jr. said. "Althea could beat up anyone. When she was only thirteen, she reached up and gave a black eye to a six-footer who had said something about me that she didn't like."

Having a play street on the block came as a relief to Althea's parents because it kept her in their sights more often. One summer morning, Althea came barreling down the three stories of stairs, stepped outside, and spotted something that would change her life. "I saw two bats and a sponge rubber ball lying on the ground," she recalled. "So, this friend of mine, who I called in those days, my 'boon coon,' because we played together, we started hitting the ball back and forth and it got good to us. So, we would anticipate every summer morning being the first on the paddle tennis court—practicing, hitting balls, enjoying it. As a matter of fact, it got to where we owned the paddle tennis court. Nobody could get on the court but us."

Althea's paddle tennis prowess caught the eye of Buddy Walker, a local musician and bandleader who worked as a supervisor on the play street to earn extra cash. He gave her a secondhand tennis racket with real strings and had her hit a ball repeatedly against the wall of a handball court. The rhythm and force of Althea's hitting impressed Walker enough to contact a friend at the Cosmopolitan Tennis Club on 149th Street and Convent Avenue. Althea's raw talent was due for an upgrade. Paddle tennis was for the street; tennis was for the elite.

Even unrefined athletic ability is an impressive sight. The doctors, lawyers, educators, religious leaders, businesspeople, and their spouses who composed the membership of the Cosmopolitan club were so enamored with Althea that they helped her find a coach who would not charge the family for lessons. Fred Johnson, a one-armed tennis enthusiast, taught her the basics of the serve and how to hit using the continental grip whether she was striking the ball from the forehand or backhand side. On public courts near the Harlem River on 150th Street and Seventh Avenue, courts that today bear his name, Johnson taught Althea as much as he knew about tennis. The Cosmopolitan club members also paid her annual membership fee of $7 and signed her up for ATA junior tournaments. School was still as unfamiliar as a desert to the teenage Althea, but every day she worked hard and advanced her education in tennis. Finally, she had found an activity at which she was good that would not get her into trouble.

At age fifteen, Althea won her first tennis title, the ATA New York State Junior Championship, at the Cosmopolitan club. In the final, she defeated Nina Irwin, a fifteen-year-old Jewish girl from Manhattan. Althea created a buzz about her potential throughout the national ATA network of clubs and the historically black colleges and universities where ATA tournaments were often held. At one such school, Central State University in Wilberforce, Ohio, Althea competed in the 1946 ATA final against Roumania Peters, at the time a student at Tuskegee Institute in Alabama and already half of a dominant doubles team with her sister, Margaret. Althea lost the match in three tough sets but commanded the attention of two prominent men in ATA circles—Dr. Robert Walter Johnson of Lynchburg, Virginia, and Dr. Hubert Eaton of Wilmington, North Carolina. They saw something special in Althea's athleticism, speed, quickness, power, and determination. She tried to crush the ball with every stroke, and tennis strategy was largely foreign to her, but those flaws could be corrected through better coaching. She lacked refinement in her tennis game and her comportment, but again, Johnson and Eaton saw those as easy fixes if Althea was willing to work at them.

The doctors offered Althea a Pygmalion deal for which she would not have to pay a cent: she could live with Eaton's family during the academic months and, in effect, attend finishing school to gain a formal education and learn social graces, and then live at Johnson's home in the summer, where he had a clay court in the backyard, and attend his ATA junior development program. Althea took the deal. She entered Williston Industrial High School as a sophomore and graduated tenth in her class. At Florida A&M University (FAMU) in Tallahassee, she earned a bachelor's degree in physical education. "From what I heard, she was quite the pool shark too," said Alvin Hollins, the sports information director at FAMU. "When the basketball team went on the road, she would look for a pool hall. A lot of guys, with their male egos, didn't think there was any way a woman could beat them. She showed those guys. They would walk away saying, 'Man, that chick can play.'" An even longer list of her tennis opponents could have said the same about Althea, especially on the ATA circuit. Her loss to Roumania Peters at Central State would be her last against a black woman in a competitive match.

Althea won the ATA national championship a record ten consecutive years. She teamed with Johnson to win the ATA championship in mixed doubles seven times, and she was a major force in women's doubles with whomever she wanted to partner. It was perfectly clear to everyone who watched Althea that she was too good for the ATA, and good enough to merit an opportunity to compete against the best white players at the four Grand Slam events—Wimbledon, and the U.S., French, and Australian Nationals. Johnson, as he would do a decade later on behalf of Arthur Ashe, lobbied the United States Lawn Tennis Association, respectfully but persistently, to try to pry open the doors to the white-run tournaments for Althea. Yet the gatekeepers were obstinate. To Althea and her many ATA supporters, she needed only an opportunity to prove herself on the biggest stages. Whenever she spoke to her tennis peers, she never lacked confidence. "I saw a lot of Althea back then, and she was tough," said Robert Ryland, a former ATA champion. "The way Muhammad Ali used to call himself 'The Greatest,' Althea used to talk about herself that way. You didn't hear any other women talking about themselves the way Althea did."

Despite the best efforts of Johnson and the rest of the ATA community, Althea still had the gates closed to her. She needed a sponsor, a white sponsor, to whom the gatekeepers would actually listen. She soon had one in Alice Marble, then the world's top-ranked player. By 1944, Marble, a four-time U.S. Nationals champion and the 1939 Wimbledon champion, had heard about Althea through the tennis grapevine. She sought to find out more. In 1944 Marble and British star Mary Hardwick played an unprecedented mixed doubles exhibition match with ATA stars Ryland and Dr. Reginald Weir at the Cosmopolitan Tennis Club. Afterward, over drinks, Marble inquired about Althea. "Alice asked me if I thought Althea could make it in the major tournaments, and I said that she definitely had the talent to do it," Ryland said. "I told her Althea was strong and had a good head for the game. She just lacked the experience, that's all." Change hardly came swiftly to major tennis. Efforts to eradicate racial discrimination never do. But by 1950, Major League Baseball, the National Football League, and the National Basketball Association had been integrated. Furthermore, white fans of boxing, a hugely popular sport at the time, had become used to seeing black world champions such as heavyweight Joe Louis and middleweight Sugar Ray Robinson. So, in 1950, Marble opted for public shaming of the tennis establishment. She had not yet met Althea, but she penned an open letter in the June issue of the influential *American Lawn Tennis Magazine* to lobby for racial inclusion.

"If tennis is a sport for ladies and gentlemen, it's also time we acted a little more like gentle people and less like sanctimonious hypocrites," Marble wrote. "If there is anything left in the name of sportsmanship, it's more than time to display what it means to us. If Althea Gibson represents a challenge to the present crop of women players, it's only fair that they should meet that challenge.... The entrance of Negroes into national tennis is as inevitable as it has proven to be in baseball, in football, and in boxing."

A confluence of factors—strong advocacy from the ATA, the Marble letter, and a somewhat more enlightened public—compelled the USLTA to finally let Althea play. In 1950 she competed first in a tournament at the Orange Lawn Tennis Club in East Orange, New Jersey, and then in other USLTA-sanctioned events. Her performances made it impossible for the USLTA to deny her one of the fifty-two slots reserved for women at the U.S. Nationals. At the age of twenty-three, Althea made her major tournament debut. As one New York newspaper reporter wrote, "In many ways, it's an even tougher Jim Crow-busting assignment than was Jackie Robinson's when he stepped out of the Brooklyn Dodgers' dugout. It's always tougher for a woman."

Althea controlled her nerves in her U.S. Nationals debut and unleashed her potent serve-and-volley game to defeat Barbara Knapp of England, 6-2, 6-2. She next faced Louise Brough, the three-time Wimbledon champion and the 1947 U.S. Nationals champion. In a compelling rollercoaster of a match, Althea led, 1-6, 6-3, 7-6, before a violent thunderstorm toppled one of the stone eagles near the court and postponed play until the following day. (In those days, tiebreaks did not exist. A player had to win each set by at least two games.) Althea could not find her groove the next day, dropping all three games and the match, 9-7. But she had sent an unmistakable message to the tennis world that a black player could compete favorably at tennis's highest level.

Although she had become a fixture in major tennis in the 1950s, and other blacks from the ATA circuit, including Ryland and Weir, had joined her at the U.S. Nationals, Gibson did not take over women's tennis right away. She faced such indignities as being denied entry into the women's locker room at some venues, having to instead change her wardrobe in a car, and she had to get used to dining alone at many tournaments. If she did not always face overt racism from the stands, she often was greeted with coldness or indifference by spectators. But the indignity that may have hurt her the most came from the USLTA. In that era, the U.S. Nationals singles and doubles championships were played in two different cities—the singles at Forest Hills in New York, the doubles at Longwood Cricket Club in Boston. Players had to be invited to each event. Even though Gibson began competing in singles at the U.S. Nationals in 1950 and had achieved a world top ten ranking by 1952, she was not invited to the U.S. Nationals doubles event until 1957, when she had reached world No. 1 in singles and was a national sensation. Considering Althea's prowess in women's doubles and mixed doubles, the racist decision by the USLTA to bar her from the annual doubles event in Boston for the first seven years of her career in major tennis denied her the opportunity to win as many as fourteen additional major titles. She won eleven majors in her career—five in singles, five in doubles, and one in mixed doubles.

As for Gibson's game, she covered the court better than any of the other women, and her serve-and-volley style proved formidable. But in her early years in major tennis, her strokes were not as technically proficient or consistent as those of the top white players—Brough, Shirley Fry, Doris Hart, Nancy Chafee, and Maureen Connolly, who in 1953 became the first woman to win the Grand Slam. Gibson's world rankings in singles were impressive—No. 9 in 1952, No. 7 in 1953, No. 13 in 1954. But the black media wanted more. She never called herself "the Jackie Robinson of tennis." Indeed, she bristled from such comparisons. But others so labeled her, and they were disappointed when she did not immediately dominate in tennis as Robinson had in baseball. *Jet* magazine, a popular black weekly, labeled Gibson "the biggest disappointment in tennis." Also, tennis was an amateur sport, and Gibson was not getting the kind of under-the-table payments to appear in tournaments as the top male players. To earn a living, she taught physical education at Lincoln University in Jefferson City, Missouri. A male friend there encouraged her to quit tennis and join the Women's Auxiliary Air Corps. She might have done it had she not reconnected with an old friend from her ATA days, Sydney Llewellyn, who convinced her to stick with tennis. Llewellyn, a Jamaican-born

New Yorker, became her coach and improved her strategic approach to the game. He also changed her grip from the continental to the eastern grip, which improved her racket control. She also added more topspin and slice to her game, which made her less predictable and less prone to errors.

Gibson's game flourished when she was invited by the State Department to take part in a goodwill tour in 1955 that allowed her to compete in tournaments in India, Ceylon, Pakistan, and Burma. The tour's main objective was to try to improve America's image abroad because the world had begun to see media reports about the mistreatment of black Americans in their own country. Having a black woman as part of the tour allowed the State Department to put a positive spin on race relations. Joining Gibson on the tour were white players Karol Fageros, Hamilton Richardson, and Bob Perry. While on tour, Gibson won nine consecutive tournaments and fifteen of eighteen during an eight-month period. When she entered the 1956 French Nationals, she was ready to slay.

Three months shy of her twenty-ninth birthday, Gibson defeated Britain's Angela Mortimer in the final, 6–0, 12–10, for her first major title. She also won the doubles title alongside another Englishwoman, Angela Buxton, who became a lifelong friend. "Neither of us had partners and we were very friendly, so we decided to try it together," said Buxton, who had been ostracized by other British players because of her Jewish faith. "My British peers felt that something was a little off. They didn't say anything. At the very most, they raised their eyebrows because I was playing with an American, and particularly a black American."

The two tennis outsiders decided to play doubles together again three weeks later at Wimbledon. Gibson got a decidedly frosty reception from the spectators. Wrote Scottie Hall of London's *Sunday Graphic* newspaper, "Shame on the Centre Court. I accuse the Wimbledon crowd of showing bias against Miss Gibson. . . . It wasn't anything that was whispered. It wasn't anything that was shouted. . . . It was just an atmosphere, tight-lipped, cold." Buxton felt the same chill when she and Gibson took the court in doubles. "When the tennis world saw Althea and me on court together, they were flabbergasted," Buxton said. "I was playing with a black player who the audience didn't really want to see." Although Gibson lost to Fry in the semifinals in singles, she and Buxton won the doubles championship for their second major title as a team.

What did the British press say about Gibson becoming the first black player ever to win a title on Wimbledon grass? "Not a lot," Buxton said. "Looking back on it, it was as if the press felt, 'Maybe she'll go away.' When we won the doubles title, there was in one of our major papers in England a small column in thin type, 'Minorities Win.' That was it."

Winning the French Nationals in singles and two more major titles in doubles placed Gibson among the game's elite in 1956. But to the casual sports fan, she had yet to break through. The two tennis tournaments that garnered the biggest headlines in the United States were Wimbledon and the U.S. Nationals. Gibson fell short in her first U.S. Nationals final in 1956, losing to Fry, 6–3, 6–4. She would never fall short again on her sport's two grandest stages, which proved inspirational to a future legend. "She had great presence, and I could tell the other women were intimidated by her," said Billie Jean King, who first saw Gibson play in 1956 when King was thirteen. "With her wingspan, power, and shot production, she was awesome. She mixed power and spin and had great placement. She seemed to glide on the court."

On July 6, 1957, the afternoon of the Wimbledon women's final, the Centre Court temperature measured ninety-six degrees Fahrenheit. Gibson was even hotter. Within minutes she led 4–0, and she routed Californian Darlene Hard, 6–3, 6–2. "Althea Gibson fulfilled her destiny at Wimbledon today and became the first member of her race to rule the world of tennis"—so began the *New York Times* article. Adding more distinction to Gibson's triumph, Queen Elizabeth made her first appearance on Centre Court to present the golden championship plate, the Venus Rosewater Dish. "At last! At last!" Gibson exclaimed as she held the plate aloft amid cordial applause from the crowd. Gibson later teamed with Hard to win the Wimbledon doubles crown as well. (Gibson played with Hard because Buxton suffered a wrist injury that eventually ended her tennis career.)

When Gibson returned home she received a ticker tape parade up Broadway, from Battery Park to City Hall, an area known as the Canyon of Heroes, and she received a key to New York City from Mayor Robert Wagner. "If there were more wonderful people like you, the world would be a better place," Wagner told the crowd. Gibson remains the only black woman to receive her own ticker tape parade along the Canyon of Heroes. She achieved yet another rarity for a black woman: she graced the cover of *Time* magazine on August 26, 1957, accompanied by the article, "That Gibson Girl." But closer to her heart, three thousand people greeted her when she returned to her childhood home on West 143rd Street in Harlem. Apartment buildings along the block were adorned with streamers, and a WELCOME HOME banner extended across the street.

Cementing her status as the best female player in the world, Gibson overwhelmed Brough, 6–3, 6–2, to win her first U.S. Nationals crown. Vice President Richard Nixon presented Gibson with the trophy. Weeks before, she appeared as the mystery guest on the popular CBS quiz show *What's My Line?* The panelists wore eye masks, but easily guessed her identity. When Gibson came out, the studio audience did not applaud wildly, so the panelists knew she was not a star in movies or on television. When journalist and panelist Dorothy Kilgallen asked if Gibson was in athletics and the answer was yes, the game was over. There were very few recognizable female athletes in 1957, and the sport for which a woman would most likely be recognized was tennis.

Gibson's star continued to ascend in 1958, as she successfully defended her titles at Wimbledon and the U.S. Nationals. At Wimbledon, she defeated Britain's Angela Mortimer in the final, 8–6, 6–2, and then partnered with Brazil's Maria Bueno to win the doubles crown. That made Gibson the first woman in tennis history to win three consecutive Wimbledon doubles titles with three different partners. In the U.S. Nationals final, she rallied to subdue Hard, 3–6, 6–1, 6–2. Gibson had become a full-fledged celebrity. Society columns in the black press ran stories of her attending parties with heads of state and business leaders. Always an enthusiastic singer, she released an album of jazz and blues standards, *Althea Gibson Sings*, for Dot Records. On May 25, 1958, she sang "Around the World" on CBS's highly rated Sunday night program *The Ed Sullivan Show*. She had a small and stereotypical part as a servant girl in *The Horse Soldiers*, a 1958 film about the Civil War starring John Wayne and William Holden.

Gibson had fame. But fame combined with indigence is a cruel twist of fate. For that reason, she retired from amateur tennis in 1958. "I am still a poor Negress," she told a New York newspaper, "as poor as when I was picked off the streets of Harlem and given a chance to work myself up to stardom. I have traveled to many countries, in Europe, in Asia, in Africa, in comfort. I have stayed in the best hotels and met many rich people. I am much richer in knowledge and experience. But I have no money."

Unfortunately for Gibson, she was also at odds with the press. A number of journalists, particularly black journalists, found her gruff and standoffish. That she was unwilling to speak out on behalf of the civil rights movement and steadfastly refused to regard her tennis victories as triumphs for her race kept the black media from ever embracing her. Wrote Russ Cowans of the *Chicago Defender*, an influential black newspaper, "Instead of presenting Althea with a trophy, the Queen [of England] would have done the field of sports a real service if she had given her a few words of advice on graciousness." Columnist Wendell Smith from the black-owned *Pittsburgh Courier*, who was a tireless advocate for integrating Major League Baseball in the 1940s, harshly criticized Gibson for "her curt manner and insulting responses to friendly writers of all papers in Chicago." Lee Fischer, a white reporter for the white-owned *Chicago American*, wrote, "Someone ought to tell Althea that graciousness is as much a quality of a real champion as the ability to play the game well." The white-owned *New York Post* wrote this about Gibson on September 1, 1957: "When a woman reporter asked if she was proud to be compared to Jackie Robinson, she said, 'No. I don't consider myself to be a representative of my people. I am thinking of me and nobody else.'"

Gibson chose to fire back only at her critics in the black press in her 1958 autobiography (with writer Ed Fitzgerald), *I Always Wanted to Be Somebody*: "I have always enjoyed a good press among the regular American newspapers and magazines, but I am uncomfortably close to being Public Enemy No. 1 to some sections of the Negro press. I have, they have said, an unbecoming attitude. They say I'm bigheaded, uppity, ungrateful, and a few other uncomplimentary things. I don't think any white writer ever has said anything like that about me, but quite a few Negro writers have, and I think the deep-down reason for it is that they resent my refusal to turn my tennis achievements into a rousing crusade for racial equality, brass band, seventy-six trombones, and all. I won't do it. I feel strongly that I can do more good my way than I could by militant crusading. I want my success to speak for itself as an advertisement for my race." (Gibson wrote a second autobiography with writer Richard Curtis, *So Much to Live For*, in 1968.)

Try as she did, and Gibson certainly tried, she was unable to turn her tennis fame into a reliable source of revenue. During the height of her tennis career, she had an endorsement deal with Henry C. Lee tennis rackets for $75 a month, and she received $25,000 a year to endorse Tip Top Bakeries bread. Abe Saperstein, the owner of the Harlem Globetrotters, offered her a deal reported at "nearly $100,000" in 1958 to travel as an opening act for the "clown princes of basketball." Karol Fageros, her friend and traveling companion on the State Department trip in 1955 and 1956, was paid $40,000 to be the opponent. A makeshift tennis court, not of regulation size, was placed over the basketball court, and Gibson won 114 of the 118 one-set matches. But Saperstein chose not to renew the contracts because of what he considered a lack of interest in the matches.

In 1960 Gibson played against Pauline Betz in an event called the World Pro Tennis Championships at Cleveland Arena. It bombed at the box office. Llewellyn, her coach, then persuaded Gibson to invest in a traveling series of exhibitions in which she played tennis and basketball. That, too, flopped at the box office. Her resources depleted, Gibson pursued a career in golf, a sport she had played for recreation at FAMU. She qualified for the Ladies Professional Golf Association tour in 1963. "I had to make a living; I had to make money to live, so I decided to give professional golf a fling," she said in an interview. Golf, like tennis, is a sport associated with the country club set. Gibson encountered racial prejudice on the women's tour as well. "There were tournaments where she wasn't even allowed to use the restrooms; she had to change her shoes in the car," said Renee Powell, who in 1967 became the second black woman on the LPGA tour.

Gibson played in 171 LPGA events from 1963 (when she was thirty-six years old) until 1977 and did not win any. Her best result was a second-place finish at the 1970 Immke Buick Open in Columbus, Ohio. Her total prize money from her golf career was $24,437. But Kathy Whitworth, who won a record eighty-eight tournaments (including six majors) in a Hall of Fame career, said that Gibson would have fared much better had she played golf seriously at an earlier age. "Time ran out on her," said Whitworth, a friend of Gibson's on the LPGA tour. "There's no question she would have been one of the greats otherwise."

The gates of the International Tennis Hall of Fame in Newport, Rhode Island, opened to Gibson in 1971. In an interview at the ITHF twenty-one years later, she told interviewer Bud Lessor that she was available to give tennis lessons for a fee and that she hoped to open a tennis academy. The tennis academy never came to fruition. Instead, she became the New Jersey state athletic commissioner in 1975. But she resigned two years later, saying, "I don't wish to be a figurehead."

Gibson married twice, but some have said those relationships were more platonic than romantic. William Darben, her husband from 1965 to 1976, supported her financially during her tennis and golf careers, and was considered her dearest male friend. Sydney Llewellyn, her former coach, a man two decades older, was her husband from 1984 to 1988. He was a Jamaican national living in New York, and some speculated that the marriage was arranged to make him a U.S. citizen.

Shortly after Gibson's job teaching sports to children through the New Jersey Commission on Physical Fitness was eliminated in 1990 because of state budget cuts, a profound sense of loneliness beset her. On August 3, 1995, she phoned Angela Buxton, then living in Florida. "She said, 'I can't cope,'" Buxton recalled. "'I've got all these bills—they're hitting the ceiling. I'm not feeling well. I haven't got any more money. As you know, I wasn't able to save very much. I can't pay the rent. I can't buy food. I never had health insurance. I need medication, and I'm not able to buy it. So, the easiest way is to do away with myself.'"

Buxton helped Gibson financially, and she told her tennis friends, including journalist Bud Collins and *Inside Tennis* editor Matt Cronin, about Gibson's plight. Money began to pour in, more than $1 million all told, from the tennis community and fans around the world. Unfortunately, Gibson's health continued to decline. She suffered a stroke in 1995 and a heart attack in 2003. She died on September 28, 2003, in East Orange, New Jersey, at the age of seventy-six. The official cause of death was pneumonia.

Frances Clayton Gray, a devoted friend of Gibson's for more than thirty years, now manages her estate. Gray said that Gibson told her after the outpouring of public affection and generous contributions, "Now, I know that people love me." Gray served on the committee assembled by Adams and the USTA to create what they promised would be a fitting memorial to a legend who would be so incredibly rich if she played today, a legend whose trailblazing life was marked by such unprecedented triumph and insurmountable sadness that no one interested in tennis should ever have to ask, "Why didn't I know about her?"

6 | U.S. Open Money

> When you win you can earn a lot of money,
> but you also spend a lot of money.
>
> HEATHER WATSON

A Brink's truck would be needed to carry all the money that Althea Gibson could have made in tennis today with her eleven major titles, including five in singles, five in women's doubles, and one in mixed doubles, as well as her world No. 1 ranking in singles for two years running. Because of the efforts of pioneers such as Gibson and Arthur Ashe, and global superstars like Serena and Venus Williams, tennis has a more diverse fan base than ever. That is why the revenues for Grand Slam events such as the U.S. Open continue to rise. The 2018 U.S. Open generated approximately $350 million—the most of any tennis event in history—according to *Forbes* magazine.

A major reason for the rise has been the $600 million face lift that the USTA Billie Jean King National Tennis Center underwent in this decade. In 2016 a retractable roof was built over Arthur Ashe Stadium, which ensured that no day of play would be rained out and the global networks that televise the event would always have live matches to show. Players say the roof has also reduced the wind currents at the stadium, which used to wreak havoc on matches. However, some players now complain about the humidity when the roof is open. After twenty-time Grand Slam champion Roger Federer of Switzerland lost in a shocking fourth-round upset to Australia's John Millman, he said that he found it difficult to breathe on court. Novak Djokovic, the 2018 U.S. Open champion from Serbia, and American quarterfinalist John Isner agreed with Federer, so the USTA may need to make some modifications at Ashe.

However, there have been no complaints about the 8,125-seat grandstand, which debuted as the U.S. Open's No. 3 court in 2017. A fabric canopy surrounds two-thirds of the grandstand, ensuring that nearly every seat is in the shade during day matches. Perhaps the most raved-about feature at the 2018 Open was the renovated Louis Armstrong Stadium. At a cost of $200 million, Armstrong seats fourteen thousand, has a retractable roof, and offers great sight lines.

The two-week U.S. Open generates more revenue for New York City each year than any other sporting event. According to David Dinkins, New York City's first African American mayor from 1990 to 1993 and a current USTA board member, a 2013 study of the U.S. Open's economic impact showed that the tournament added more to the city's coffers each year than baseball's New York Yankees and New York Mets, football's New York Giants and New York Jets (both teams actually play in New Jersey), hockey's New York Rangers and New York Islanders, and basketball's New York Knicks combined. (Basketball's Brooklyn Nets were the New Jersey Nets in 2013 and not part of the equation.) So how does the Open bring in so much money? Tennis attracts a wealthier fan base with more disposable income than fans of other sports. Those who visit New York for the Open almost always book hotel rooms in Manhattan, where the rates are among the most expensive in the world. A room costing more than $400 a night in Manhattan is quite common. Those who can afford that rate also spend top dollar at Manhattan's restaurants and shops, and they do it day after day after day.

Fans visiting the Open also pay handsomely for meals on site and souvenirs. Fifty dollars for a U.S. Open T-shirt is the norm. As the big spenders keep the cash registers humming at the tournament, the sport's superstars are being paid more than ever.

The 2018 men's and women's champions each received a record-setting payout of $3.8 million. The runners-up received $1,850,000 each. A loser in the semifinal round received $925,000. Each quarterfinal-round loser got $475,000. A fourth-round loser took home $266,000, a third-round loser $156,000, a second-round loser $93,000, and a player who lost in the first round received $54,000. There was also equal prize money in men's doubles and women's doubles, where every match is a best-of-three-set affair. The championship team split $700,000. Each team that lost in the first round split $16,500. In mixed doubles, the champions split $155,000. Every team ousted in the first round split $5,000. The payout in mixed doubles is comparatively low because so few stars compete in the event nowadays. Why should a marketable tennis star run the risk of getting injured in mixed doubles when there is so much more money to be made in singles? It used to be a given that the top women and men in singles would also compete in doubles. Not anymore. The pursuit of bigger paychecks in singles tennis has convinced nearly all of the elite players to bypass the doubles. Fans who watch doubles tennis at the professional level still see a high quality of play; the matches are competitive and often exciting. But do not expect to see Federer or Spain's Rafael Nadal or Serena or Venus in too many doubles matches at major events. The stars are saving their bodies for singles.

While the tennis elite get richer, other players find the U.S. Open fortnight more of a financial challenge. Players must pay for their own transportation to New York, as well as their own lodging and any meals outside of the National Tennis Center. U.S. Open players and journalists covering the event can get a discounted rate (still more than $300 a night) at the tournament's official hotel, the Grand Hyatt, on Forty-Second Street on Manhattan's East Side, or at another hotel with which the USTA has cut a deal. But even a discounted hotel room does not make a dollar stretch far enough for a tennis pro who is not among the elite.

Sachia Vickery, an African American player who lives in Miramar, Florida, ended 2018 ranked No. 103 in the world. She shuns Manhattan whenever she plays at the U.S. Open. Instead, she stays with a friend in the Jamaica section of Queens, not far from the National Tennis Center. Each pro who competed at the 2018 U.S. Open received a per diem of $400. It makes more sense for a player like Vickery to save those dollars rather than splurge on a Manhattan hotel and meals at four-star restaurants. "I prefer to stay close to the tennis center because the trip back and forth is much easier, and Manhattan is expensive and crowded," said Vickery, who is twenty-three years old. "Manhattan is too hectic. It's overwhelming."

In today's brand of women's tennis, Vickery is an undersized player at five foot four, but her speed and tenacity make her a formidable competitor. Her tennis idols are Hall of Famer Martina Hingis, also an undersized player at a slender five foot six, and Venus and Serena, who are not undersized at all. "People have told me I'm too small, my game is not big enough, and I don't have any weapons," Vickery said. "But winning at this level is all about fighting for points. I'm quicker than a lot of girls on the tour, and I have that as a weapon." Vickery was born into sports. Her father, Rawle Vickery, was a pro soccer player. Her mother, Paula Liverpool, ran track in high school, and her brother, Dominique Mitchell, played college football at South Carolina State University. But Vickery does not come from a family of means. She was reared by her mother, a woman of Guyanese descent who came to America at age twenty, and her grandmother, Vilma Liverpool. Vickery began playing tennis with other kids in a local park, but the cost of equipment and travel to youth tournaments was often prohibitive. "My grandmother used to come to tournaments with me when I was younger because my mother was always working," Vickery said. "My mom was single, and she worked three jobs to keep me in tennis. It was very difficult early in my career because hiring a coach was too expensive." Although money was scarce, Vickery had the good fortune to meet Richard Williams, the father of Venus and Serena, when she was eight. "For three years, I trained with him sometimes, which was a big thrill because his daughters were my favorite players," Vickery said. "Even today, he gives me advice when I see him in Florida. He's very positive. He'll remind me that young girls are watching me and looking up to me. I used to be one of those young girls who looked up to Venus and Serena."

The Williams family has not assisted Vickery financially, nor has she asked. In 2013 she won the USTA girls' eighteen-and-under national championship, which earned her an automatic spot in the U.S. Open. There, she defeated veteran Mirjana Lucic-Baroni of Australia in the first round and cracked the world's top two hundred. Then her momentum stopped. For several years, she traveled the pro circuit alone because she could not afford a full-time coach. Her playing schedule became a combination of WTA tour events and smaller pro tournaments on what is known as the Challengers circuit, where total prize purses are in the range of $10,000–$20,000. How well she fared in one Challengers event would often determine if she could afford to play in the next one. "I would just practice here and there, but I didn't have any kind of structure," she said. The goal for Vickery is to play well enough on the Challengers circuit to achieve a world ranking well inside the top one hundred, which would enable her to play on the WTA tour full-time.

At Wimbledon 2018, Vickery began working informally with a British coach, Matthew Evans. She reached the second round, for which she pocketed $86,773 and improved her world ranking by seventy points. "It's going well," she said. "We've done a lot of work on the serve—that's been the main priority. He's also worked with me on a lot of strategic things on court, hitting high-percentage shots, things that I've never really worked on before." The work is paying off. In a hardcourt victory in 2018, Vickery slammed a career-high fifteen aces. "I'm adding to my game to become more of an all-around player," said Vickery, who had been known as a counterpuncher.

Were it not for one error that still bugs her, Vickery may have been able to afford a full-time coach immediately after the 2017 U.S. Open. She won three matches in the qualifying tournament that year to earn a spot in the 128-player main draw, and then won her first-round match. While holding a match point in the second round against fellow American Sofia Kenin, Vickery missed a swinging forehand volley with the court wide open. She ended up losing the match in a third-set tiebreak, 7–0. That defeat was the difference between an $86,000 payout for losing in round two and the $144,000 minimum she would have been paid for reaching the third round.

In March 2018, Vickery showed her considerable potential in the second round of the BNP Paribas Open in Indian Wells, California. She rallied from a set down and 0–3 in the second set to upset Garbiñe Muguruza of Spain, a former world No. 1 with major titles at Wimbledon and the French Open. "After I won my first game in the second set and the crowd saw how I was still fighting, they got behind me 100 percent," said Vickery, who won thirteen of the last sixteen games in a 2–6, 7–5, 6–1 victory. She celebrated the win on court by crossing her arms into an "X"—the Wakanda salute from *Black Panther*, an Academy Award–winning film that finished No. 1 at the box office in 2018. The image of Vickery's black empowerment pose went viral, attracting favorable attention from two of the movie's stars, Chadwick Boseman (who portrayed "Black Panther") and Letitia Wright (who, like Vickery, is of Guyanese heritage). Unfortunately, the pose also prompted some people to attack Vickery on social media for supposedly bringing "racial politics" into tennis. Vickery shrugged off the critics, saying they did not understand the meaning behind the gesture. "I think one of the main reasons I did it was because I wanted to show people how proud I am to be a black athlete," she said. "I think sometimes we don't express it a lot or talk about it enough. I think it's really, really important, especially to the younger kids that are coming up. While I'm on the tennis tour, this is something that I'm always going to be passionate about."

Something else about which Vickery is passionate is a program she has run for several years in her mother's native country, Guyana. Vickery visits once or twice a year, bringing tennis rackets, clothes, and shoes to Guyanese children. "I literally just bring everything that I can to try to help out," she said. Because of her program, rumors circulated that Vickery was going to begin representing Guyana in pro tournaments instead of the United States. Not true, she said. "I'm passionate about Guyana, but I'm an American and I'm going to be representing the United States." Nevertheless, Vickery has a goal of opening a tennis academy someday in Guyana. To ensure that she will have enough funds, she will likely continue to avoid Manhattan and its sky-high prices during future U.S. Opens.

Quite unintentionally, Heather Watson has found a way to greatly reduce the costs of lodging in New York City during the U.S. Open. In 2018 Watson, formerly England's top-ranked player, lost in the first round for the eighth consecutive year. Hugely disappointing for a player who became the first British champion of a WTA tour event in twenty-four years when she won in Osaka, Japan, in 2012. Watson is the daughter of a black woman from Papua New Guinea and a white Englishman. She began playing tennis at age seven. When she was twelve, her parents had the financial means to send her to Nick Bollettieri's tennis academy in Bradenton, Florida. Today, Watson splits her time between Bradenton and West London. She achieved a career-high ranking of No. 38 in 2015. That same year, she was two points from defeating Serena in a third-round match at Wimbledon. While her singles results have been disappointing recently—she ended 2018 ranked No. 92 in the world—she has achieved success in doubles. To the delight of her countrypersons, she partnered Henri Kontinen of Finland to the Wimbledon mixed doubles crown in 2016. A year later, she and Kontinen lost a tough three-set match in the Wimbledon final. She began 2019 with a world ranking of No. 46 in doubles and a renewed determination to get her singles game back on track. "I am definitely a singles player first; that's where my main focus is," said Watson, who also won singles titles in Monterrey, Mexico, in 2016 and Hobart, Australia, in 2015. At age twenty-six, Watson closed out 2018 with career tennis earnings of $3,222,163. "When you win you can earn a lot of money, but you also spend a lot of money," said Watson, who began 2019 as England's No. 2 player behind Johanna Konta. "Every match I play, I pay for my coach, my trainer, and my physiotherapist to travel with me. Tennis is an expensive sport, and I would never have got as far as I have without my parents supporting me. It's not a sport you can even get into if you don't have financial help."

Former champion Younes El Aynaoui of Morocco is another player who cultivated his skills at the Bollettieri Academy. El Aynaoui, who won five ATP titles in a career that began in 1990, arrived at the academy at age eighteen determined to make it as a pro, but without the means to pay for coaching. That is, until he started working at the academy. He cleaned courts and the gym. He drove the bus. He strung rackets. He even babysat younger players. His hard work, off the court and on, paid dividends. He reached his first ATP tour final in Casablanca, Morocco, in 1993, and won his first title six years later in Amsterdam, Holland. He reached the quarterfinals of the 2000 Australian Open, and won his second title in Bucharest, Romania, in 2001.

El Aynaoui had his best year on the pro tour in 2002 at the age of thirty: he won tournaments in Casablanca; Doha, Qatar; and Munich, Germany; and reached the quarterfinals of the U.S. Open, losing to defending champion Lleyton Hewitt. El Aynaoui, who achieved a career-high world ranking of No. 14 in 2003, may be best remembered by tennis fans for an epic match he lost. He battled Andy Roddick for five hours in a 2003 Australian Open quarterfinal at Rod Laver Arena before succumbing 4–6, 7–6, 4–6, 6–4, 21–19. (It was the longest fifth set in major-tennis history until John Isner defeated France's Nicolas Mahut 70–68 at Wimbledon in 2010.) Given the high cost of tennis, players representing African nations are still rare in the sport. Yet El Aynaoui did it with distinction. He made $3,867,667 in career earnings, received a gold medal from King Mohammed VI, and the main court at the Royal Tennis Club in Marrakech is named after him.

Like El Aynaoui, former tennis pro Ronald Agenor was born in Rabat, Morocco. But the well-traveled Agenor learned the game in France as a teenager, and he eventually represented Haiti on the ATP tour because his father was a United Nations diplomat and minister of agriculture for the Caribbean island. Agenor, who won his first pro title in Athens, Greece, in 1989, was sometimes mistaken for Yannick Noah, the 1983 French Open champion. Agenor often played in dreadlocks, a bandana, and multicolored shirts. Like Noah, he had a flair for spectacular shotmaking. That's why Agenor was nicknamed "the Haitian Sensation." He ranked a career-best No. 22 in 1989, and won three singles titles—Athens, Greece, in 1989; and Genoa, Italy; and Berlin, both in 1990. He also posted victories over eventual Hall of Famers Noah, Jimmy Connors, Mats Wilander, Michael Stich, and Andre Agassi.

Agenor, tired of life on the road, left the pro tour in 1996 only to return two years later. He hoped to receive a wild card into the 1998 U.S. Open. But the USTA instead offered a wild card to Patrick McEnroe, who was ranked No. 664 in the world at the time; Agenor was ranked No. 275. Although McEnroe declined the wild card, Agenor bristled at the racial inequality that he believed led to the snubbing. In his 2007 autobiography, *Tilted Courts: The Power Politics of International Tennis*, he wrote, "For Ronald Agenor, making a comeback on the international professional tennis tour would prove twice as difficult as it would be for Patrick McEnroe of the United States. Haiti, the poorest country in the Western Hemisphere, does not even host a satellite or Challengers event. It has no presence in the upper echelon of the international tennis hierarchy that is controlled by Americans, Europeans, and Australians. So, in crucial moments, such as when decisions have to be made about awarding wild cards, I would be an outsider." Agenor, now a U.S. citizen, lives in Beverly Hills, and runs his own tennis academy in Los Angeles—his version of the American dream. Yet he does not forget from whence he came or the racial slights he endured on the pro circuit. He recalled two of them: at a tournament in Holland, the driver of a players-only courtesy car refused to take him back to his hotel; also, he believed the officials were biased against him in a match against Connors at the 1991 French Open. "Of course, there were some other things that happened, but those things are part of daily life and not related to tennis," he said. "I feel in some way lucky that I did not grow up with the upfront racism that dominates in the United States, as I was able to focus fully on tennis."

The year 2018 ended with the news that 2017 U.S. Open champion Sloane Stephens and her coach, Kamau Murray, would be taking "a break" from each other. But just months after Murray was hired to coach Monica Puig, the 2016 Olympic gold medalist from Puerto Rico, and Stephens hired Sven Groeneveld of Holland to coach her, Stephens and Murray reunited. Also, Darren Cahill, the Australian coach of then world No. 1 Simona Halep of Romania, announced that he would take leave from coaching in 2019 to spend more time with his family and do tennis commentary for ESPN. Since player-coach relationships are often ephemeral, the Halep-Cahill tandem is not guaranteed to reunite, especially if the player enjoys a higher level of success with a different coach. An elite player travels with a full-time coach, a hitting partner (who often acts as an assistant coach), a trainer, and a physiotherapist. The player's agent or manager may also be part of the entourage. That means one expensive hotel room in Manhattan during a possible two-week run at the U.S. Open is not nearly enough for a tennis star. Many players use their celebrity status to barter for free rooms at the swankiest hotels in exchange for promotional shout-outs on social media. Having a tennis superstar mention a specific Manhattan hotel as their home away from home during the Open, along with a photo or two of the venue, is worth more in free publicity to the hotel than the cost of a few rooms. Serena, for instance, had 10.9 million Twitter followers and 11 million Instagram followers as of June 2019. She could introduce her vast social-media network to a hotel in New York City about which they had never heard—a hotel where they may choose to stay in the future. For the record, Serena and Venus stayed at the Lotte New York Palace during the 2018 U.S. Open. So did Rafael Nadal and Australian star Nick Kyrgios. Each of the stars took part in a badminton exhibition to further promote their association with the Palace. Sam Querrey, an American formerly ranked in the world top ten, has stayed at the Tuscany St. Giles hotel during the Open in exchange for agreeing to appear at events such as a cocktail party or a breakfast for invited guests and media. Naomi Osaka, a two-time major champion and a player of Japanese and Haitian heritage, and Kei Nishikori of Japan both stayed at the Kitano Hotel, the only Japanese-owned hotel in New York City. Caroline Garcia of France, the Open's No. 6 seed, settled into The New Yorker hotel in exchange for promotion on social media. "It's an easy deal," she told the *New York Times*. "It's not like they ask you to post 10 pictures. They were happy with one or two."

How do the star players and the swanky hotels find each other? Soon, there may be an app for that. But for now, fixers, otherwise known as player agents and managers, are handling the task. John Tobias, a player agent with TLA Worldwide who represents Sloane Stephens, said that an elite player will typically get a free room or rooms in exchange for two or three social media posts about the hotel. "You've got to be a reasonably highly marketable player or [the hotels] are not going to be interested," he said. "They'll take a look at your social media following to see if the type of audience you have is even worth it."

Fabien Paget, whose company 02 Management represents several tennis pros, said he worked with eight to ten Manhattan hotels to connect them with players competing at the 2018 U.S. Open. One of his players, Nicolas Mahut, received two free rooms at the Quin Hotel and a discounted rate for two other rooms, so Mahut's coach, trainer, and physiotherapist could join him. Other guests at the Quin were offered a rate of $1,995 a night—seriously—which included "an exclusive opportunity to meet with several of the players" staying at the hotel throughout the tournament, "subject to availability."

Presumably, the hotels that enter into these deals provide enough security to ensure the athletes' safety. It would be a shame if a player's decision to overshare on social media in exchange for free rooms at a luxury hotel during a tennis tournament resulted in an unfortunate incident. The upscale bartering between athletes and hotels is yet another example of what an enormous moneymaking venture the U.S. Open is—for a relative few. At the highest level, New York City's economy benefits, the tennis stars benefit, and the highest-ranking executives of the USTA benefit—even though the USTA is actually a 501C3, a nonprofit organization. But not every nonprofit organization has an executive director making $1.37 million a year while its president and chair—the public face of the organization—is paid $40,485 in the same calendar year. Not every nonprofit organization has been sued by several of its black employees alleging racial, gender, and age discrimination, only to be compelled by a state attorney general to create a plan to remedy the problem, a plan that included hiring someone to be in charge of diversity and inclusion until that same person ended up suing the same nonprofit organization for racial discrimination. There is something quite strange happening within the chief governing body for tennis in America, and a man whom that organization once called "one of the best umpires in the world" would like the public to know all about it.

1. Serena Williams and Venus Williams shake hands with Jelena Ostapenko (*left*) and Yulia Putinseva after a doubles match at the 2016 French Open. Courtesy of Jimmie 48 Tennis Photography.

2. Serena and Venus at the 2017 ASB Classic in Auckland, New Zealand. Courtesy of Jimmie 48 Tennis Photography.

3. Venus Williams at the 2018 Miami Open. Courtesy of Jimmie 48
Tennis Photography.

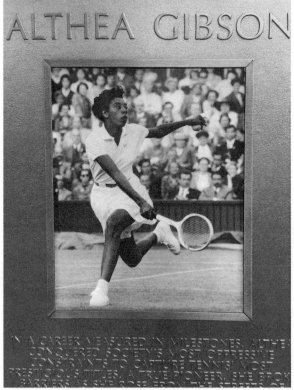

ALTHEA GIBSON

IN A CAREER MEASURED IN MILESTONES, ALTHEA
CONQUERED SOCIETY'S MOST OPPRESSIVE
CONSTRAINTS TO CAPTURE TENNIS' MOST
PRESTIGIOUS TITLES. A TRUE PIONEER, SHE BROKE
BARRIERS AS SHE ROSE FROM HER HUMBLE

4. (*opposite top*) Arthur Ashe (*right*) in a 1991 photo with Bob Davis, president of the Black Tennis Hall of Fame. Courtesy of Bob Davis.

5. (*opposite bottom*) Althea Gibson's plaque at the U.S. Open's Court of Champions. Courtesy of the author.

6. (*above*) 2018 U.S. Open champion Naomi Osaka. Courtesy of Jimmie 48 Tennis Photography.

7. Heather Watson signs an autograph at the 2018 U.S. Open.
Courtesy of the author.

8. Sloane Stephens at the 2018 WTA Finals in Singapore.
Courtesy of Jimmie 48 Tennis Photography.

9. James Blake (*right*) with former tour pro Tommy Haas.
Courtesy of the author.

10. Sloane Stephens with fans at the 2018 U.S. Open. Courtesy of the author.

11. (*opposite top*) Sachia Vickery after practice at the 2018 U.S. Open. Courtesy of the author.

12. (*opposite bottom*) Scoville Jenkins, a former tour pro, is the associate head coach of men's tennis at Oklahoma State University. Courtesy of Oklahoma State Athletics.

13. (*above*) Kamau Murray coached Sloane Stephens to the 2017 U.S. Open title. Courtesy of the author.

14. 2017 U.S. Open finalist Madison Keys. Courtesy of Jimmie 48 Tennis Photography.

15. 2018 U.S. Open runner-up Serena Williams and 2018 champion Naomi Osaka, with the then USTA president Katrina Adams (*far left*) and ESPN sportscaster Tom Rinaldi (*far right*). Courtesy of Jimmie 48 Tennis Photography.

7 | Black Umpires

They let you get only so far.

TONY NIMMONS

Tony Nimmons could hardly bring himself to watch the 2018 U.S. Open. Not after something that had been such an important part of his life had been taken away in such abrupt and painful fashion. He did his best to ignore what was happening at the USTA National Tennis Center during the Open fortnight. At first, he didn't comment on Serena's surprisingly lopsided 6–2, 6–1 rout of big sister Venus in the third round. He even managed to suppress his thoughts after the great Roger Federer lost in the fourth round to unheralded Australian John Millman.

But Nimmons is an African American, one who appeared on the verge of making history for someone of his ethnicity. So, as the final weekend of the Open drew near, when it became clear that Serena, America's most celebrated tennis champion, would advance to the final to face another woman of color, either Madison Keys or Naomi Osaka, Nimmons checked his disappointment at the door and engaged in the tennis conversations at his current job at the Indian Point nuclear power plant, some thirty miles north of New York City.

"There are a lot of tennis fans at my job, and the U.S. Open is a big thing," said Nimmons, a nuclear officer who helps to secure Indian Point from trespassers or potential evildoers. "For a while, I could not stomach tennis anymore. I couldn't bring myself to watch it. I'd play tennis and then I'd have to stop. But then, I felt like I needed to comment on what was going on."

Nimmons is forty-nine years old, six feet, three inches tall, brown skinned, strapping, and bald. He could easily be mistaken for a former defensive lineman in pro football. He could be intimidating to those who stereotype men of his physical stature. But he also possesses a warm smile and a friendly, helpful demeanor. His talent and professionalism once allowed him to move swiftly up the ranks of tennis umpires. But after filing a lawsuit against the United States Tennis Association alleging racial discrimination and then appealing to the Equal Employment Opportunity Commission to have his day in court, Nimmons was fired by the USTA in 2016.

The job of umpire was a dream come true for Nimmons, a native of Brooklyn, New York. He certainly did not do it for the money. A tennis umpire's travel, lodging, and meals are paid for, but the salary is paltry compared to that of umpires and referees in other sports. That is because, unlike Major League Baseball umpires, pro basketball referees, and officials in pro football and pro hockey, tennis umpires don't have a union. According to a survey by BBC Sport, a highly rated tennis umpire, one with a gold or silver badge, makes anywhere from $65,000 to $78,000 a year. Most umpires make roughly $39,000 a year, and a linesperson receives about $28,300 a year. According to one former umpire, the International Tennis Federation (ITF), which supervises tennis officials, paid the top umpires $1,500 a week on a twenty-week contract in 2018 that covered a period including the U.S. Open from late August through mid-September and matches in the Davis Cup and the Fed Cup. (The Fed Cup and the Davis Cup are international competitions among nations. The women compete for the Fed Cup, the men for the Davis Cup.)

An opportunity to travel the world and officiate matches involving tennis's best players held great appeal for Nimmons. While sitting in a high chair at courtside between two players or teams, he dutifully kept track of the score, announced the score after every point, used his deep and resonant voice to convey authority, controlled the crowd, kept players in line, settled disputes, issued penalties to players who misbehaved or dawdled during play, kept tabs on video replay challenges, made sure new balls were used at the appropriate time, ensured that different crews of linespersons rotated onto the court and off at designated times, and overruled a linesperson's call if necessary. The job requires sound judgment, a thorough knowledge of the rules, and patience.

A 2011 article on USTA.com referred to Nimmons as "one of the best umpires in the business." That also appeared to be the sentiment of the ITF. Nimmons officiated more than two thousand matches, including U.S. Open matches for twenty consecutive years (1995–2014). He served as an umpire in six U.S. Open finals doubles matches. He also officiated at seven Australian Opens, six French Opens, five Wimbledons, and seventeen Davis Cup events. If anyone seemed qualified to sit in the high chair and preside over a U.S. Open singles final—considered the crowning accomplishment for an American-born umpire—Nimmons would have fit the bill. But the USTA never gave him the opportunity. The USTA has never given any African American man that opportunity. The USTA has given only one African American woman that opportunity, and it happened more than a quarter century ago. Distressing as it was for Nimmons to endure those annual slights from the USTA, he paid an even greater price for complaining. Because of a series of events that he found bizarre and infuriating, Nimmons lost his standing in tennis and then his dream job. His racial-discrimination lawsuit is nearly identical to one filed against the USTA a decade ago by Cecil Hollins of New York City and Sande French of California, both African American umpires. That lawsuit alleged systemic discrimination based on race, gender, and age.

"There's a racist culture at the USTA," Nimmons said in the office of his attorney, Gary Ireland, on Broadway in Midtown Manhattan, across the street from the Ed Sullivan Theatre where a crowd stood in line to attend a taping of *The Late Show with Stephen Colbert*. "The

USTA does not have a culture that is built to bring up and support a person of color such as myself. They let you advance only to a certain point and that's it."

Nimmons was once mentored by Hollins. The two met while playing tennis on opposite courts in Queens. Nimmons, inexperienced at playing the sport, kept hitting errant shots that interrupted Hollins's match. Hollins helped his protégé break into umpiring, and, once Nimmons began officiating matches, advised him on how to report incidents of racial prejudice, whether it came from a player, another umpire, or a tennis official—and both men were subjected to verbal abuse from all three groups.

On September 11, 1993, Sande French served as the umpire for the U.S. Open women's final. Steffi Graf of Germany, the No. 1 seed, dismissed No. 12 seed Helena Sukova of the Czech Republic, 6–3, 6–3. While tennis fans have applauded nine U.S. Open singles titles won by African Americans since then—six by Serena, two by Venus, and one by Sloane Stephens—they have not seen another African American umpire in a U.S. Open final.

French and Hollins eventually reached an out-of-court settlement with the USTA, and both signed nondisclosure agreements that prevent them from discussing their case publicly. But in a series of interviews in 2006, Hollins explained why he and his coplaintiff took legal action. For example, he said the USTA relegated French to lesser matches in the thirteen years after the Graf-Sukova final.

"In 1994, the year after she worked the Open final, she was assigned to work only the lines at [U.S. Open] matches," Hollins said then. "She didn't get to sit in the umpire's chair. She went in to complain to Rich Kaufman, who had replaced Jay Snyder as the [USTA] chief of umpires. She asked, 'How come I've been demoted from chair umpire to the lines?' And Kaufman told her, 'You didn't deserve to do that women's final last year.' That's outright racism. Sande is still the only woman to work a Grand Slam final who has not been promoted by the USTA or the ITF."

In the early 1990s, Hollins, an attorney at the time, approached Snyder to find out how to become a tennis umpire. Hollins learned that there is a finishing school for umpires, and a person had to be recommended for the school by his or her country's tennis federation. There are different color-coded designations for umpires as they move up the ranks. Someone who learns the basics of umpiring gets a white badge. The next highest levels are bronze, silver, and gold. According to the ITF, here is what the different badges allow an umpire to do:

Gold badge: Can work any tennis match anywhere in the world.

Silver badge: Can work any match anywhere except a Davis Cup or Fed Cup final.

Bronze badge: Can work any match anywhere except a semifinal or final at a Grand Slam event, or a Davis Cup or Fed Cup final.

White badge: Can officiate matches but not in the main draw at a Grand Slam event.

French held a bronze badge when she worked the Graf-Sukova final in 1993. Under current rules, she would not be permitted to work a major final. The lawsuit had alleged that the USTA prevented her from moving up the ranks by limiting the number of later-round matches she could work. Hollins, meanwhile, had moved swiftly up the ranks, and by 1994, he was the only African American umpire to officiate matches at Wimbledon. Later that year, he became the first African American umpire with a gold badge.

"I remember having Cecil work some of my matches, and he did an excellent job," said Roger Smith, a black former player and Davis Cup captain from the Bahamas. "He stayed on top of things, he was very decisive, and he was an umpire you could talk to. Some umpires act like they're above talking to players. He was never like that."

Yet despite his gold badge and fine reputation among players, Hollins never officiated a U.S. Open singles final, or even a U.S. Open semifinal. Nimmons has worked a U.S. Open men's semifinal. In Hollins's case, each year when the U.S. Open field narrowed to the final four players in singles, he got passed over for the plum assignments. For him, the final indignity occurred at the 1997 U.S. Open. Early one morning, he played a friendly match on one of the tournament courts with another black umpire, Al Pendleton. Such an activity was common among tennis officials as long as they got off the court before the real matches began at eleven o'clock in the morning. While other officials were playing tennis on other courts, Hollins said a white male groundskeeper walked up to him and Pendleton and said, 'We gotta get this court ready. You n——s gotta get off the court.'" Hollins said that when he and Pendleton complained to chief of umpires Rich Kaufman, they were told, "You're both lucky to be working this tournament. When a groundskeeper tells you to get off the court, you get off the court. Don't come in here bothering me with this. Get out of my office."

After Hollins and French filed their lawsuit, his badge was downgraded from gold to silver. As a gold badge umpire in 2006, Hollins said he made $60,000. Tennis umpires are not in the business for the money. Hollins left the sport and now serves as an administrative judge in New York City. Sande French continues to work as a tennis umpire—at the lowest level. As part of the out-of-court settlement with the USTA, she accepted a downgrade of her badge from bronze to white.

However, the lawsuit was not the only action taken by Hollins and French. The plaintiffs also contacted the office of then New York state attorney general Eliot Spitzer, whose office launched an investigation in late 2005 into USTA hiring and promotion practices. Spitzer's office announced these major findings from the investigation in 2006:

1. Few black umpires are chosen to officiate U.S. Open matches, especially the more prestigious later-round matches. A significant reason: the USTA consistently neglects to recommend black umpires for admission into badge schools, which are a prerequisite to advance in the sport. An umpire's badge level determines his or her assignments and level of pay in the sport.
2. There were stark gender disparities in assignments given to chair umpires at major tournaments. Women, for example, almost never worked men's matches. Between 2001 and 2005, no woman umpire worked a U.S. Open quarterfinal, semifinal, or final-round men's match, but male umpires worked later-round women's matches every year. (At the 2018 U.S. Open, Alison Hughes, a

British woman, officiated the men's final in which Novak Djokovic of Serbia defeated Juan Martin del Potro of Argentina.)

3. Duties of an umpire for women's and men's matches are identical, but the USTA simply preferred to assign more men to marquee matches than women.

4. The USTA violated Section 63(12) and Section 296(1) of the New York State Executive Law and Section 8-107(1) of the New York State Administrative Code, as well as Title VII of the Civil Rights Act of 1964, by its repeated and persistent violations of these statutes.

Particularly because of the fourth finding, the attorney general compelled the USTA to agree to hire someone to oversee diversity and inclusion policies for the organization. The person that the USTA selected for the job was Nimmons, even though he had been spending more than half the year on the road as an umpire. By then, Nimmons had worked his way up the officiating ranks and held a silver badge. He also held fast to his goal of working a U.S. Open singles final.

"I was already doing a number of things for the USTA when I was on the road," Nimmons said. "As the USTA's officiating coordinator, I'd meet with people interested in becoming umpires, and I'd put out brushfires, like the time gold badge umpires were threatening a boycott of the U.S. Open because of the scheduling of assignments and the financial compensation. In my off time, I was the fixer, the buffer, the bag man, the janitor, all these things. I investigated a number of things for the USTA around officiating."

Because he kept the goal of working a U.S. Open final uppermost in his mind, Nimmons said he did not dwell on the ugly racial episodes he endured in tennis. From the lawsuit: during one match, he said, a white player whom he would not name called him "a black piece of shit." Nimmons penalized the player for a conduct violation but did not default the player for verbal abuse, which would have been within his authority. At another tournament in an American southern state, Nimmons overruled a call by a white linesman. Afterward, he said, the linesman told him, "Tony, you need to go back to the ghetto."

Nimmons said another white umpire once asked him, "Hey, Tony, if you were a monkey and you were hungry and I told you there was a watermelon in a tree, what would you do?"

"When things like that happened, I would always follow protocol and report it to my supervisor," Nimmons said with a shrug. "It's not like anything was ever done about it, but I would report it, leave it in the USTA's hands and move on."

At the end of 2012, Nimmons said he felt certain that the USTA would recommend him for gold badge school. That year, he officiated matches at all four Grand Slam events, plus Olympic tennis, which was held at Wimbledon, and the Davis Cup. But nothing changed. For two consecutive years, he was taken aside by Kaufman and U.S. Open tournament referee Brian Earley and told that he would be the standby umpire for the men's final. But in each year, the umpire actually selected for the job did not break his leg in the shower, or walk in front of a bus, or accidentally slit his throat while shaving, so Nimmons did not get the job.

"A good friend of mine, a gold badge umpire, told me if the USTA wanted me to do the final, all the USTA had to do was tell Brian Earley, the tournament referee, 'We want Tony to do the final this year,'" Nimmons said. "Then, they would set it up and it would be done. But I heard that the excuse was, 'Well, if we give the final to Tony and something [bad] happens, then people will say, 'Why did you give it to this silver badge umpire when you have all these gold badge umpires here?' There's no support in the USTA hierarchy for any black umpire who is deserving of the opportunity. The problem is, they let you get only so far."

For Nimmons, who said the USTA had promised it would help him get a gold badge, the annual snubs became increasingly annoying. Although the International Tennis Federation technically oversees the officials at the four major tournaments, the ITF does not tell the U.S. Open, French Open, Australian Open, or Wimbledon whom it must assign to officiate the marquee matches. Each tennis federation gets to make that call. Hence, if the USTA had truly wanted Nimmons to work a U.S. Open singles final, he would have done so.

Coincidentally, one factor that has limited the chances of African American umpires to officiate U.S. Open finals has been the dominance of the Williams sisters. Grand Slam events rarely assign an umpire from the host country to officiate a championship match involving a player from the host country. From 1997, when Venus reached the U.S. Open final, to 2018, when Serena played for the title, a Williams sister has appeared in eleven of the twenty-two women's finals. In two other women's finals not involving a Williams sister, another American player won the title match—Lindsay Davenport in 1998 and Sloane Stephens in 2017. However, there have been many opportunities in the past two decades for the USTA to assign an African American umpire to officiate a U.S. Open men's final. No American man has won the U.S. Open since Andy Roddick in 2003, and no American man has played in a U.S. Open final since Andre Agassi in 2005.

"If the USTA wants something to happen, it's going to happen," Nimmons said firmly. "Several years ago, before they put the roof over Arthur Ashe Stadium [in 2016], the USTA scheduled the men's final for a Monday two years in a row. They did that because rainouts in previous years pushed the men's final from Sunday to Monday. The ITF objected. The whole tennis community objected because the weekend after the U.S. Open is a Davis Cup weekend, and the men playing in the final would have one fewer day to rest and prepare for Davis Cup. The umpires didn't like it either because we're flying all over the world after the U.S. Open. But the USTA did it anyway for two years, because they could. I remember one year, Norm Chryst, a white umpire, had worked the final, and he told me after the match, 'Tony, that should have been your final.' He knew what was happening to me behind the scenes.

"The USTA can do whatever it wants," Nimmons continued with barely suppressed anger. "They can't [cite] the ITF as the reason Cecil Hollins had a gold badge and never worked a U.S. Open final or semifinal and he's now out of the sport, or that I didn't get the gold badge that I was promised and didn't get to work a U.S. Open final and now I'm out of the sport."

When contacted for comment, Jasmine Sheppard, a spokeswoman for USTA president and chair Katrina Adams (whose tenure ended on December 31, 2018), responded, "Katrina will not be discussing or generating a statement on the case due to pending litigation."

In 2014 Nimmons continued to officiate matches all over the world. Still, the USTA did not recommend him for gold badge school, as it had promised. Soon, the USTA would take actions that would essentially end Nimmons's career. In 2014 the USTA hired Francis Gilbert to be Nimmons's supervisor. Gilbert also ran the newly created officiating department. Nimmons said Gilbert promptly limited his travel, thus preventing him from working the amount of matches necessary for gold-badge consideration, and threatened to fire him in front of colleagues at meetings. When a black female employee complained to Nimmons that a vendor had placed a hangman's noose on her desk, he reported the incident to Gilbert but no action was taken. According to Nimmons, the USTA later claimed the noose was a lasso that had been placed on the woman's desk as a joke. When another USTA employee mentioned to Gilbert at a Super Bowl party in 2015 that Nimmons had contacted the Equal Employment Opportunity Commission regarding workplace discrimination, Gilbert revoked Nimmons's travel privileges.

Suddenly one of the top umpires in tennis—in the USTA's own words—and the sport's best-known African American umpire was completely off the circuit. The ITF did not intervene, according to Nimmons, because it viewed the situation as a USTA matter. Nimmons was demoted to video editor. He had not been trained for that position, nor was he interested in it. After his dream job was taken away, Nimmons developed stress-related problems and went on disability. The USTA fired him on June 30, 2016. He then filed the discrimination suit, despite a comment he had heard from USTA general counsel Daniel Malasky: "What we do to those who complain is bury them in paperwork. They usually can't afford the legal fees and drop the case."

In his lawsuit, Nimmons seeks unspecified monetary damages to cover his loss of income from tennis umpiring and working as a diversity officer; loss opportunities and benefits; compensatory damages from emotional distress and mental anguish; recoupment of attorney's fees and costs of litigation; and reinstatement to his previous status as a silver badge umpire. If he is reinstated, Nimmons said he will advocate for the formation of a tennis umpires union. "The umpires are underpaid and discriminated against," he said, "and if you complain, you're out."

The USTA's reluctance to develop and promote African American umpires and assign them to the U.S. Open's most important matches has been a major problem for decades. The problem has been particularly painful for Nimmons because from 2014 to 2018 the public face of the USTA as its president and chair was an African American.

Katrina Adams is a Chicago native and a Northwestern University graduate who excelled in professional tennis for more than a decade, ranking a career-best No. 8 in the world in doubles and No. 67 in singles. Adams partnered with Zina Garrison, a 1990 Wimbledon singles finalist, to win seven of her twenty professional doubles titles. Adams won three more doubles crowns alongside Lori McNeil, who, like Garrison, emerged from a public tennis program in Houston to earn a world top-ten ranking in singles. "When I played with Zina, I was the put-away player at the net," Adams said. "Zina and I worked better together because she was the set-up player. Lori and I played a similar style."

After Adams retired in 1999, she coached in the USTA player development program before making a highly successful transition to tennis administration. She was appointed to the USTA board, and she also became the executive director of the Harlem Junior Tennis and Education Program. The HJTEP is part of the National Junior Tennis League cofounded by Arthur Ashe and Sheridan Snyder in 1969 to use the sport "to gain and hold the attention of young people in the inner cities and other poor environments." Promoting education and teaching life skills are of primary importance to NJTL chapters such as the one Adams runs. She has also put her communications skills and sports knowledge to good use as a commentator on Tennis Channel and as a panelist on CBS Sports Network's women-led show *We Need to Talk*. In 2015 she was elected to a two-year term as the USTA's first black president, chair, and chief executive officer. On her watch, the

USTA completed a five-year, $600 million face lift of the National Tennis Center, including a remodeled, fourteen-thousand-seat Louis Armstrong Stadium, and in 2016 it opened the USTA national campus in Orlando, Florida, which includes one hundred fully lit courts and tennis programs for youths through senior citizens and wheelchair athletes.

Unfortunately, Adams did not appear to be in position to rectify the USTA's problem of discrimination against African American umpires. While she was the public face of the association, she did not run the actual day-to-day operation. That was handled by Gordon Smith, the executive director. Smith, a white male, is a salaried employee. Adams is a per-diem employee.

The USTA is a 501C3, a nonprofit organization. In 2017, the last year for which the USTA's financial records could be obtained, here were the five highest-salaried employees of the association followed by Adams's financial compensation for comparison:

Gordon Smith, executive director and chief executive officer:
$1.37 million
Lew Sherr, chief revenue officer: $911,554
Andrea Hirsch, chief administration officer: $807,745
Kurt Kamperman, chief operating officer of community tennis:
$852,281
Ed Neppl, chief financial officer: $625,798
Katrina Adams, president and chair: $40,485

According to a former USTA board member, Adams agreed to relinquish the title of chief executive officer at the end of her first term in late 2016 in exchange for a second two-year term as president and chair. Smith, who retired at the end of 2019, held the title of CEO in 2017–18, which gave him more authority over the direction of the USTA.

Had Adams given a public voice during her first term to the issue of systemic discrimination against African Americans within the USTA, she most likely would not have been appointed by the board to a second term. Indeed, it could be argued that appointing Adams to a second two-year term, through the year 2018, was a tactical move by the USTA to have an African American woman as the face of an organization that has been served with two racial-discrimination lawsuits from African American umpires in the past two decades. Adams's two terms have come and gone. Allegations of racial discrimination against the USTA remain. Nimmons, who has known Adams since her playing days, seemed loathe to criticize her for a lack of intervention on the issue.

Choosing his words carefully, Nimmons said in an October 5, 2018, interview, "I want to protect Katrina. I think what she's doing is good for tennis. I'm hesitant to talk about what we may have said to each other personally, if you can understand that." He then tapped his fingers on the table in the conference room in his attorney's office and exhaled before continuing. "Yes, I am disappointed that Katrina has not stuck her neck out. But I can also understand that this is her legacy as well, and the USTA had not had an African American in her position before."

"But wouldn't it be a tremendous legacy if she took corrective action?" his attorney, Gary Ireland, asked. "If she used her position to fix this problem on behalf of African American umpires?"

"It certainly would," Nimmons said.

From 2015 through 2018, the USTA could point to an accomplished black female as its president and chair as a means of blunting any criticism that the organization does not appoint and promote black people. On April 9, 2015, New York City Councilman Daniel Gorodnick wrote a letter to Adams to inquire about the USTA's hiring practices. The USTA responded with a letter that included the name of every nonwhite salaried employee within the USTA, rather than specifically listing the USTA's black salaried employees.

Perhaps because the USTA's marquee event, the U.S. Open, generates $350 million a year for New York City's economy, local politicians are unwilling to address the issue of two racial-discrimination lawsuits against the USTA in the past two decades—including a lawsuit filed by the person whose hiring as the diversity and inclusion officer resulted from findings by the New York State attorney general of systemic discrimination a decade earlier.

The office of New York City mayor Bill de Blasio did not respond to requests for a comment. Calls and emails to the office of Letitia James, who became New York State attorney general on January 1, 2019, were not returned. Calls and emails to the New York City Commission on Human Rights also were not returned. Jacob Tugendrajch, a spokesman for New York City Council speaker Corey Johnson, said, "Respectfully, Speaker Johnson will decline to comment on this ongoing lawsuit."

In the first U.S. Open after the Nimmons lawsuit, the USTA used Carlos Bernardes, a brown-skinned Brazilian, and Kader Nouni, a black Frenchman, on some high-profile matches in an apparent effort to deflect criticism of its treatment of African American umpires. Seeing men of color in the umpire's chair may have created the impression that the issue prompting the lawsuit had been rectified. But that is not the case. The distressing fact remains that no African American has been selected to officiate a U.S. Open women's or men's final since 1993.

Nimmons said he yearns to return to tennis umpiring. But first, he wants his day in court. He is convinced that the USTA is stalling, hoping to drain his resources and his resolve until he accepts a financial settlement and goes away, as Hollins did, or accepts a financial settlement and a massive demotion, as French did. Nimmons said he is determined to leave a lasting mark on his profession and fulfill his long-held dream of working a U.S. Open singles final in his home state.

"You could ask the question, 'Tony, you did the U.S. Open for twenty consecutive years; why didn't you speak up earlier?'" he said. "The reason is, I take people at face value. If someone is telling me, 'Tony, you're going to get this job and then you're going to get your gold badge,' then that's what I think is going to happen. That carrot was dangled in front of me by the USTA during the case brought by Cecil and Sande."

Nimmons said he does not know if there is an African American umpire working matches today in whose face the USTA may be dangling that same carrot. Nimmons lives in Lake Carmel, New York, close to his job at the nuclear plant. He also serves as an emergency medical technician and a volunteer firefighter. He said his grown children, Anthony and Basia, no longer worry about their dad because they are convinced that his ordeal with the USTA has not crushed his spirit. He remains hopeful that a local politician will lead an effort to reexamine New York City's relationship with the USTA since the U.S. Open is staged each year on city-owned land supported by taxpayer dollars. The EEOC sent Nimmons a letter on January 30, 2018, affirming his right to sue the USTA for conduct it has deemed unacceptable. That, he said, is what gives him hope.

8 | Sloane Stephens

Everyone was, like,
"Oh, she's a one-hit wonder."

SLOANE STEPHENS

Sloane Stephens flashed her beatific smile when she heard the question. She had just silenced all of her critics, people who want to see things done on their own schedule rather than whenever the athlete is ready. She had just authored the biggest win of her twenty-four-year life when a female journalist asked if this example of outrageous success was something that she would be hungry to achieve again.

"Of course, girl!" Stephens said, making an interview room full of reporters and photographers seem like an intimate chat room for friends. "Did you see that check that lady handed me?" The room then seemed to shake with laughter, and Stephens laughed the loudest of all. She had 3.7 million reasons to laugh. She had just stunned the tennis world, seven months after surgery on her left foot, by winning the 2017 U.S. Open and a then record first-prize check of $3.7 million. The wide-eyed, open-mouthed look of astonishment on Stephens's face when she received the check was priceless. That the check was presented as Katrina Adams, the first black female president and chair of the United States Tennis Association, and two U.S. Open finalists of color, Stephens and Madison Keys, stood side by side, created a moment rife with cultural significance. But the moment on September 9, 2017, truly belonged to Stephens, who had elevated herself into a select group: major tennis champion. "Man, if that doesn't want to make you play tennis," she said, "I don't know what will."

Stephens became the first black woman not named Williams to win a major title since Althea Gibson captured her second straight crown at the U.S. Nationals in 1958. A winner's check then was nonexistent, for the game Gibson played was considered amateur tennis. Stephens, like Venus and Serena, is enjoying the fruits of Gibson's labor. Stephens earned her financial windfall by playing the best tennis of her life during the U.S. Open fortnight. Not only did she defeat Keys, her friendly rival, in the first U.S. Open final between two women of color since 2002, when Serena beat Venus, but she also dismantled Keys, 6–3, 6–0.

Two days before the final match, Stephens passed another significant test. She defeated Venus in a rites-of-passage semifinal, 6–1, 0–6, 7–5. Venus had been in excellent form, turning back the clock at age thirty-seven and coming off a superb quarterfinal-round victory over Petra Kvitova of the Czech Republic that was decided in a third-set tiebreak. Venus shut out Stephens in the second set of their semifinal, but Stephens refused to fade away. At 5–5 in a fiercely contested third set, Stephens seized the momentum and, ultimately, the match with an exquisite backhand passing shot down the line. "That was, like, the point of the tournament," said Stephens, who often likes the word "like." As in, "Playing Venus in the semifinals, that was, like, my favorite match."

Venus tested Stephens' ability to make shots under pressure, and asked questions about the younger woman's fitness, about heart, about determination, about resilience—and Stephens came up with the right answers. All of her athletic gifts were in full bloom during those two weeks in New York City—her speed, which, arguably, allows her to cover the court better than anyone in the women's game; the easy power that she uses to startle opponents who think they are in a well-contested rally before a winning stroke whizzes past them; and her fighting spirit, which could take her to world No. 1 if she ever draws upon it consistently in tournaments.

Stephens had come so far after persistent foot pain in 2016 finally compelled her to have an operation in January 2017. "When I had surgery, I was not thinking that I would be anywhere near a U.S. Open title," she said with refreshing honesty. "Nor did I think that I was going to be anywhere near the top one hundred in the world."

Players who miss significant time because of injury or suspension routinely see their world ranking plunge. Stephens decided to come back for Wimbledon 2017, not because she thought she could actually win the event, but to test her foot and her game against most of the best players in the world. (Serena played only the Australian Open in 2017, which she won while pregnant.) Stephens, who had been ranked No. 36 before her surgery, used a protected ranking to get into Wimbledon's main draw without having to endure the qualifying tournament in which a player must win three matches in three days to reach the main draw. In effect, Wimbledon placed Stephens into its field of 128 women based on her reputation. But she lost in the first round. She then entered hardcourt events in Toronto and Cincinnati to test her foot. After she competed pain-free and reached the semifinals in Cincinnati, where rainouts forced her to play two matches on the same day, she felt encouraged about her chances at the U.S. Open. Not super-confident, but encouraged. Just to make sure she would be fit enough to handle a two-week run at the U.S. Open, she withdrew from the Connecticut Open at Yale University. That decision, seven days before the U.S. Open, proved wise.

"I worked hard to get here," Stephens said, the silver U.S. Open championship trophy made by Tiffany glistening on the table beside her. "I was able to play free and run and compete and just get out there and get after it in every match."

Some believe champions are born. Others believe they are made. The correct answer may lie somewhere in between. But it is probably a safe bet to believe that if no one in your family tree has ever shown a considerable amount of athletic ability, or achieved something of significance in an athletic endeavor, then it is highly unlikely that you will become a champion in an individual sport. Not impossible. Just highly unlikely. Fortunately for the five-foot-seven, 140-pound Stephens, when she dove into the athletic gene pool, she came up big.

Sybil Smith, Sloane's mother, grew up in Fresno, California, and attended Boston University, where she became the first African American female swimmer to achieve All-American status at the highest level of competition, Division I. She was a four-time All-American at BU and the finest female swimmer in school history. Her specialties were the backstroke, the butterfly, and freestyle. The Boston University Athletic Hall of Fame enshrined her in 1993. She then attended graduate school at Harvard University, earning a master's degree in counseling and consulting psychology while also serving as an assistant coach of the women's swim team.

As a celebrated black athlete in a predominantly white sport, Smith prepared Stephens well for the quizzical stares and questions she would face as a black girl who plays tennis. Let your accomplishments speak for themselves, Smith taught her daughter. Nobody will think it's unusual to see a black swimmer or a black tennis player if you show them your ability. Skin color will be what they see first, but your ability and your character will leave a stronger impression.

John Stephens, Sloane's father, debuted in the National Football League as a running back for the New England Patriots. Following a successful collegiate career at Northwestern State University in Louisiana, he became the American Football Conference's Rookie of the Year with the Patriots in 1988. That year he made the Pro Bowl (the NFL's all-star game) when he gained 1,168 yards. He ran with force and abandon until a game on October 22, 1989, when his helmet-to-helmet collision with San Francisco 49ers defensive back Jeff Fuller left Fuller paralyzed. John Stephens seemed to lose a certain zest for the game after that. He spent six years in the NFL, four with the Patriots followed by stints with the Green Bay Packers, Atlanta Falcons, and Kansas City Chiefs. In a noteworthy achievement off the field, he won the NFL's first Gale Sayers Humanitarian Citation for his work on behalf of a community health center in Roxbury, Massachusetts. His life then took a tragic turn. He was charged with raping a woman in Kansas City in 1994. He pled guilty to sexual assault, was sentenced to five years' probation, and was required to register as a sex offender. Sybil Smith, from whom he had been estranged, severed the relationship and took Sloane with her to Fort Lauderdale, Florida. John Stephens was then arrested in Kansas City for carrying a concealed weapon, and later apprehended in Texas for not properly registering as a sex offender. He later became stricken with a degenerative bone disease, which prompted him to reconnect with Smith and connect with Sloane, the daughter he had not truly known. But in 2009, he faced yet another rape charge in Louisiana, and could have been looking at up to eighty years in prison when his life abruptly ended. On September 1, he lost control of his Ford pickup truck while driving at a high speed and without a seat belt on Highway 17 in Shreveport, Louisiana. According to local law enforcement officials, he lost control of the vehicle, and as it flipped over several times, he was ejected and struck a tree. He died at the age of forty-three. Sybil Smith and Sloane attended the funeral in Louisiana.

In the NFL, a running back gets hit—hard—on virtually every play, and he needs stamina and resilience to keep coming back for more. A tennis player, in the ebbs and flows of a tight match, needs to display those same qualities. John Stephens and Sybil Smith were able to imbue Sloane with those qualities. Unfortunately, her father did not live to see her professional success.

Sloane Stephens began playing tennis at age nine, when her stepfather, Sheldon Farrell, a business consultant, and her mother introduced her to the sport. (Farrell died of cancer in 2007.) Sloane began playing at the Sierra Sport and Racquet Club in Fresno, California. Coach Francisco Gonzalez saw her potential and urged Smith to get Sloane into a tennis academy. Once mother and daughter had relocated to South Florida, they went in search of a program. In Florida, there is no shortage of parents with the financial means to try to make a child's tennis dream come true, if only it were that easy. Smith was a professional woman with an Ivy League graduate degree and a daughter with athletic genes. Yet Sloane did not exactly hear high praise during a visit with one tennis coach. "When I was eleven, my mother and I went to a tennis academy, and one of the directors told me I would be lucky if I was a Division II player and got a college scholarship," Stephens said. That did not stop Stephens from aiming high and pursuing her dream of becoming a tennis star, doubters be damned. She displayed enough speed and power while learning the game at the Nick Saviano High Performance Tennis Academy in Key Biscayne, Florida, that she acquired the nickname "Diesel." That same speed and power eventually made her a major champion and the No. 3 player in the world in 2018. Determination and work ethic, combined with good genes, have made her an elite player. "She's got a good gene pool, but she's taken it to a whole other level," said her uncle, Tony Smith, a former pro golfer. "It just makes me so proud of what she's accomplished and where she came from."

Stephens's ascension to the upper echelon in women's tennis did not come fast enough for some. As far back as June 2013, she was called "Serena's Heir" in a *Time* magazine article. It's not unusual for a news organization to try to beat the competition by identifying "the next big thing"—and then hoping that everyone forgets the prediction if it turns out to be wrong. Before going pro, Stephens won junior doubles titles at the French Open, Wimbledon, and the U.S. Open, and at the age of eighteen, she became the youngest player ranked in the world top one hundred in singles. *Time* was banking on its prediction based on those facts plus Stephens's quarterfinal-round upset of Serena at the 2013 Australian Open and her appearance that summer in the Wimbledon quarterfinals.

Heading into the 2013 Aussie Open, the media pushed a false narrative that Serena had been mentoring Stephens, as if all black champions automatically mentor younger blacks on the tour. "We're not besties," Stephens told the media. "I would never message her [to say], 'Oh, let's go to dinner' or anything like that." The two were not at odds. It's just that Stephens knew her place. Her achievements to that point were in no way comparable to Serena's, so if anyone needed to make the first move to befriend the other, it would have to be Serena. But instead of becoming besties, the two black women became rivals of sorts. When they faced each other in an Australian Open tune-up event in Brisbane, a match Serena won in straight sets, Stephens expressed annoyance to the media about Serena's grunting and shouts of "come on!" during play. "That's insane," Stephens said. "Just intimidation. That's just what happened. That's what she does. She scares people."

Those choice words lent a certain intrigue to their match in the Aussie Open quarterfinals, which Serena played with a heavily bandaged left foot because of an injury earlier in the tournament. Serena was not moving as well as usual, but there's an old tennis adage: "If you play, you're not hurt. If you're hurt, don't play." Hence, Serena made no excuses. Stephens played her best match in only her third year on the WTA tour and upset Serena, 3–6, 7–5, 6–4. In the postmatch interview, Serena referred to Stephens only as "my opponent," while calling her "a good player" and offering virtually no public praise. Stephens felt slighted. Four months after the match, she told ESPN the Magazine, "She's said not one word to me, not spoken to me, not said hi, not looked my way, not been in the same room with me since I played her in Australia, And that should tell everyone something, how she went from saying all those nice things about me to unfollowing me on Twitter."

The day after the match in Melbourne, Serena sent a picture of her swollen foot out to her millions of Twitter followers, implying that *this* was the reason she had lost. In the semifinal match, Stephens did not play with the same level of efficiency or composure, and she fell to defending champion Victoria Azarenka of Belarus, 6–1, 6–4. Azarenka then went on to win the championship, just as Marion Bartoli of France had done after defeating Stephens at Wimbledon in 2013. It would take another four years for Stephens to reach another major semifinal, and then her first major final, and then her first on-court celebration as a major champion.

Stephens was 1-5 against Serena through June 2019. They will likely face each other again. It should be compelling and highly entertaining since they are two of the finest athletes in the sport, and there still seems to be an edge between them. Serena plays against history now, her status as a tennis icon long ago assured. Stephens, a major champion now, may still believe she has something to prove. But whether she has what it takes to win big matches is no longer in doubt. Asked about Serena at the 2018 U.S. Open, Stephens, who ended the year ranked No. 6 in the world, said in an even tone, "She's one of the greatest players to ever play, if not the best of our generation."

To the victor go the spoils, and on August 24, 2018, when Stephens walked into the refurbished Louis Armstrong Stadium to take part in media day some seventy-two hours before the start of the U.S. Open, someone should have played the University of Michigan fight song, "Hail to the Victors."

Kids holding oversized tennis balls squealed as Stephens strode onto the court. They clamored for autographs and selfies as the U.S. Open allowed fans to watch and listen to reporters interview the superstars of the sport—Roger Federer, Rafael Nadal, Simona Halep, Novak Djokovic, and now Stephens. (Serena missed the media event because her daughter, Alexis Olympia, was, according to her camp, "under the weather.")

For the moment, all eyes were on Stephens in her return to New York City for the first time since winning a major title as an unseeded player. She is a marquee player now, and likely to remain one. "I think I've handled it the best that I could," she said with her usual high-wattage smile. "I've just made the most of it, tried to keep tennis first. That's really all you can do."

Stephens plays in Nike gear now, one significant change since her 2017 U.S. Open triumph. Spectators at the 2018 Open also saw a life-sized photo of Stephens next to a Mercedes-Benz SUV since she has become the fourth "brand ambassador" for the luxury car company. The other three are Federer, race car champion Lewis Hamilton, and golf star Rickie Fowler. Stephens even got a new Mercedes as part of the deal. "There's always a lot of extra things that happen after winning," she said. "Obviously, an American winning the U.S. Open is pretty big. Definitely a lot of things to do. A lot less down days for myself. But that comes with the territory."

With a major title on her resume, Stephens—attractive, well-spoken, black, and young at age twenty-five—has become an advertiser's dream. "She just checks a lot of boxes for brands that are multicultural, looking for multicultural angles, female empowerment, that whole thing," said Stephens's agent John Tobias of TLA Worldwide. "She is an athlete in the most high-profile sport for women, and it is a global sport."

Stephens began 2019 with seven endorsement deals: Nike, Mercedes-Benz, Head tennis rackets, Colgate toothpaste, Target department stores, doTerra therapeutic body oils, and the Milk Processor Education Program (Milk PEP), which features Stephens in television commercials and print advertisements as part of its Built with Chocolate Milk campaign. The ads promote chocolate milk as an energy drink and show Stephens touting its supposed benefits to her tennis. "Sloane transcends tennis," Miranda Abney, Milk PEP marketing director, told *Sports Business Journal*. "If you look at her Instagram feed, she is quite the fashionista. She was in the [2018] *Sports Illustrated* swimsuit issue. This is bigger than the tennis court."

The exact amount of compensation in any player's endorsement contract is a well-guarded secret in tennis circles. It is known, though, that contracts are incentive laden—aside from a yearly base salary for endorsing a product, bonus money will kick in if the player reaches the quarterfinals of a tournament, with more if she reaches the semifinals, more if she reaches the final, and even more if she wins the tournament. Since the four Grand Slam events are the most important, success in those tournaments leads to higher bonus payments. Win a Grand Slam event, get a bonus. Win two Grand Slam events in a row, get a bigger bonus. Win three in a row, rake in even more bonus money. Win four, and you're Serena and you've struck advertising gold. Stephens's seven endorsement deals are expected to bring in annual revenue in the high seven figures ($8–$9 million), and if she wins tournaments, especially a major tournament, in 2020, the deals could be worth more than $10 million a year, according to *Sports Business Journal*.

Entering 2019, Stephens had received $13.4 million in prize money in her career, including $5.1 million in 2018 alone.

For winning the 2017 U.S. Open, and looking smashing while doing it, Stephens joined the top tier of female athlete endorsers, trailing only Serena, fellow tennis star Maria Sharapova, and retired race car driver Danica Patrick. Stephens has also become half of an attractive sports couple—her fiancé is soccer star Jozy Altidore, a forward for the U.S. men's national team and Major League Soccer's Toronto Football Club. Stephens's higher global profile has allowed her to promote ventures in which she was already involved before the advertising world started calling. Her charitable program Soles 4 Souls: Stamping Out Poverty collects and distributes footwear to people in need. That includes children who need sneakers for sports. Stephens has earned a Bachelor of Science degree in business administration from Indiana University East as part of a free program that the WTA makes available to players. Also, the Sloane Stephens Foundation sponsors an annual play day for kids in Compton, California (where the Williams sisters grew up). The kids are invited to the Dignity Health Sports Park, a multiuse sports complex on the campus of California State University in Carson, for a day of tennis, relay races, dance contests, food, and fun. "I started the foundation because I love kids," she said. "I think tennis has given me a lot in life—given me a lot of opportunities to travel the world, see the world, free education through the WTA. I've been able to meet incredible people. Tennis has done a lot in my life."

Although Stephens did not win a major title in 2018, she conquered a world-class field to capture the Miami Open in Key Biscayne, at the same tennis complex where she once played as a junior. In the final, Stephens outslugged 2017 French Open champion Jelena Ostapenko of Latvia to claim the $1.34 million winner's check. The victory was her sixth singles title:

2018—Miami
2017—U.S. Open

2016—Auckland, Acapulco, Charleston sc (on Althea Gibson
Court)
2015—Washington dc

In 2017 Stephens also played on the USA's Fed Cup championship
team. Never mind that she lost both of her singles matches in the
final against Belarus. And never mind that Stephens lost ten consecutive matches after winning her U.S. Open title. "Tennis is definitely
a rollercoaster, but I have learned to not panic," she said in a January
15 interview at the Australian Open after a first-round loss to China's
Zhang Shuai, the eighth defeat in her ten-match drought. "There are
always going to be times when you're on an extreme high. I think for
me now it's not that great, but it's nothing to panic about." The primary reason for Stephens's occasional struggles on court is that she
lacks a strong serve. Much like Chris Evert in the 1970s and 1980s,
Stephens's serve is just a means to begin a point. Since Stephens does
not get free points with aces and service winners, she has to work
harder than, say, Serena or Venus to hold her serve. Fortunately for
Stephens, her all-around game is usually solid enough for her to win
without a strong serve.

After Stephens survived the ten-match losing streak, she came very
close to winning another major title in June. She led by one set and
one service break in the French Open final against world No. 1 Simona
Halep until a determined Halep used airtight defense and superior
court coverage, usually Stephens traits, to win the clay-court match in
three sets. Stephens lost another three-set battle to Halep, 7–6 (8–6),
3–6, 6–4, in a hardcourt final in Montreal in August that was voted
the Match of the Year by the wta. It was Halep's sixth consecutive
victory against Stephens, and seventh in their nine career matches.

The sight of Halep across the net should always prove motivating
for Stephens, as should the desire to win another major. Her U.S. Open
defense in 2018 ended in a 6–2, 6–3 defeat to Anastasija Sevastova of
Latvia in the quarterfinals. Stephens had opportunities to take the
lead in the first set, but failed to convert on seven break-point chances.
"When you don't play the big points well, the match can get away from

you—that's what happened today," she said. Stephens, the No. 3 seed, put a positive spin on losing to a player seeded sixteen slots below her. "I could have shit the bed in the first round, and that would have been really bad," she said. "So, the fact that I made it to the quarterfinals and played some really good matches and just competed as hard as I could, I mean, like, that's a lot to be proud of."

In her final event of 2018, the WTA Finals Singapore, Stephens hopped on a roller coaster for a ride of extreme highs and lows at an indoor event that featured the top eight players of the year and a prize purse of $7 million. She used speed, solid defense, deft passing shots, and sheer determination to win three-set matches against Naomi Osaka, Kiki Bertens, and Karolina Pliskova. That sent Stephens into the championship match against Elina Svitolina of Ukraine. Stephens's forehand was the dominant stroke in the first set, which she won, 6–3. But Svitolina, figuring she had nothing to lose, played with more aggressiveness, and it paid off as she won the next two sets, 6–2, 6–2, and the title.

"It's not the way I wanted to finish, but I worked really hard to get here, and I can be really proud of my result," said Stephens, who received $590,000 for finishing second. Svitolina pocketed $1.75 million.

Being an avid consumer of social media, Stephens is well aware of comments about her from critics who tend to focus more on her defeats than her victories. The online trolling may intensify if Stephens does not win another major title. She and her coach of three years, Kamau Murray, split after the 2018 season, then reunited in 2019. Sylvester Black, an African American who first worked with Stephens when she was twelve years old, coached her in Singapore. Sven Groeneveld, a Dutchman, coached her briefly in 2019.

"Everyone was, like, 'Oh, she's a one-hit wonder, she'll never do anything again,'" Stephens said in Singapore, verbally placing a chip on each shoulder. "I want to have some better results in the bigger tournaments and just do better and show that I'm, you know, I'm a top ten player or a top whatever player."

9 | James Blake

I became an accidental activist.

JAMES BLAKE

"Standing while black" should not be hazardous to one's health. But on September 9, 2015, James Blake found out how troublesome standing while black can be in America. On a sunny afternoon in New York City, Blake, once the fourth-best tennis player in the world, waited in front of the tony Grand Hyatt hotel on Forty-Second Street for a courtesy car to take him through the Midtown Tunnel and on to the National Tennis Center for a day of meetings at the U.S. Open. Blake, a retired champion with ten pro titles, had not spent as much time in the tennis community in 2015 as he once had. Just a year earlier, he was a fan favorite on the ATP tour, particularly at the U.S. Open, not far from his birthplace of Yonkers, New York, or the city where he spent his formative years, Fairfield, Connecticut. A handsome man with light brown skin and a shaved head, Blake has the look of an actor. By 2015, a year after he retired as a player, his main associations with tennis were as a commentator with Tennis Channel and as chairman of the USTA Foundation, the organization's charitable arm. He had business to attend to that day, so he checked his smartphone just like countless others in busy Manhattan and waited for the courtesy car. Trouble arrived instead.

At first, Blake thought that he recognized the white man with the shaved head and hulking build who ran aggressively toward him. He thought it may have been one of his old wrestling teammates from Fairfield High School, where he had made many friends and where they named the school's tennis courts after him. The local boy made good. It's just another ex-classmate, Blake thought. Until he received a most unceremonious greeting. Without saying a word, the white man picked up Blake and body-slammed him to the concrete sidewalk as horrified bystanders looked on. The man then pounced on top of Blake, pushing his knee into the small of Blake's back to hold the startled former champion in place. Blake then saw the man produce a pair of handcuffs. Figuring no one could be that kinky, Blake presumed that it had to be an undercover police officer pinning his body to the pavement.

"This is a mistake," Blake told the man who still had not said a word. "I'm in tennis. I'm going to the U.S. Open. You can check my ID." The man yanked Blake to his feet but still did not identify himself as four other officers swooped in and surrounded Blake. Had Blake shown enough righteous indignation to demand an explanation for being body-slammed in broad daylight on a crowded city street, the brutality could have escalated and he may have ended up dead. Blake could have been severely injured, perhaps permanently injured, by the body slam had he not been in fine physical condition. Had he talked back to the undercover cop who failed to identify himself that day, or exchanged harsh words with one of the other officers who rushed in, he could have been killed. Video footage of brutal interactions between people of color and law enforcement officers, confrontations that sometimes end in death, has become more prevalent.

This was not the first time Blake had been singled out by police, he said. When he was nineteen, he signed his first endorsement contract with Nike for clothes and tennis shoes. He said he spent some of that money on "a couple of nice cars." Since Blake wore his hair in dreadlocks at the time and was young and brown skinned and driving a nice car, he must have set off sirens within the department of racial profiling. Several times, he said, officers pulled him over "for nothing." Hence, his list of encounters with police includes these trumped-up charges:

Driving while black: 1990s
Standing while black: 2015

One of the officers on Forty-Second Street (not the body-slammer) told Blake that he fit the description of a man wanted for credit card fraud. It is hard to imagine that even in the most lawless metropolis, a suspected credit card fraudster would be body-slammed onto concrete and then surrounded by five other officers. As Blake tried to urge the police to walk him back to his hotel room at the Hyatt so he could produce more definitive proof that he was not a con man, the body-slammer would only say in a tone of distrust, "We'll see. Yeah, we'll see." Finally, an older man arrived, most likely a detective, who ordered Blake uncuffed. He apologized to Blake. The body-slammer did not.

Blake, who in his playing days projected a gentlemanly image reminiscent of his tennis hero Arthur Ashe, wanted to put this stunning example of racial profiling behind him. He called his wife, Emily, who was back home in San Diego, with their two infant daughters. "I just want to forget about it," he told her. But Emily, emotionally distraught after learning of the assault, asked, "What if that had happened to me?" Emily Snyder Blake is white. James Blake is the product of an interracial marriage between an African American man and a white British woman. White women in America are not nearly as likely as men of color to be subjected to racial profiling. Still, Emily's point had hit home: What if your loved one had suffered this way? Would you want to just forget about it?

"You have to do something," she told him. "You can't just let it go."

Blake learned that the New York Police Department (NYPD) had concocted a version of the incident that did not jibe with the facts, or the surveillance footage from a camera outside the hotel. The NYPD said Blake had not been body-slammed and had been in police custody for no more than five minutes before he was released with an apology. The video camera showed otherwise. Once Blake arrived at the U.S. Open that day, he used his voice in a way he never had before.

No way, he said, am I the only black man who has been treated so brutally by law enforcement officers—physical abuse followed by an official story that gave a falsified version of what had occurred.

"I became an accidental activist," Blake said. "I realized this is something that has happened to so many other people, people who don't have the voice that I do, so it wouldn't be fair to stay quiet. I could have just gone back to my comfortable life in San Diego with my wife and two daughters, but that wouldn't be fair because, then, it would just happen more and more. Then I would have felt guilty about not doing all I could to make a difference."

Since that terrible experience on a busy Manhattan street, Blake has done all he can to give voice to those who are routinely ignored, those who are assumed guilty because of how they look, how they sound, or whom they choose to love. He has chosen in tennis retirement a path charted by Ashe throughout the latter's stellar tennis career. Blake has fought hard, and publicly, to try to get the body-slammer removed from the NYPD. When news reports revealed that the officer who attacked him (James Frascatore) had a record of at least three previous civilian complaints, including a charge of punching a man in the face, Blake believed a modicum of justice would eventually be served. Instead, in a departmental trial, the NYPD ruled that Frascatore would lose five vacation days. That's all. Blake launched a fierce verbal volley in response. "Losing a few vacation days for the use of excessive force, following a history of repeated civilian complaints, is not meaningful discipline," he told reporters. "It is this continued failure of the NYPD's disciplinary system that perpetuates police abuses, brutality, and misconduct, and leads to the unjust killings of civilians."

In a bizarre twist, Frascatore, perhaps emboldened by the lenient penalty handed down by the NYPD board, sued Blake, alleging that the negative publicity had made his life "a living hell." But in an act of sanity, a judge tossed out the frivolous lawsuit. Blake, meanwhile, has continued to use his voice and celebrity to amplify issues of social justice, issues about which he would not have commented during a fourteen-year professional tennis career.

During an interview on August 24, 2018, at Yale University in New Haven, Connecticut, before he would face Tommy Haas, a retired player from Germany, in a one-set "legends" match, Blake spoke firmly in support of Colin Kaepernick, the former San Francisco 49ers quarterback who has been shunned by the National Football League since the end of the 2016 season for taking a knee during the national anthem to call attention to issues of police brutality. "What's happened is extremely sad," Blake began. "The initial protest by Kaepernick clearly stated that it was about police brutality, injustice, and racism. It has been switched, thanks in part to the White House, saying that it's about the anthem, it's about the flag, it's about veterans, when it was clearly stated that those things had nothing to do with it."

Blake took issue with Donald Trump, the forty-fifth and least likely president of the United States, for arguing that what NFL owners should say about a player who does not stand for the anthem is, "Get that son of a bitch off the field!" Kaepernick, Blake said, "has given up in upwards of $30 million that he would have been entitled to in his career as a quarterback in a league that has clearly blackballed him. And still, he's putting his money where his mouth is by donating more than $1 million—$25,000, $50,000, $100,000 at a time—to various grassroots organizations that are making a big difference, and he's encouraging other people to do so." Indeed, a list of organizations to which Kaepernick has made donations includes Mothers Against Police Brutality ($25,000), Communities United for Police Reform ($25,000), The Mni Wiconi Health Clinic Partnership at Standing Rock Reservation ($50,000), Meals on Wheels ($50,000), and Imagine LA ($20,000, with a matching donation by Serena).

"All the pro football players are trying to do is protest injustice," Blake concluded. "It's similar in a way to Rosa Parks breaking a rule by sitting in the front of the bus [an act that sparked the Montgomery, Alabama, bus boycott in 1955]. That law was clearly unjust, and people silently and forcefully protested against it. That's what I feel the NFL players are doing. For it to be done during the anthem is what has brought the issue to many people's attention. That's why it's still being talked about two years later. Having the emphasis shift to being about the flag and the anthem is really unfortunate. That's clearly not what the players are doing. In fact, what servicemen fought for is freedom of speech. There are so many freedoms that we have in this country, including the freedom to speak up, and not do it violently. There's nothing going on where the players are attacking police officers. The players are going about their business and still competing on the field. I think it needs to get back to a conversation about police brutality. I wish it would get back to talking about the number of arrests, the number of deaths, the mass incarceration of African Americans in this country. It's something that's out of control and needs to be stopped."

To journalists who covered Blake during his tennis career, these comments are surprising. Not because his comments are not thoughtful and informed. He was always one of the smartest and most well-spoken players on the pro tour. He left Harvard University after his sophomore year to turn pro when he was America's No. 1 collegiate player in 1999. But what is surprising about Blake's outspokenness now, at the age of thirty-nine, is the degree to which he assiduously avoided controversy during his career. That, he says now, was largely by design.

"In my final press conference as a player, I said I didn't have any regrets about my career," he said. "I did everything I could to be as good a player as I could. That was my main goal—go about my business and do everything I can to win, have kind of a one-track mind to be focused only on tennis. I guess the only regret I have now is not that I didn't have more success, financially or rankings-wise, but that my voice didn't have more gravity. To be able to speak up about things that maybe aren't right in the world. I used to mention that LGBT [lesbian, gay, bisexual, and transgender] athletes were not getting the right kind of treatment by others. There were still derogatory things being said about them, and there were laws on the books that were exclusionary. I didn't think I would be saying much about these things, but then what happened to me in 2015 happened."

Since being brutalized for standing while black, Blake has more closely aligned himself with Ashe. In an homage of sorts to Ashe's 1993 memoir, *Days of Grace*, which highlighted the tennis legend's decades-long dedication to the struggle for human rights and social justice, Blake in 2017 wrote *Ways of Grace: Stories of Activism, Adversity, and How Sports Can Bring Us Together*. Blake's book highlights other athletes who have used their status as public figures to focus attention on important issues and advocate for social change. Included in the book are the stories of how Serena and, especially, Venus helped bring about equal prize money for women players at Wimbledon, and the heavy price paid in the United States by black sprinters Tommie Smith and John Carlos for their one-gloved "Black Power" salute on the podium at the 1968 Summer Olympics in Mexico City.

As tennis's most talented black male player through much of his career, Blake often fielded questions about whether he was "the next Arthur Ashe." But with Blake, the Ashe comparisons went further because of their similarities in on-court demeanor and off-court character and graciousness. In 2008 Blake received the Arthur Ashe Humanitarian Award from the ATP during a pro tournament in Miami. The year before, Blake released *Breaking Back: How I Lost Everything and Won Back My Life*. The book, which reached No. 15 on the *New York Times*'s best-seller list, recounted the first twenty-eight years of Blake's life—from being the second son of biracial parents who met as tennis singles in Yonkers, New York; to being diagnosed at age thirteen with severe scoliosis, which required him to wear a back brace for eighteen hours a day during his teenage years; to overcoming that bout with adversity to put himself on the radar as a pro prospect from Fairfield, not exactly a hotbed of tennis talent; to making an inspiring professional comeback after fracturing vertebrae in his neck in May 2004 when his head hit an unforgiving net post while playing a practice set in Rome with fellow American Robby Ginepri; to losing his father, Thomas Sr., to cancer in July 2004. Years spent watching his father battle cancer compelled Blake to launch an annual event in 2003 that has raised millions of dollars through the Thomas Blake

Sr. Memorial Research Fund at Memorial Sloan-Kettering Cancer Center in New York City.

Like Ashe, Blake acquired a reputation in the tennis community for not publicly revealing whatever distress he may have felt from racial slights on the court. Ashe, for example, did not visibly erupt when Ilie Năstase of Romania, a future Hall of Famer and an incorrigible bad boy, spewed, "That goddamn n——!" during a match against him. Ashe also defused a potentially combustible situation before a doubles match when his playing partner Năstase, in a misguided attempt at humor, walked onto the court in blackface.

Blake himself had a memorable moment when he could have exploded on August 31, 2001, during a second-round match at the U.S. Open against the No. 4 seed, Lleyton Hewitt of Australia. The players had split the first two sets, with Blake often bringing the partisan crowd to its feet after hitting winners with his biggest weapon, the forehand. Foot speed, which Blake used to cover the court and set up his finishing strokes, and the forehand were his key strengths, and he employed them to good effect against Hewitt. An upset did not appear out of the question—until a close line call went against Hewitt early in the third set. Since video replay technology to decide close calls would not come to pro tennis until 2006, players were still taught to rely on the competence, integrity, and professionalism of the umpire and linespersons. But on this day, Hewitt threw tennis etiquette into the trash bin. He went for the race card simply because a black linesperson, Marion Johnson, had made a close call in Blake's favor. Hewitt made a beeline toward the umpire's chair, pointed to Johnson, and shouted, "Look at him!" He then pointed at Blake and shouted, "Look at him! You tell me what the similarity is!" Hewitt has never revealed whether he acted out of fear that he could lose in an upset to an American at America's Grand Slam event, and Blake chose not to find out. Regardless, Hewitt made the ugly insinuation that a black linesperson had made a call in Blake's favor because of race. During the outburst, Blake's on-court demeanor was that of someone who had not heard Hewitt's remarks. But the crowd certainly heard them—there was a boom microphone just below the umpire's chair. The fans booed Hewitt vociferously for the remainder of the match, and cheered wildly for Blake, especially after he won the third set for a two-sets-to-one lead. The Aussie appeared ready to be knocked out if Blake had continued to take the fight to him. However, Blake suffered physically in sets four and five. Dehydration and stomach cramps caused him to vomit on the court, and he received three bags of intravenous fluid after losing the controversial match, 6–4, 3–6, 2–6, 6–3, 6–0.

Afterward, Blake admitted to reporters that he had heard what Hewitt said, and he had clearly understood the insinuation. He simply chose to discuss it with Hewitt, one-on-one. "We talked about it in the locker room, and he did apologize," Blake said. "What he said was wrong. And he said he didn't mean for it to come out the way it did. I didn't know him well at all at the time. But I knew we would both be on the tour for a long time, and I told him that if he said anything like that again, I wouldn't be so kind. I'm not a pushover. I just made the decision that I was going to give him the benefit of the doubt that time."

Blake's older brother, Thomas Jr., and his parents attended the Hewitt match. His parents told a courtside reporter in a live interview on USA Network that James tries to ignore issues of race. Since that statement conjured an image of Althea Gibson in her heyday saying that she did not focus on racial issues, Blake provided a clarification after the match. He told reporters that he did not ignore racial issues but instead tried not to focus on them during a match because trying to beat a world-class player such as Hewitt was difficult enough. Still, Hewitt's insinuation in 2001 has long left a sour taste in the mouths of Blake's fans, especially considering that Hewitt went on to win the U.S. Open that year.

On November 20, 2006, Blake rose to a career-high world ranking of No. 4. He also helped lead the United States to a Davis Cup championship in 2007. He earned $7.98 million in prize money in his career. Yet he could have achieved more. He is arguably the most talented player to never reach the semifinals of any major tournament. "I would have thought James Blake would have won a major; I thought he had the game," said MaliVai Washington, a former ESPN commentator whose appearance in the 1996 Wimbledon final is the last by an African American male at a Grand Slam event. "As an announcer, I was analyzing James's game. I saw him winning a major, but for whatever reason, it didn't happen. That he never got to a major semifinal is mind-boggling." Perhaps Blake was too nice as a player, not possessive of a Serena-like killer instinct that is needed to fight off all comers and stand alone at the top. At major tournaments the men play best-of-five-set matches, so it is noteworthy that Blake's career record in five-set affairs was 4-15. In the deciding set of matches (either best-of-three or best-of-five), his record was 103-104. In matches on clay, the surface of doom for American men, Blake was 46-54. On grass where his speed and groundstrokes should have served him better, he was 32-29. On hardcourts he shined brightest, compiling a record of 283-166. But in championship matches on all surfaces, his record was 10-14.

Largely because of his speed and forehand, Blake gave an annual dose of hope to his fans in the tristate area (New York, New Jersey, and Connecticut) who attended the U.S. Open. Approximately a dozen of them regularly came to U.S. Open matches in matching T-shirts and full voice, and they called themselves "the J-Block." Cheering and chanting whenever Blake won a point and consuming enough mass quantities of beer to rival *Saturday Night Live*'s Coneheads, the J-Block did its best to try to get their man onto the champion's podium at Flushing Meadows. But it never happened.

Blake's best chance to win a major title occurred at the 2005 U.S. Open. He looked the part of a champion in his first four matches, as well as in the first two sets of his quarterfinal match against another popular American, Andre Agassi. Blake won the first two sets, 6-3, 6-3. But Agassi, a brilliant ball-striker, raised his game and won the next two sets, 6-3, 6-3. In an intense, thoroughly entertaining fifth set, Blake went ahead with an early service break only to have Agassi storm back behind a flurry of baseline winners to grab a 5-3 lead. Blake then rallied to force a final set tiebreak in a match with enough ebbs and flows to rival a heavyweight championship bout. Blake smacked a forehand winner that left him two points from victory, two points from a first career major semifinal. However, Agassi unleashed a final and decisive flurry of winners from the baseline, earning four of the last five points to seize the tiebreak, 8–6, and the match. "My heart dropped a little bit," Blake said. "Obviously, you want to win, but you feel it in your stomach, once you realize it's over. You've got to just walk up there and congratulate Andre." (Agassi went on to lose in the U.S. Open final to top-seeded Roger Federer.) Blake, for all his tennis gifts, never came that close to a major semifinal again. Thus, he had to confront the question, "Are you just too nice to be No. 1?"

"I think you can be a nice guy and be No. 1," he replied. "Roger Federer is No. 1, and he's as nice a guy as you could ever meet. I think he proves that you can be nice to people, and respect other people, and have friends in the sport, and still be No. 1."

It has become almost a reflexive response from Blake's fans that he did not win a major title because he had the misfortune of playing much of his career at the same time as three true legends: Federer, who holds the men's record with twenty major titles; Rafael Nadal, who is second with nineteen after winning the French Open and U.S. Open in 2019; and Novak Djokovic, who owns sixteen, including 2019 titles at the Australian Open and Wimbledon. But Andy Murray of Scotland, not as gifted a player as Federer, Nadal, or Djokovic, has still won three major titles in this era. Stan Wawrinka of Switzerland, also not as gifted as Federer, Nadal, or Djokovic, nevertheless has won three major titles. Furthermore, Juan Martin del Porto of Argentina and Marin Čilić of Croatia have each won a major title during the reign of Federer, Nadal, and Djokovic. What Murray, Wawrinka, Čilić, and del Potro have done that Blake, unfortunately, could not, is elevate their games at the biggest tournaments and maintain that high level of consistency for an entire fortnight. Those players have not done it nearly as often as Federer, Nadal, or Djokovic. But they have done it. When a major tournament reaches the quarterfinals, each of the eight remaining players has won four matches and has built some momentum and confidence.

From that point on, anything can happen. Often, there is no telling who will be the hottest player on the court in those final three rounds. Occasionally, major champions have to defeat players ranked ahead of them to win titles. They have to score upsets. Blake did not do it often enough. His career record against players ranked in the world top ten at the time was 19-55.

Blake is quite busy these days. In 2018 he became the tournament director of the Miami Open, a two-week hardcourt event in which the top female and male players compete. Aside from making the rounds daily to make sure that players, fans, VIPs, sponsors, officials, and media were happy—and taking steps to correct whatever problems may arise—Blake was also the public face of the tournament. He fielded questions from reporters in 2018 about the event's move to a new facility at Hard Rock Stadium, the home of the NFL's Miami Dolphins. After thirty-four years in Key Biscayne, the tournament relocated to a much larger facility in the name of progress, Blake said. Among his other duties before the 2019 event in March was to announce the extension of a deal with Itau, Latin America's largest privately owned bank, to continue as the Miami Open's major sponsor through 2024. The tournament has a total prize purse of $7.97 million. Sloane Stephens and John Isner won the titles in 2018, each taking home $1.34 million from an event that guarantees equal prize money for men and women.

"We work closely with the ATP and the WTA at my tournament in Miami, and we all want the same thing—greater prize money for both sides," Blake said. "The only argument that people seem to make about gender equity in tennis is that the men play three out of five sets at the majors and the women play two out of three sets. But in our tournament, both the men and the women play two out of three sets, so, of course, they should be paid the same. People see the work that the players are doing on the court in the matches. But I don't think people realize how much work the players do off the court, in practice and in workouts, to earn that money. They deserve every dollar they get."

As a post-retirement player, Blake proved worthy of top honors in the 2018 Invesco Legends Series, an exhibition tour in which retired male stars played one-set matches in the semifinals and the final round in ten different cities (nine in the United States and one in Toronto, Canada). Blake, displaying more court speed and quickness than the other seniors, finished in first place against a field that also featured John McEnroe, Lleyton Hewitt, Jim Courier, Michael Chang, Todd Martin, Robby Ginepri, Tommy Haas, Mardy Fish, and Mark Philippoussis. (The legends series awarded no prize money, according to an event spokesman.) When the series came to Yale University in August 2018 for matches during the WTA Connecticut Open, Blake defeated Haas in the semifinal, and then outlasted the fifty-eight-year-old McEnroe in the final, 6-4.

"It's a ton of fun; I still love playing," Blake said at Yale. "Part of what you miss about the pro tour is the locker room. The other players have become my friends. You get to have different conversations with people than you used to. Tommy Haas and I have four daughters between us. We talk more now about changing diapers and about playdates instead of—well, I'll spare you what we talked about in the locker room when I was twenty-two or twenty-three. Now, we go out there and beat each other up and then come in here and have a beer together."

Blake's daughters, now six and four, are well past the diaper-wearing stage. Indeed, they may soon be ready for what many black parents call "the talk"—potentially lifesaving advice on what a child should do in an encounter with a police officer. Blake's father gave him and Thomas Jr. the talk when they were teenagers in Fairfield. "He explained that the city where we lived was 98 percent white, and if I was at a party at midnight and the cops showed up and saw sixty kids and one tall black kid, I would get singled out," Blake said. "Our dad didn't want us in a bad situation. He didn't allow us to play with toy guns—no water guns, no cap pistols, no guns allowed. He didn't want us in a situation where someone would mistake a toy gun for the real thing."

Since there have been too many painful episodes in too many American cities because an interaction between a person of color and a law enforcement officer has gone horribly wrong, Blake said his daughters will someday hear the talk. "There will be something about police, about profiling, and how we treat people," he said. But perhaps he will wait until his girls are old enough to watch the video of their father being body-slammed on a New York City street for no reason by an undercover cop. Perhaps he will let them see it and then ask questions about it.

Blake had filed a lawsuit against New York City and the NYPD, but he withdrew the suit in June 2017 and instead asked the city to establish a legal fellowship that would advocate for people who have had unpleasant encounters with the NYPD. "I wanted to move to something positive, and I wanted to provide help to people who don't have a voice or the resources," he said. The fellowship began in January 2018 and will be funded by New York City for six years. Funds will be made available to lawyers making a minimum salary of $65,000 a year who want to represent clients who would otherwise be unable to afford legal services. The city also agreed to reimburse Blake for $175,000 in attorney's fees and travel costs. "If the fellowship serves a purpose and helps the citizens of New York, hopefully there will be pressure on future politicians to keep it going," he said. "The hope is that it makes a difference for people who need legal help."

However accidental his activism may have been, Blake in tennis retirement is bearing a much closer resemblance nowadays to his role model, Arthur Ashe.

10 | Tournament Director

A lot of people in tennis don't believe in tennis.

DALE CALDWELL

The best way to develop a love affair with tennis is to start playing the sport and then watch it played well. So many people did not have tennis on their radar until they saw Venus and Serena ply their trade on the biggest stages in the world. Now, those folks are not only fans of the Williams sisters, or whomever their favorite players happen to be, but they are also devotees of the sport. Many of them signed up for tennis lessons, and—once they learned to consistently keep a rally going for more than four hits—they became players themselves. Better still, they shared their newfound love of the game as if it were an elixir with family and friends. Trips to the neighborhood tennis courts or the indoor club with the fancy bubble on top that lets them play year-round became a healthy obsession. Tennis became the common denominator that turned strangers into fast friends, if not lovers, or creators of future champions.

One day, on a public tennis court on Central Park Avenue in Yonkers, New York, an African American man named Thomas met a white British woman named Betty. Their shared forehands, backhands, and verbal volleys led to romance, and then marriage, and then the birth of two sons. One of those sons, James Blake, became a Davis Cup champion for the United States and the winner of ten singles titles. He also became known as a gentleman of sterling character, in the Arthur Ashe tradition, which spoke well of his parents and the sport they fancied. That is how tennis is discovered and cherished by so many. That is how many black people since the last decade of the twentieth century have found tennis. It was no longer an activity just for the rich. It was no longer some "sissy sport." Tennis became cool because a pair of black sisters made it so. Those newly minted tennis fans still remember images of the seventeen-year-old Serena, her braided hair adorned with white beads, exclaiming, "I can't believe it!" while pressing her left palm against her chest after winning her first major title, a straight-sets victory over then world No. 1 Martina Hingis at the 1999 U.S. Open final. On that sunny September afternoon, it appeared as if Serena would win tennis trophies forever—and she just might. Many fans have a similarly indelible memory of Venus celebrating like a human pogo stick, bouncing all over the grass on Wimbledon's Centre Court following her first major title, a straight-sets triumph over fellow American Lindsay Davenport in the 2000 final. Give yourself extra credit if you remember that Serena and Venus each won their first major singles championship by the same scores, 6-3, 7-6. It is perfectly fine to be a tennis fan, and to encourage others to join you. One New Jersey man is on a quest to create more tennis fans, and more players, and more opportunities for players who are not blessed with the athletic skills of a Serena or Venus to make a living in the sport.

Bringing tennis to the masses is what the United States Tennis Association purports to do, but too many Americans still have not been so introduced. Dr. Dale Caldwell is determined to change that. He is an educator who in 2011 became the first African American to serve as president of the USTA Eastern Section, which covers New York City, New Jersey, and southern Connecticut. Caldwell saw this as a golden opportunity to cultivate new tennis players and fans in the Northeast region, and he had definite ideas on how to do it. Unfortunately, the

USTA board did not share his vision for taking tennis to the masses instead of encouraging individuals to join clubs supported by USTA funds. After he served on the USTA board in 2011 and 2012, he left in 2013, unhappy with the association's player development strategy.

"The USTA has more of a connection with corporate interests and less of a connection with people who play tennis," said Caldwell, a certified tennis teaching professional for more than thirty years. "Our country should be developing more players who can make a living in the sport and win championships. The USTA says, 'We're doing our best as a non-profit organization.' The USTA has a net profit of $180 million a year, so how it is a nonprofit?" Referring to Martin Blackman, USTA general manager of player development, Caldwell said, "The job of the USTA should be to empower Martin to give money to promising tennis programs and coaches in American communities. If the USTA gave Martin $3 million a year to distribute to tennis programs and coaches where there are talented players who need that additional assistance, then America would produce a lot more players than we're seeing now." Too many talented youngsters in urban cities walk away from the sport, Caldwell asserts, because the USTA does not provide enough resources to help keep programs and facilities sustainable.

Blackman, a black former ATP player who grew up in the Bronx, New York, said the USTA's player development program, which includes a one-hundred-court training complex in Orlando, will eventually produce more American stars. "Orlando is a huge asset because it allows us to say 'yes' to more players, and our training center in Carson, California, is an asset for developing players based on the West Coast," he said. Although the USTA is long on optimism, the results have still come up short.

John McEnroe is among those in the United States attempting to duplicate the European model of year-round academies where kids receive a private-school education while eating, sleeping, and drinking tennis. Caldwell does not believe that approach will produce many future champions here. "The McEnroe model might work for upper-middle-class kids, but it won't work for kids in the 'hood,'" he said. "Why would it? You're taking inner-city kids away from their loved ones and friends and isolating them in an unfamiliar environment. That's culture shock. If kids can't grow up playing a sport they enjoy with their friends and near their families, then it's unlikely that they will enjoy that sport enough to stay with it."

Caldwell devotes much of his life's work to the study of human behavior. There is plenty of the Ivy League on his resume, specifically an undergraduate degree from Princeton University and an MBA from the Wharton School at the University of Pennsylvania, as well as a PhD in education. He is the executive director of the Rothman Institute for Innovators and Entrepreneurs at Fairleigh Dickinson University in New Jersey. He also runs a company called Strategic Influence, and he has created a program called Intelligent Influence, which is a framework for developing effective human interaction. In 2010 he received the Tennis Educational Merit Award from the International Tennis Hall of Fame. He was the cocurator of *Breaking Barriers*, an exhibit on the history of blacks in tennis, which debuted at the ITHF a decade ago. He is the founder of the Black Tennis Hall of Fame, which exists not in a physical space but in cyberspace at www.blacktennishistory.com, and he is the coauthor of *Tennis in New York: The History of the Most Influential Sport in the Most Influential City in the World*. He credits tennis with helping him overcome extreme shyness as a boy. The son of a Methodist minister who would sometimes strategize with Dr. Martin Luther King Jr. during America's civil rights movement in the 1950s and 1960s, Caldwell got used to his family moving from one city to another. Through success in tennis, he developed self-esteem, pursued positions of leadership, and made friends. Hearing the stories of how whites would not allow his father to share tennis courts with them in some southern cities made him more determined to play the sport. He starred on teams he captained in high school and college and competed in USTA-sanctioned events but did not play on the ATP tour.

As Caldwell knows, there are many people who are not talented enough for the ATP or WTA tour but can play tennis with a high level of proficiency. Those players are skilled enough to entertain crowds and influence others to take up the sport. Now, he wants to provide a showcase for them. "The No. 76 player in the world is a very talented player who is traveling all over the world, competing mostly in smaller tournaments for the ranking points, and he may have $200,000 in earnings and $150,000 in expenses," he said. "Since tennis players are responsible for their own travel, lodging, and expenses, a player who's making $200,000 a year doesn't have that amount in his pocket at the end of the year. That player would be better served playing in tournaments closer to home where he could make that level of income and acquire the ranking points he needs to move up." Caldwell wants to create a series of tournaments for rising male and female players, collegiate players, and other unsung players with skills. His goal is to launch events in the Eastern Section in the future, including the Central Park Open in New York City, and the Newark Open, New Brunswick Open, Jersey City Open, and Trenton Open in New Jersey. His plan is to eventually expand the circuit nationally and into the Caribbean.

Caldwell intends to brand these tournaments as the People Up tour. "Yes, People Up, as opposed to top down," he said with a grin. "Tennis will grow from the grassroots level up. Tennis needs to do a better job of introducing the sport to people. That's where the future generations of tennis players and fans have to come from." His vision includes combining the matches with live concerts to give spectators a chance to watch potential stars in tennis and music in their forma-tive stages. Caldwell has reached out to tennis facilities, potential sponsors, and people well connected in music and entertainment to introduce his concept of People Up. The responses have been encour-aging, he said. "There is plenty of undiscovered talent out there," he said. "These events will allow talented athletes and artists to be seen up close, in front of their family and friends, and in front of people who will become their new fans."

Victoria Duval is an athlete and artist who could showcase her talents on a People Up tour. At the 2013 U.S. Open, Duval, then seventeen, thrilled a capacity crowd at Ashe Stadium with a first-round upset of Samantha Stosur, the 2011 Open champion. In 2014 Duval was ranked a career-high No. 87 in singles. But while competing at Wimbledon, she was diagnosed with Hodgkin's lymphoma. However, the Miami native has persevered, drawing upon strength similar to that shown by her father, Jean-Maurice, a doctor who survived a 2010 earthquake in his native country of Haiti that left him with broken legs, cracked ribs, a broken arm, and a punctured lung. Duval has been cancer-free since September 2014. She designs T-shirts—a percentage of each sale goes to cancer research. "Art has been a big part of my life for many years," she said. "It's gotten me through a lot of obstacles." She began 2019 ranked No. 353 with a goal of returning to the top one hundred. Regular exposure in People Up events might just boost her ranking and her business.

Caldwell sees a People Up tour as an extension of the New York Open, a professional tennis event he staged for two years earlier in this decade during Fourth of July weekend. The first New York Open took place from July 4 to 7, 2013, at the historic West Side Tennis Club in Forest Hills, which, until 1978, hosted the U.S. Open. A mix of amateurs and professionals competed in the New York Open, and, in a homage to Wimbledon, the players wore tennis whites. Since the West Side Tennis Club bears a resemblance to the All England Lawn Tennis and Croquet Club in Wimbledon, England, spectators must have felt as if they had stepped into a time machine. With Caldwell serving as the tournament director, fans came away from the New York Open impressed with the quality of the matches. Winston Lin, a member of the Columbia University tennis team, won the men's title, but, as an amateur, he was unable to accept the modest winner's check of $2,000. However, he got to keep the silver championship plate. The women's title was won by Nini Lagvilava, a professional player from Georgia—not the American state, but the country at the intersection of Europe and Asia. Since the event quite rightfully offered equal prize money, she walked away with $2,000 and a silver plate. The New York Open also included a book festival, a film festival, jazz musicians, food vendors, and a slew of volunteers.

From July 3 to 5, 2014, the tournament moved to the Central Park Tennis Courts on West Ninety-Third Street and Central Park West in

Manhattan, so the tournament could accommodate more spectators and allow Caldwell and his nonprofit organization, Tennis in New York, Inc., to offer free tickets. Owing to its new venue, the event included supervised hikes in Central Park, yoga classes, and lectures on tennis and mindfulness. A skilled networker, Caldwell partnered with the New York chapter of the National Autism Association to include an autism support festival as part of the weekend, which brought even more people into the park to sample the tennis. Every attendee received a free tennis lesson.

After the 2014 event, Caldwell was approached by a group that wanted to buy the name "New York Open" to stage its own tennis tournament. Caldwell, less married to the name than to the concept of bringing talented yet unsung tennis players to the public in a free weekend tournament that also featured music, local artists, booksellers, and educators, sold the name for a fee "in the low six figures," he said.

The 2018 version of the New York Open was staged in February as a weeklong men's indoor tournament on an all-black court inside the Nassau Veterans Memorial Coliseum on Long Island. Opening night featured exhibition matches with Sloane Stephens and John McEnroe. The tournament also unexpectedly featured racial controversy. During a match between Donald Young, a black player from Georgia, and Ryan Harrison, a white player from Florida, Young accused Harrison of uttering a racial slur. Harrison vehemently denied the accusation. Both players had exchanged heated words during the match. Afterward, in conversations with tournament officials, the umpire, and a ball boy near the scene of the on-court confrontation, no one admitted to hearing a racial slur. Both Young and Harrison have since declined to discuss the matter publicly. Those who believe any publicity is good publicity would more likely remember the 2018 New York Open than Caldwell's controversy-free predecessor. However, the 2013 and 2014 New York Opens made a more positive impression. A black educator and former USTA board member with no previous experience as a tournament director successfully staged two tennis events featuring professional players in an intimate, fan-friendly setting. Each event was community driven, not corporate led, and the concept holds considerable promise for black people, indeed all people, who are interested in making inroads on the business side of tennis—a $5.57-billion-a-year industry in the United States, according to the Tennis Industry Association.

"I'm creating minor-league tennis," Caldwell said with a broad smile. "A player in the People Up tour can make $50,000 a year. Granted, you won't make a lot of money, but you can make a living. It takes a financial commitment in the six figures to put a tournament on the ATP or WTA schedule. That means there are a lot of people in America who are not getting to see professional tennis players compete in person. And the ATP and WTA both want to limit their events to the top three hundred players in the world rankings. If you fall below that level, you're relegated to the minors. If you're not a star, it's tough to make a living now in tennis. So, we're going to provide those players— talented tennis players who don't have rankings high enough to play a full year on the ATP or WTA tour—with a chance to play tennis for a living. At our events, you're going to see players with a very high skill level. The fans just won't know their names yet. We'll have players with many different styles—bombers, spinners, slicers. A lot of young players tend to play in the same style: hard hitting from the baseline. It will help those players to compete in our events against more experienced players who know how to use slice and topspin. That's how you learn. That's how you grow and get better."

On today's pro circuit, it is common for the nonelite players to share hotel rooms at Challengers events or at WTA and ATP events to save money. Other players will find a friend or a host family to provide lodging to limit expenses. Caldwell said his People Up events will be even more cost-effective. "For our events, lodging won't really be an issue," he said. "Players will already live in the area, or they'll have friends and relatives to stay with, or they'll be able to rent a place Airbnb-style."

Caldwell envisions each event on the People Up tour having a field of sixteen men and sixteen women ranging in age from seventeen to their late thirties. The total prize purse would be in the range of

$7,500–$10,000 with the tournament winner receiving $3,000 and the runner-up $1,500. There would be no entry fee. Men and women would receive equal prize money for competing in best-of-three-set matches played in the morning and afternoon, Friday through Sunday.

"On a Friday or Saturday evening during the tournament, we'll have a music concert," Caldwell said. "We'll connect with people in the area who are involved in the music scene and know who the up-and-coming artists are. Those artists will have the same opportunity as the tennis players to showcase their talent and increase their fan base." In this era of live streaming, the events could be available for viewing online, just as WTA and ATP events are now for fans without televisions. Local colleges or entrepreneurs with a media background could provide the equipment for broadcasting the events.

To those accustomed to watching professional tennis in a stadium at $100 or more per ticket, or on television as part of a monthly cable or satellite fee, the People Up concept may sound far-fetched. But why can't it work? There are Challengers events that attract tennis pros to places such as Dothan, Alabama, and Tyler, Texas, and to such countries as Tunisia and Mozambique. There is no reason that minor-league events for money and rankings points cannot be staged in more American cities, so a new crop of fans can be cultivated. As exciting an event as the star-driven U.S. Open is, many fans cannot afford to attend. "The thing I found when I was on the USTA board was, a lot of people in tennis don't believe in tennis," Caldwell said. "What I mean is, those people believe in star players. Well, it's easy to support Roger Federer, Rafael Nadal, Venus, Serena. They're stars. The USTA will promote stars, but the USTA doesn't promote tennis. The support network is lacking. What is needed is a system that will bring tennis to more people and allow young people especially to be around their friends while they play the game and get better at the game. That's how to grow tennis in America and create more opportunities for people who want to make a living in tennis."

11 | Coaches

Tennis is still the domain of the wealthy.

BOB DAVIS

When Sloane Stephens, at the age of twenty-four, won the 2017 U.S. Open, among the kudos she handed out during the trophy presentation was a sincere thank you to what she called "my village." Although she did not mention the village keeper by name at that precise moment, he was right there at Arthur Ashe Stadium, in Stephens's friends' box, savoring the moment. For Kamau Murray, the village keeper, it was a highly impressive entry on his career resume. In his third year as Stephens's coach, he had essentially transformed a player with vast potential but no significant titles into a major champion.

"Sloane and I have a good perspective on wins and losses," Murray said during an interview in his hometown of Chicago. "We avoid the finger-pointing and the blame game. She and I have had a clear idea of why things have happened since we began working together in 2015. It's important to react to a win or a loss, but not to overreact. Not overreacting to things, whether they're positive or negative, helps us to maintain a positive working relationship."

Murray became Stephens's coach at the beginning of 2015 at the request of Stephens's mother, Sybil Smith, a former All-American swimmer at Boston University. "Sybil and I came to an agreement that Sloane needed a little bit of counseling as well as coaching," Murray said. "It certainly helped that we won the first tournament we went to, in Auckland, New Zealand."

But on the eve of the biggest match of Stephens's career, the 2017 U.S. Open final against Madison Keys, Stephens had an anxiety attack. She called Murray's hotel room and asked to speak with him in person. Her calmed her by illustrating on paper the way to beat Keys, using a strategy no one else had attempted. After hours of watching video of the power-hitting Keys, Murray became convinced that she didn't like to hit a forehand while moving to her right. So, the plan was to make Keys do precisely that. Take Keys, who had dominated opponents in her first five matches, out of her comfort zone. Stephens was skeptical at first, but she bought in.

Murray's strategy worked. Keys made five times as many unforced errors as Stephens, thirty to six, the vast majority of them from Keys's forehand. On point after point, Keys was forced to hit forehands while moving to her right. The errant shots accumulated like fallen leaves, resulting in a surprisingly lopsided 6–3, 6–0 victory for Stephens.

Thanks to the village keeper, Stephens's life has changed dramatically. She will be forever known as a major champion. A coach, the right coach, can make a profound difference. For Murray, Stephens is the success story that we know. Murray, thirty-eight years old, with a microscopically thin layer of black hair, smooth brown skin, and a big smile, appears poised to produce more success stories.

Murray is on a mission to establish a world-renowned tennis academy in what had been the site of one the largest public housing areas on Chicago's South Side. Situated on 13.5 acres, Murray's XS Tennis Village opened in 2018 and houses twenty-seven regulation-sized tennis courts (eleven indoors, sixteen outdoors), four smaller indoor courts for kids ages twelve and under to learn the game, a basketball court, a fitness center, a gymnasium, a boxing ring, and a classroom, where volunteers from the University of Chicago provide academic instruction and tutoring. XS exists on the same turf where the Robert

Taylor Homes housing project—infamous for gang-related violence, rampant drug use, and random killings—stood before most of the high-rise structures were finally bulldozed. Murray bought the land and raised millions of dollars from donors who shared his vision of a facility that would make Chicagoans proud, especially South Siders. His village is a model for what an inner-city tennis academy and educational center should be.

The term "village" conjures images from the Nigerian proverb "It takes a village to raise a child." The proverb means it takes a community of people to make children feel safe, nurtured, and loved so they can become their best selves. Through exposure to tennis and first-rate education, XS aims to develop future athletes, professional men and women, and better citizens.

"I call the village 'XS' as a play on the word excess, which means greater than normal, better than average," Murray said in the gym as a steady rain fell outside on the first day of December 2018. "We needed a facility with a roof. In a city like Chicago, when it's pouring rain or it's twenty degrees outside, you need a roof."

Murray's father was a college basketball player who became an attorney and then a judge in Chicago's Cook County. His mother is an educator in the Chicago public schools. All four of their children earned athletic scholarships to college. Kamau began playing tennis, somewhat by accident, at age seven. After the family returned from a summer trip to the African nation of Senegal, Kamau's parents sought to enroll him in a day camp for the rest of the summer. "Every camp in the neighborhood was full, except tennis camp," he said with a laugh. "The program cost $12 and they had space, so whether I wanted to play or not, I was going to play tennis." After Kamau attended Whitney M. Young Magnet High School, where he basically coached the tennis team after the actual coach quit, he enrolled at Florida A&M University, the alma mater of Althea Gibson. He left FAMU with his tennis letters, a bachelor's degree, and a master's degree in finance. But after less than a month on the men's pro tour, he knew he was not going to make it big as a player. He returned to Chicago and worked in sales for the pharmaceutical giant Pfizer while coaching youth tennis on the side.

"I didn't go to school to get into tennis coaching, but once I started working with kids and seeing how much they were enjoying it, I wanted to continue coaching," he said.

Coaching soon became Murray's passion. His first XS tennis program was housed in what had been a health club. Under his tutelage, black girls and boys from the South Side began to win local and statewide tournaments against white kids from well-to-do families. Before long, many of the white parents signed their kids up for lessons with Murray. Now at XS Tennis Village Murray and his twenty employees, including a staff of coaches, are nurturing, pushing, encouraging, and persuading even more kids to be better than they ever thought they could be. There were as many white kids as black kids receiving tennis instruction at XS during the December 1 visit, and that represented a typical Saturday session. Sometimes, Murray brings in special guests to share their expertise with the kids. Sloane Stephens has been to the village. On December 1 the kids met Renee Stubbs, the former Australian star who won six major titles in doubles. Former president Bill Clinton and his daughter, Chelsea, visited XS in November 2018 for an educational event. Neither former president Barack Obama nor Michelle Obama—who both used to call Chicago home—visited XS in 2018, but there is a video touting XS on Michelle's Instagram page.

Considering how busy Murray had been since the opening of XS, it did not come as a shock that he and Stephens discontinued their working relationship at the end of 2018. He did not accompany Stephens to Singapore for the WTA Finals in November—because Bill and Chelsea Clinton visited XS that week. In February 2019 Murray began coaching Monica Puig of Puerto Rico, the 2016 Olympic gold medalist. However, as if to prove that the only constant in tennis is change, Murray and Stephens reunited in August 2019.

At XS, Murray tries to make tennis instruction as affordable as possible. An individual lesson costs $80. If a child cannot afford the full amount, the family can pay on a sliding scale. Murray has already sent forty players from his program to college on tennis scholarships. One of them, Zoe Spence, became the first African American to earn a full tennis scholarship to the University of Notre Dame. As a sophomore in the 2017-18 season, Spence went 15-8 in her spring singles matches and made the Atlantic Coast Conference All-Academic Team.

Black players on predominantly white teams at the highest level of college tennis, Division I, is no longer unusual said Scoville Jenkins, who played on the pro tour for seven years and is now the associate head coach of men's tennis at Division I Oklahoma State University.

"If you look at the rosters in major college tennis, there is at least one black player on every team now," said Jenkins, who is black. "I just came from a men's tournament at the University of Tulsa, and there was a black kid playing for Tulsa, a black kid playing for the University of Nebraska–Lincoln, a black kid playing for the University of Nebraska–Omaha, and a black kid from England playing for the University of Iowa. I think the Williams sisters have done a lot to change the perception of tennis in the eyes of a lot of young black people."

Murray opened eyes in the tennis community a decade ago while coaching Taylor Townsend, a Chicago native who became the world's No. 1 junior before joining the pro tour at age sixteen. Although Townsend eventually moved to Atlanta to reunite with her original coach, Donald Young Sr., the split from Murray was amicable. "I'm a big fan of what Kamau is doing in Chicago at the XS Tennis Village," said Townsend, who won her first WTA tour doubles title in 2018. "He does a great job of coaching and motivating players."

Now that Murray's vision of a massive tennis facility on Chicago's South Side has become a reality, he seems convinced that he will produce other champions. His XS program may well challenge the notion that top junior players in America have to come from high-priced tennis academies in Florida or California to become successful pros. After all, Townsend and Donald Young Jr., both of whom became world No. 1 as juniors, come from Chicago—and they achieved that ranking before XS ever existed. "I don't know if we're an alternative to the academies in Florida and California, but we're something else,"

Murray said. "We need more opportunities for kids to play tennis. I think we fill a void. Those academies are needed. Tennis cannot afford to lose any existing programs, no matter how much they cost. But our program can fill a void for those high-performing young athletes whose parents cannot afford some of those other programs."

Chicago is known not only as the Windy City, but also as "the City of Broad Shoulders." An argument can be made that learning to play tennis in a more challenging environment could produce players who are tougher, mentally and physically. Where an infamous housing development once stood on the South Side a tennis oasis stands today. There are plans to build dormitories on the XS site as well. People who love tennis or want their children to become immersed in a tennis and educational environment may consider the XS Tennis Village as an alternative to, say, an academy in Florida that costs up to $80,000 a year per child. Honestly, are the sun-drenched climates of Florida and California really the ideal spots to develop players who are tough enough to win at tennis's highest level? Or do we just assume that they are because those are the high-priced goods we have been sold? For more than a decade, America has not been relevant on the global stage in men's tennis. Whenever Serena and Venus hang up their rackets, a gaping hole will exist in American women's tennis. Future stars need to be developed and nurtured somewhere. It appears that Murray is at once offering a new option for kids and their parents and throwing down a gauntlet to the USTA.

The best investment a young tennis player, or the parent of one, can make is to hire a coach. Playing tennis is not the kind of skill that you learn entirely by yourself. There is no such thing as a "natural player." You have to master the different strokes and grips before having any chance to succeed at the junior level, collegiate level, or professional level.

But what about Richard Williams, you might ask? Didn't he first convince his then wife, Oracene Price, to have two more daughters and then teach those newbies everything they needed to know to play tennis well and, eventually, revolutionize the sport? Well, not exactly.

First, Williams pored over stacks of tennis books and videotapes, and he took tennis lessons himself from a mysterious figure in the Compton section of Southern California, a "Mr. Oliver," who he said accepted payments in the form of whiskey. Only after Williams had been coached by others did he attempt to pour what he had learned into Venus and Serena. And once his daughters progressed beyond the level at which he could help them improve, he turned them over to professional coaches such as Rick Macci, Robert Ryland, and Nick Bollettieri for further development.

Williams and Price, a small businessman and a nurse, successfully executed a plan that produced a pair of global tennis superstars and sports icons. Most tennis parents with high aspirations for their child would not attempt the Williams-Price strategy. Those parents firmly believe that, rather than going the do-it-yourself route, their child needs quality coaching from day one to have any chance at a career in tennis or a tennis scholarship to college. Their approach to achieving the dream could be why the term "pay through the nose" was invented.

"There are kids in tennis academies in Florida whose parents are spending $80,000 a year," said veteran coach Bob Davis, who does not run such an academy. "Tennis is still the domain of the wealthy. Ninety-nine percent of those kids are not going to make a dime playing tennis. But the social benefit to being involved in tennis is a good thing. And if the kid gets a college scholarship, then those parents will believe it was all worth it."

Davis has spent a lifetime in tennis. Back in the 1950s, when the sport was still largely segregated, he played junior doubles alongside Arthur Ashe in the black-led American Tennis Association. In 1982 Davis became one of the few blacks to own and operate a tennis academy. Located in upstate New York, the facility was called Taromar (the first letters from the names of his daughters, Taryn and Robin, and his then wife Mary). Althea Gibson would sometimes visit to do some coaching. Taromar had dormitory space for forty people, two tennis courts, and an agreement to lease another fourteen courts from the nearby State University of New York at New Paltz. But there were not enough interested black families who could pay for tennis instruction. Alas, that spelled the end of Taromar.

In 1988 Davis and Ashe teamed with Nick Bollettieri to start the Ashe-Bollettieri Cities (ABC) program, which used tennis as the hook to attract inner-city youngsters for life skills training. ABC morphed into the Safe Passage Foundation, a scholarship program for youngsters, which is now run by the USTA. Davis, who lives in Bradenton, Florida, is still coaching and providing ways for those who cannot afford the high price of tennis instruction to learn the game. In the mid-1990s, he founded Black Dynamics, a company that provided funds for talented junior players to receive coaching. Two of those teenagers, Shenay Perry and Jamea Jackson, later played on the WTA tour and represented the United States in the Fed Cup. There were other success stories as well, especially after Davis was convinced to change his company's name.

"A potential donor told me, 'Your company is Black Dynamics. You should be getting money from blacks,'" Davis said. "I wanted donations from all people to help as many kids as possible. I changed the name to the Panda Foundation. A panda is a black and white bear from Asia. So, we're still around, helping kids learn the game and train against the best junior players in the world."

The big Florida-based academies such as IMG in Bradenton (formerly the Bollettieri Academy), Saddlebrook in Tampa, and Evert Tennis Academy in Boca Raton (run by Chris Evert and her brother, John) are far beyond the financial means of most American families. If learning tennis was more affordable, then it is likely that Americans would have more professional success in the sport. No American man has won *any* of the four Grand Slam events since 2003, when Andre Agassi won the Australian Open and Andy Roddick took the U.S. Open. Parents paying top dollar for a child's tennis lessons may produce a happier child who plays tennis for life and then passes on that love of the game to their children and grandchildren. That's one way to grow the sport. But it is not producing any American champions on the men's side. Nevertheless, parents who can afford to pay the freight will continue to pay, in the hope that their child may someday follow in the well-heeled footsteps of Serena and Venus.

"A director of one of the Florida academies told me he charges $44,000 a year for a child to be in his program," Davis said. "That doesn't include housing or food. Just tennis. Just on-court coaching. $44,000. That's a black family's income for an entire year!" (Actually, the average annual income for an African American family in 2018 was considerably less: $36,651.)

"If a child goes to IMG Academy for tennis coaching and private schooling, that's $80,000 a year," Davis continued. "Other academies take in children who are homeschooled, and their education is scheduled around the tennis instruction."

James Blake, once the No. 4 player in the world, grew up in Fairfield, Connecticut, far from the big academies. He takes a certain pride in not coming to tennis via a traditional route. "You don't have to go to the academies as a junior to make it to the pros," he said. "During the winters, I used to practice indoors, or before school, or late at night, whatever I had to do to stay competitive." But the route that Blake took to get to the pros would not have kept him there. Once he turned pro after his sophomore year at Harvard, he relocated to Florida and trained at Saddlebrook Academy.

A higher level of coaching, fitness training, and mental conditioning has been known to turn a pretty good junior into a major champion. Scoville Jenkins witnessed this transformation in 2004 from two of his former peers, Novak Djokovic, now a sixteen-time Grand Slam champion, and Juan Martin del Potro, who became the 2009 U.S. Open champion. Jenkins partnered with Djokovic in junior doubles at the 2004 Australian Open. At the time, both were ranked in the thirties in singles. After the event, Djokovic said goodbye to junior tennis. He was able to secure funding to move from his native country of Serbia to a tennis academy in Germany run by Rainer Schuettler, then the No. 5 player in the world. "When I saw Novak again, at the U.S. Open that summer, he was a man—not a kid anymore—a man," Jenkins said. "His forehand and his serve had been weak. Now his whole game was solid. He got the best coaching, the best physical training, the best mental training at that academy. He was a brand-new player, the Novak you see today. Same with del Potro. He went from Argentina to an academy in Europe. Before, his forehand was weak. I'm not kidding. You could attack it. Now, he kills you with his forehand. All of a sudden, I was way behind those guys."

Jenkins won the USTA boys' eighteen-and-under national championship in 2004, earning a wild card into the main draw of the U.S. Open. But like every other promising American junior a decade ago, Jenkins never caught up to Djokovic or del Potro. Could the USTA do what European academies are doing to transform promising juniors into champions, particularly at the USTA's sprawling tennis complex in Orlando, Florida, which features one hundred fully lit courts?

"I think the USTA always gravitates toward kids whose families have money, kids who can afford to travel to a lot of junior tournaments and have good results," Jenkins said. "Those are not necessarily our best prospects, or the ones who could use the assistance the most."

Former ATP and WTA players often become coaches. They coach as private instructors; or as teaching pros at clubs, academies, or resorts; or as mentors of a WTA or ATP player; or at the collegiate or private school level. In 2018 Jenkins joined the coaching staff at Oklahoma State University after spending the previous four years as an assistant at the University of Wisconsin. He has also coached at the University of Washington and Kennesaw State University in Georgia.

"A lot more people are getting into college coaching because the pay is going up," Jenkins said by phone from the OSU campus in Stillwater. "A Division I college head coach, if it's a highly ranked program, can make anywhere from $100,000 to $1 million a year. Schools will pay big for top coaches and recruiters now. Athletic directors now don't just say we want our football team to win championships, or our basketball team to win championships. They want all the athletic teams to win championships. But if you don't win, they'll fire you. It's just like coaching a nationally ranked football team now."

Jenkins declined to reveal his salary as an associate head coach, saying only, "Associate coaches are getting paid very well now. There are assistant coaches making six-figure annual salaries." As college coaches' salaries rise, the job appears to offer much more stability than coaching a professional player.

College coaching certainly involves far less travel than life on the WTA or ATP tour. The 2020 major professional tour opened in the Asia-Pacific region, highlighted by the Australian Open in January. That was followed by a pair of major hardcourt events in Indian Wells, California, and Miami in March and April. After that comes the clay-court season, with nearly all the matches in Europe, concluding with the French Open from late May to early June. Next comes a three-week grass-court season in Europe that ends with Wimbledon during the first two weeks in July. Then the summer hardcourt season is contested in the United States (except for a one-week tournament in Canada), ending with the U.S. Open from late August until mid-September. Afterward, the women spend the rest of September and October playing hardcourt events or indoor tournaments mostly in Asia. The men's tournaments are more spread out geographically until a season-ending event for the top eight players in London in November.

The opportunity to earn a salary comparable to that of a coach on the WTA or ATP tour while spending enough time in one city to actually call it home is making college coaching an increasingly attractive option. In addition to Jenkins, the list of blacks now coaching at Division I schools includes Traci Green, the women's head coach at Harvard University; Bryan Shelton, the men's head coach at the University of Florida; Rodney Harmon, the women's head coach at Georgia Tech University; Mark Beckham, the women's head coach at the University of Louisville; Torrie Browning, the women's head coach at George Washington University; Keith Puryear, the women's head coach at Navy; Rance Brown, the associate women's head coach at UCLA; Ike Kiro, the men's assistant coach at the University of Detroit Mercy; Nelo Phiri, the women's assistant coach at St. John's University; Breaunna Addison, the women's assistant coach at Miami University of Ohio; and Kris Powell, the women's assistant coach at the University of Chicago.

"I get to actually coach college players—on the pro level, I think a coach has to make a player feel better, which is more important than the actual coaching," Jenkins said. "A friend of mine, Jesse Levine, who I played with on the pro tour, coached Madison Keys for six months. That ended when she told him one day, 'It's just not working out.' A pro coach can get fired at any time." When Levine and Keys parted company after the Madrid Open in Spain, Levine had to book his own flight back to Florida. He was unemployed for several months before landing a job coaching tour pro Jessica Pegula, a Buffalo, New York, native (whose parents own the National Football League's Buffalo Bills and the National Hockey League's Buffalo Sabres) who ended 2018 ranked No. 112 in the world.

There have been much quicker breakups among pro players and their coaches than the Keys-Levine partnership. In August 2017 future Hall of Famer Maria Sharapova fired Hall of Famer Jimmy Connors after one match—Sharapova's loss to African American Taylor Townsend in Cincinnati. In the player-coach dynamic, chemistry means infinitely more than either person's resume. For that reason, a coach of a pro player should get as much in writing as possible before taking the job.

"A pro coach of an up-and-coming player, or someone who's not a star, may have a contract that guarantees a weekly salary plus bonuses if the player achieves a certain ranking—top 200, top 150, top 100," Jenkins said. "But if the player is more established, the coach may get 10 percent of a player's winnings plus a bonus. For someone who's coaching a star, the coach may get a straight salary plus a bonus if the player wins a major tournament."

A player's endorsement contract with a sponsor typically includes bonuses for advancing deep into a tournament, and a bonus for winning a major tournament, so it is understandable that a player-coach contract would be structured the same way. But whether the player is elite, or a veteran tour pro trying to advance, or a youngster just starting out, there is no substitute for having a quality coach. However, quality is expensive. This is tennis, after all.

"The player is expected to pay for all of a coach's expenses, and the coach doesn't want to work for $20,000 a year—he wants some money," Jenkins said. "A player who is just starting in the pros should try to get a coach from a good federation, like the French federation, because when you're a young player, the federation will take care of a lot of the coach's expenses for you."

The French tennis federation has been known to establish a time period, say three years, for how long it will provide financial support to a coach working with a young player who is not of financial means. Such was the case with Gael Monfils, a supremely athletic black Frenchman who was the world's No. 1 junior before turning pro in 2004. Although Monfils, at age thirty-two, is arguably the best player never to win a major title, his career has more than justified the French federation's investment in his future. In February 2019 he won his eighth career title at a tournament in Rotterdam, becoming the second black man to win the event, after Arthur Ashe. Monfils has been ranked in the world top ten and has earned more than $16 million in prize money.

Monfils and another black Frenchman, Jo-Wilfried Tsonga, have been solid contenders on the pro tour for more than a decade. Tsonga, a superb athlete who bears a striking resemblance to Muhammad Ali, began 2019 as the last black man to compete in a major singles final, losing to Novak Djokovic at the 2008 Australian Open. Tsonga has received more than $21 million in prize money in his career. Although he has not won a major title, he has reached the quarterfinals or better in five Australian Opens, four Wimbledons, three French Opens, and three U.S. Opens. He began 2019 promisingly, winning the title at an indoor event in Montpelier, France, in February.

But Tsonga withdrew from a tournament in Indian Wells in March and made the stunning announcement that he had been diagnosed five years earlier with sickle cell disease—an affliction more common among blacks and Hispanics, according to the Cleveland Clinic. Tsonga, who turned thirty-four in April 2019, is on medication. "When I fly, it takes me two or three days to recover, to be good physically," he told the French newspaper *L'Equipe*. "In everyday activities, [sickle cell disease] does not stop me from doing anything." Tsonga, who is married and the father of an infant son, achieved a career-best ranking of No. 5 in 2012.

Monfils, who ranked a career-high No. 6 in the world in 2016, ended 2018 ranked No. 29. Both he and Tsonga face a unique form of pressure every spring because no Frenchman has won the French Open title since Yannick Noah in 1983. That is also the last time a black man won a major championship in singles.

Perhaps a future winner of a Grand Slam event is a foreign-born player on an American college campus today. Certainly, international players are filling rosters at Division I schools. At Oklahoma State, for instance, only one player on the 2018–19 men's team was born in America.

"Schools want the best players and best coaches, regardless of where they're from," Jenkins said. "You're not going to find a men's tennis team ranked in the top ten today that has a majority of its players from America. International players are being recruited heavily by American colleges, and the pro game has changed the rules regarding what tournaments those players can compete in, so college players can compete in ITF Futures events to earn some money while maintaining their college eligibility. That's something any college tennis player can take advantage of now, American or international."

Clearly, American college tennis is a meritocracy. There is no "America First" rhetoric that determines who gets scholarships to play at the top schools. College coaches—in their zeal to win championships and retain their jobs and their rising salaries—are putting the best players on the team, regardless of nationality. For this reason, coaches of tennis-loving American youngsters—whether those coaches work at high-priced academies in Florida and California, or at Kamau Murray's XS Tennis Village in Chicago, or anywhere else—are going to have to do a better job of nurturing and developing talent just to get those kids on the court.

12 | Contemporary Male Players

> Black men tend to look at other
> sports to find their heroes.
>
> DONALD YOUNG

Many of Scoville Jenkins's friends in his Atlanta hometown did not know he played tennis until they saw him on national television trading strokes with defending champion Andy Roddick at the 2004 U.S. Open. Why the secrecy? "Whenever kids in school found out that I played tennis, it became a running joke," said Jenkins, who spent seven years on the ATP tour. "They would say things like, 'You're a sissy.' 'You're soft.' 'Who plays tennis?' It wasn't cool to them."

The emergence of Venus and Serena Williams as tennis superstars in the late 1990s made tennis cool to an enormous number of people, especially black women and girls. However, that which inspires black women and girls to aim higher and work harder does not necessarily inspire black men and boys.

"Venus and Serena are phenomenal talents—legends—but a lot of black men need to see someone who looks like them doing something great before they begin to believe they can do it too," said Donald Young, a former teenage prodigy who has settled into a solid pro career, now in its sixteenth year. "Black men tend to look at other sports to find their heroes."

Black men and boys tend to look to the National Basketball Association, where they see the heroics of LeBron James, Stephen Curry, Kevin Durant, and literally hundreds of other black players in a league where the average annual salary is a staggering $6.2 million. And every NBA player's contract is guaranteed.

Black men and boys also look to the National Football League, where more than 70 percent of the players were black during the 2018 season. NFL contracts are not guaranteed and only a player's signing bonus and yearly salary truly count. Nevertheless, black males see an array of stars such as Russell Wilson, Julio Jones, Khalil Mack, and Aaron Donald shining every weekend and enjoying the trappings of success. Black males also look to boxing, where welterweight champion Floyd Mayweather plied his trade for more than two decades and amassed $1 *billion* in earnings. And don't forget baseball, track and field, and mixed martial arts, as well as soccer, where black athletes like Jozy Altidore (the fiancé of 2017 U.S. Open champion Sloane Stephens) and Paul Pogba, perform for huge crowds and multimillion-dollar annual salaries.

It can be hard to convince black men and boys to pursue potential riches on a tennis court when so many of their brethren are fattening their bank accounts and diversifying their portfolios through involvement in athletic endeavors that are considered more socially acceptable in the black community. Jenkins, who earned $353,515 in prize money in his career, chose tennis. At an emotional cost.

"I sacrificed friends, relationships, family because I love tennis so much," he said. "I used to miss Friday night football games during high school because I was hitting with my coach from seven o'clock to midnight."

Jenkins supplemented his on-court income with endorsement money from Babolat rackets and a trio of sneaker companies—Adidas, then Nike, and then Reebok—but he believes that he did not fare well with advertisers because of his look. Not his skin color, his look. On a tennis court or off, he appeared the polar opposite of Arthur Ashe. "I looked very different: long braids, saggy pants, earrings," he said. "I was just being myself, someone from southwest Atlanta."

That look would blend in well among the brothers on Peachtree Street, but it did not fly on Madison Avenue. Jenkins's father, Scoville D. Jenkins (the son is Scoville A. Jenkins), said in a 2006 interview that tennis unfairly stereotyped his son from the start: "When we go to Europe, they all look at black Americans the way they see us in films and on TV. They expect him to be pulling out a gun or some [marijuana]. They expect him to walk around sayin', 'What's up, motherfucker?' There's no fan reaction to Scoville when he plays abroad. They know who he is, but there's no reaction."

Those are hardly comforting words to a young black male who may be considering a career in tennis. Although the younger Jenkins does not exactly endorse his father's sentiment, he acknowledged that the way others in tennis perceived him often got in the way of what he wanted to achieve. "I wasn't what people wanted me to be," said Jenkins, who earned a bachelor's degree in sociology from the University of Washington in 2014. "I'm not what I look like. But I was considered a risk to a lot of companies. I wasn't the typical tennis player."

No black player is. The status of outsider still comes with the territory. But if you win as many prestigious championships as Venus and, especially, Serena have won, then the public will become more accepting of how you look and who you are. The six-foot-three Jenkins, an outstanding athlete who also played basketball as a teenager, would have found much more acceptance in the NBA than on the ATP tour. Despite becoming the first African American to win the boys' USTA eighteen-and-under hardcourt national championship in 2004—which earned him a wild card into the U.S. Open main draw and the aforementioned match against Roddick—Jenkins said the USTA, the governing body of American tennis, never warmed up to him. "The USTA never put me on its elite player list, even though I had the results," he said. "My family was middle class, and my parents needed some financial assistance so I could travel to junior tournaments. But when I needed the USTA most, I never got the help."

He does not believe race was a factor. The USTA's director of men's tennis at the time was Rodney Harmon, an African American from Ashe's hometown of Richmond, Virginia, who reached the 1982 U.S. Open quarterfinals and achieved a career-high singles ranking of No. 56 in 1983. So, what happened? Jenkins said that when he told the USTA that he preferred to continue working in Atlanta with his own coach, Troy Hawkins, rather than training with USTA coaches at its facility in Key Biscayne, Florida, the financial assistance never came.

Jenkins competed against the likes of Roger Federer and Rafael Nadal in his career, and he recorded victories over a trio of players then ranked in the world top twenty: Dominik Hrbaty of Slovakia, Jarkko Nieminen of Finland, and American Vince Spadea. Jenkins also played junior doubles at the Australian Open alongside future Hall of Famer Novak Djokovic. Jenkins had a career-high ranking of No. 187, a notable achievement in a sport that ranks more than a thousand pros. Still, he believes he would have risen higher if not for the economics of the sport.

"I worked my butt off in my career, but tennis is really expensive," he said. "A player has to pay for everything: coaching, travel, hotels, meals, getting your rackets strung. The average sports fan doesn't realize how expensive it is to play professional tennis. When you play a best-of-five-set match, you need to get three or four rackets strung at $150–$200 per racket. You pay for all that. And when you're growing up, tennis is a sport that you need to play year-round to develop your game. It's not like football, where you can take a semester off to play basketball and then come back to football. In tennis, you need to put in so much time and be totally committed, and still most players will never get to No. 100 in the world."

That may be a sobering fact for young black men and boys who are used to seeing athletes in other sports holding index fingers aloft and spraying one another with champagne in celebration of a championship. The relatively low return on an aspiring tennis player's physical, emotional, and financial investment may even have contributed to the decision by the sons of black men who competed in major finals to choose a different sport altogether.

Yannick Noah of France fulfilled a boyhood dream when he won the 1983 French Open, defeating then world No. 1 Mats Wilander of Sweden in the championship match before a delirious crowd at Stade Roland Garros in Paris. Born in the African nation of Cameroon, Noah became a superstar who thrilled fans around the world with his prodigious shot making. A career that culminated in his induction into the International Tennis Hall of Fame in 2005 began with a tip from Arthur Ashe to the French tennis federation to take a serious look at Noah, who was then eleven years old. One of the finest athletes ever to play tennis, Noah made winning volleys between his legs with his back to the net a full two decades before Federer did so. Noah remains the last black man to win a major singles title. His son, Joakim Noah, also a gifted athlete, grew to be six feet eleven, seven inches taller than his dad, and he chose a career in basketball. It turned out to be a wise and lucrative decision—Joakim Noah pocketed more than $104 million in the first eleven seasons of his NBA career.

MaliVai Washington is the last African American male to compete in a major final, having powered his way to the championship match at Wimbledon in 1996. Although he enjoyed competing in other sports, Washington was destined to become a tennis player. His father, William Washington, was his coach. The elder Washington sent four of his children into professional tennis: Daughters Mashona and Michaela were ranked in the top one hundred in the world—Mashona, No. 50 in 2004; Michaela, No. 81 in 1984. Son Mashiska ranked a career-best No. 290 in 1999. MaliVai, the best of the brood, was the No. 11 player in the world in 1992. Four years later, he competed for the golden trophy at Wimbledon, which the tournament itself calls the "All England Lawn Tennis Club Single Handed Championship of the World."

"Tennis places such an emphasis on the Grand Slam tournaments, so what I remember most was being one of the last two men standing at Wimbledon," said Washington, who lost to hard-serving Richard Krajicek of the Netherlands, 6–3, 6–4, 6–3. "Unfortunately, he got the one service break he needed in each set. Before the match, I felt some nervousness, but not the kind that makes an athlete say, 'Holy shit!' What I felt was a prepared nervousness, the kind that makes you say, 'Okay, let's go.' I was on Centre Court, playing for the most revered title in tennis. I was exactly where I was supposed to be. He just executed better than I did."

A versatile player who could handle any surface, Washington won four tournaments—Charlotte and Bermuda on clay; Memphis and Ostrava, Czech Republic indoors—along with $3,232,565 in prize money in a ten-year career that ended after a left knee injury in 1999. While recovering after surgery on the same knee two years earlier, he took a real estate class, then earned his license, and then bought his first property. He has excelled in the property game ever since. "Maybe it's because I always liked playing Monopoly with my brothers and sisters," said Washington, who runs Diamond Life Real Estate in Jacksonville Beach, Florida. "I love what I do. My intention is to buy one property every month. That's the track we're on."

Washington and his wife, Jennifer, have two children. Neither of them plays tennis. Thirteen-year-old daughter Zeta plays volleyball only, and sixteen-year-old son Noah (not named after Yannick Noah) plays lacrosse only. Washington exposed both of his kids to tennis, but neither embraced the sport, which has been easier on the family finances. "You could spend tens of thousands of dollars or hundreds of thousands of dollars on a youngster's development in tennis, and guess what? They get injured," Washington said. "Or they say they don't love tennis anymore. Or they peak in college and never make it to the pro tour."

Neither of Washington's children is playing a sport that offers the possibility of professional riches. That's just fine with him. He said they both enjoy what they're doing, and both could earn an athletic scholarship to college. Washington earned a tennis scholarship to the University of Michigan, and then, against the advice of Arthur Ashe, he left college at age nineteen to turn pro. "No disrespect to Arthur, but I was ready to go," he said. "I was a two-time All-American and ranked No. 1 in the country. A lot of players leave college early to turn pro, get to No. 300 or 400 in the world and realize, 'Damn, I'm not good enough.' If you're eighteen years old and you're No. 150 in the world, your best tennis years are ahead of you. But if you're twenty-eight years old and No. 150, and that's the highest you've ever been ranked, then you really need to consider doing something else with your life."

Gentlemanly and well spoken, Washington invites comparisons to Ashe without even trying. Indeed, Washington received the Arthur Ashe Humanitarian of the Year Award from the ATP in 2009, largely because of the MaliVai Washington Youth Foundation, which he founded in 1996. The foundation has taught life skills to more than twenty thousand boys and girls from kindergarteners through high schoolers in the Jacksonville area while promoting academic achievement and a healthy lifestyle through sports. Tennis instruction is also part of the program, but it is not the reason for the foundation's existence. For a time, Washington worked as a tennis commentator on network television, smoothly handling play-by-play as well as match analysis for ESPN, Tennis Channel, and CBS. He then left broadcasting to watch his kids grow, tend to his real estate interests, and help raise funds for his foundation. A recent fundraiser, to which Venus contributed an autographed racket and clothing from her EleVen fashion line, brought in enough money to build a recreational center for teenagers.

If a youngster in Washington's foundation shows promise in tennis, the former Wimbledon finalist certainly would be available to advise. But is the USTA doing enough to help develop tennis talent in areas like Jacksonville? "I think the USTA does a nice, solid job of making tennis more accessible," he said. "But tennis is not cheap. To become really good, you need to find a coach, a program, an academy, where people are willing to invest a lot of time in you. That alone is not cheap."

Washington came from a tennis family with a father who helped guide him to a successful (albeit injury-shortened) career. Despite his impressive run at Wimbledon, he did not have the breakthrough win that could have put tennis on the radar of more African American males. The sport continues searching for that player. A decade after Washington, a Chicago native became the next great hope.

When Donald Young was barely a teenager, he dominated the competition in fourteen-and-under and sixteen-and-under tournaments.

A lefthander with quick hands and a deft touch, his game invited comparisons to John McEnroe's. Young was the only athlete included in *Newsweek* magazine's "What's Next?" issue in 2004. A year later, he won the Australian Open junior title and the boys' eighteen-and-under national hardcourt title, making him the world's No. 1 junior, as well as a client of prestigious talent agency International Management Group and the recipient of a multiyear endorsement deal from Nike worth $1 million a year. Coached by his parents, Donald Sr. and Ilona, and mentored by Indian-born Suhel Malhotra, a respected coach in Chicago, Young turned pro in 2004, at the age of fifteen. Venus and Serena were only one year younger when they turned pro. But women's tennis has much more of a history of teenage prodigies living up to advance billing and excelling as professionals. It is a huge gamble to put a boy into the same arena as men in a sport that requires physicality and mental toughness. Nevertheless, Young appeared primed to become the next big thing in men's tennis, possibly the player who could entice a generation of black boys to pick up a racket, as the Williams sisters had done for so many others.

But expectations proved too high. Although Young grew to five feet, eleven inches tall and has size thirteen feet, he did not emerge from puberty with the kind of physique that would add much-needed power to his finesse-laden game. In the vernacular of sports, he did not grow into his body. Hence, players that he used to defeat in boys' matches because of his athleticism, shotmaking skills, and knowledge of the game were able to overpower him in men's matches.

This is not to say that Young is a has-been, or an underachiever. His sixteen years in professional tennis are a testament to his fitness and dedication. In 2012 he achieved a career-high ranking of No. 38. In 2017 he again cracked the world's top fifty in singles and also played in his first major doubles final. In a fiercely contested French Open title match, Young and Santiago Gonzalez of Mexico lost to Michael Venus of New Zealand and American Ryan Harrison, 7–6 (7–5), 6–7 (4–7), 6–3. The outcome was in doubt until Venus and Harrison broke serve for a 5–3 lead in the third set and then served out the match.

Courteous and thoughtful, Young never boasted publicly about the kind of player he would become. Others supplied the hyperbole that his tennis career has not met. Nike no longer pays him. IMG dropped him as a client. He began 2018 without an agent. His family relocated several years ago from Chicago to Atlanta, where they run a tennis club. The year 2018 was a downer for Young, beginning with a straight-sets loss to Novak Djokovic in the first round of the Australian Open. Young's 2004 Aussie Open juniors crown seemed a lifetime ago. Other defeats during the year along with a slew of nagging injuries caused his ranking to plummet at year's end to No. 274.

"It's tough when your career doesn't meet other people's expectations and people criticize you," said Taylor Townsend, a longtime friend and mixed doubles partner of Young's, as well as a kindred spirit. "We were both world No. 1 as juniors, and we've had ups and downs in our careers. His body didn't develop like his peers'. But I think Donald should be proud of what he has accomplished."

Young said he is indeed proud, but he would rather look ahead than backward. If he can stay healthy and somehow add some punch to his serve and groundstrokes, then his overall skills and tennis IQ could make him a late bloomer. A possible source of inspiration for Young is the career arc of Stan Wawrinka of Switzerland. Once known primarily for winning a 2008 Olympic doubles gold medal with Roger Federer, Wawrinka did not win a major title in singles until his tenth year on tour. Now, he has three majors on his resume (2014 Australian Open, 2015 French Open, 2016 U.S. Open). Young is still seeking his first pro title. He has not stopped believing.

"It definitely can happen," he said after the Djokovic loss in Melbourne. "I'm looking forward to being healthy and putting myself in position to play more matches and do some damage."

Atlanta is as close to a tennis hotbed as any predominantly black city in America. The Atlanta Lawn Tennis Association has the largest membership among blacks of any statewide amateur league in the country, and the city hosts the BB&T Atlanta Open, an ATP tour hardcourt tournament, every July. But Young said tennis still is not nearly as popular among Atlantans as it should be. "People are into the [pro football] Falcons and the [pro basketball] Hawks," said Young, who roots for both teams himself. "Tennis is cool if you play. But a lot of people still don't play. Tennis needs to be in more of the schools. Basketball is in every high school in Atlanta. Football is in a lot of high schools. Tennis is an intramural sport, if it's played at all. And the tennis coach may be just a teacher who likes tennis, not someone who can really coach it, so the kids don't get better."

Echoing a sentiment expressed by Atlanta native Scoville Jenkins, Young added, "What keeps a lot of black kids from getting into tennis is that if you really want to get better, you have to give up other sports. Boys want to play basketball, football, baseball, track and field. I think it's easier for a girl who wants to be really good in tennis to just play tennis. But for anybody who wants to play, tennis is superexpensive."

There's the rub. The high cost of tennis remains prohibitive for too many parents who can only wish their children would follow in the footsteps of Venus, Serena, Stephens, Blake, and Young. Sometimes, to have any chance at all of living that dream, to have people tout you as "the next big thing," you need the kind of luck that puts you in exactly the right place at the right time.

In 1996 Constant Tiafoe and his wife, Alphina, emigrated to America from the African nation of Sierra Leone. Three years later, he worked as a day laborer to help build the Junior Tennis Champions Center in College Park, Maryland, not far from the main campus of the University of Maryland. So impressive was Tiafoe's work ethic that he was hired to be the janitor at the club. Often, he brought his twin three-year-old sons, Frances and Franklin, to the club with him so they could play with each other and watch tennis. Frances took a particular interest in the game. Although he was not getting lessons from the club pros, he watched intently, and whenever he had a chance to take a racket and balls onto an empty court, he attempted to serve the way he had seen others serve, or he whacked forehands and backhands against a concrete wall.

Looking back on those years, Frances said, "In the beginning stages, I was just watching. I learned a lot from mimicking things and seeing little things. The next thing you know, I started to understand the game pretty well. One thing led to another. I really studied a lot, watched a lot of film. Obviously, I didn't have coaches or anything like that."

Eventually, Frances found a club member willing to coach him. Misha Kouznetsov, a Russian, was twenty-four years old when he began coaching eight-year-old Frances. In a scenario not unlike the members of Harlem's now-defunct Cosmopolitan Tennis Club making the teenage Althea Gibson an honorary member and paying her fees for lessons and junior tournaments in the 1940s, Kouznetsov paid Frances's entry fees and shuttled him to and from tournaments. With his game raw and enthusiasm high, Frances won enough junior events to get on the USTA's radar.

Before long, he was playing under new management—former tour pros Martin Blackman, the USTA director of player development; Jose Higueras of Spain, then the USTA director of men's tennis; and Nicolas Todero of Argentina, a USTA player development coach. Frances relocated to Orlando, Florida, site of the sprawling, hundred-court USTA complex. The coaches who travel with him now on the ATP tour are also former pros: Robby Ginepri, No. 15 in the world in 2005, and Michael Russell, No. 60 in the world in 2007.

"Frances has surrounded himself with a great team," Donald Young Jr. said. "He's got Robby and Mike with him, guys who played the game at a high level."

Tiafoe is six foot two and a cut 170 pounds. It is not unusual for him to practice while shirtless—his physique tends to draw considerable interest. Yet his speed is even more impressive. He has the quickness and court coverage to force an opponent to hit an extra ball to try to win a point. That speed also keeps Tiafoe in a rally until he is able to turn defense into offense and seize the point.

So far, the USTA coaches have let Tiafoe, or "Big Foe," as his fans call him, be himself on the court, which means they are trying to refine, not overhaul, the unorthodox strokes that he developed while hitting by himself over days, weeks, months, and years at the club in College

Park because no one had yet shown him the proper technique. He has known so much winning since he started swinging a racket that no one is trying to fix what is not broken.

From such humble beginnings began the career of Frances Tiafoe, born January 20, 1998. He may well develop into the next great black male tennis player. With dark brown skin, a deep voice, a gap-toothed smile, an easygoing disposition, and an intriguing power game, he seems destined for major victories and lucrative endorsement deals. Said Woody Blocher, a San Diego-based teaching pro and former tour player: "Tiafoe is a beast. If he doesn't make top five in the world, there's something wrong." Frances Tiafoe is so good that Constant Tiafoe now goes by Frances Sr., just so you know from whence the son came. Tiafoe won his first professional title in March 2018, a hardcourt event in Delray Beach, Florida, and he defeated a major champion in the process. A victory over Juan Martin del Potro in the round of sixteen gave Tiafoe a measure of revenge because del Potro had knocked him out of the 2018 Australian Open in the first round.

Nothing validates the hard work of a young tennis professional quite like a championship trophy. However, Tiafoe's coming-out party actually occurred seven months before the Delray Beach title. On August 29, 2017, in a first-round match at the U.S. Open, Tiafoe nearly shocked the tennis world and nearly defeated Roger Federer. In the end, Federer relied on his experience more than his strokes to overcome Tiafoe, 4–6, 6–2, 6–1, 1–6, 6–4. What Tiafoe's growing legion of fans found most encouraging was that the occasion was not too big for him. Except for a few rushed forehands that went awry in the final set, he could have won. "I really didn't feel nervous at all," he said, flashing the gap-toothed smile. "How many years have I been watching the U.S. Open? Since I was a little kid. I always dreamed of being on [Arthur Ashe Stadium] court, playing the best in the world. Finally, it happened, so I was ready for it."

Tiafoe already speaks like a champion. There was no, "I can't believe I did so well." Or, "If I had to lose to anybody, I'm proud to lose to Roger." Or, "Nobody expected me to win, anyway." Tiafoe talks about himself and his tennis like a young man who can see major victories on the horizon. He had no qualms about telling the international media at the U.S. Open that he had essentially let Federer off the hook. "I felt like when I was playing well, I was controlling most of the rallies," Tiafoe said. "When I was hitting the ball big, he wasn't really doing much except staying steady with me. If I stepped back a little bit, he took that and ran with it. Yeah, that's what he did. He won by the skin of his teeth."

Afterward, an impressed Federer said, "Frances has done well this year. Moved up the rankings. Got a taste of Arthur Ashe [Stadium], how it is to play against top players. He's only going to learn from a match like this and become better."

Tiafoe ended 2018 ranked No. 39 in the world. His year would have been more memorable had he not squandered a two-set lead in a third-round match at Wimbledon against Russia's Karen Khachanov. After Tiafoe lost a third-set tiebreak, frustration replaced intensity. He dropped the next two sets, 6–2, 6–1. In his other major tournaments, he lost in the first round of the French Open to American Sam Querrey, a former top ten player rebounding from injuries, and he dropped a second-round match at the U.S. Open to Australia's Alex De Minaur. Tiafoe earned $1,026,059 in prize money in 2018. In the previous three years combined, he made $902,320. He has endorsement deals with Nike and Yonex rackets. Several more deals will follow if his ascension continues. In October, he competed for Team World against a team of European stars led by Federer and Rafael Nadal at the Rod Laver Cup in Chicago. Tiafoe reached his first major quarterfinal at the 2019 Australian Open by defeating No. 5 seed Kevin Anderson and No. 20 Grigor Dmitrov. The more experience Tiafoe gets on the biggest stages, the stronger his game should become. He may yet be responsible for a wave of black boys wanting to grab tennis rackets and swing like Big Foe.

13 | Contemporary Female Players

Gosh, I love *you*, not the tennis-playing you.

AN UNIDENTIFIED FAN OF MADISON KEYS

Not all athletes whom the media and the public identify as "black" choose to describe themselves that way. James Blake, a 2010 Davis Cup champion for the United States, has one white parent and one black parent. He identifies as black. For many people, the choice is obvious, whether it is based on their physical appearance, how others perceive their physical appearance, or the group with whom the individual chooses to identify because of personal or family history. Yet for many others, the choice of racial identification is complex and nuanced. It is not remotely as simple as choosing to be on one team over another. Since it is not the intention of this author to try to usurp anyone's ability to define themselves, the term "player of color" is used here to describe any professional tennis player who has chosen publicly not to identify as either "black" or "white."

Madison Keys, then, is a tennis player of color, the daughter of attorneys—a black male and a white female—who grew up in what is hardly a tennis hotbed: Rock Island, Illinois. Her prodigious talent thrust her into the public eye in her preteens. At age twelve, she defeated much older junior players to win the prestigious Easter Bowl tournament in Miami. She turned pro at the age of fourteen, just as Venus and Serena had. Indeed, tennis was not on Madison's radar until her four-year-old self noticed a white dress that Venus was wearing on television while competing in a grass-court tournament called Wimbledon.

"Oooh, I want a dress like that," Madison told her parents.

"We'll buy one for you if you want to learn to play tennis like Venus," they said.

Rick and Christine Keys, who named their daughter after a character in the film *Splash*, bought Madison the pretty white dress and took her to the Quad City Tennis Club in Moline, Illinois, to begin the embryonic stage of a future champion. In 2009, when she was fourteen, Madison relocated to Florida with her mother and two of her siblings so she could get more advanced coaching and training at the Evert Tennis Academy in Boca Raton. In July of that year, she was deemed ready to play an exhibition set against Serena, fresh off another Wimbledon championship, at a World Team Tennis event in Florida. Under the rules of this exhibition, the first player to five points won the set. Serena took it easy on the kid. But Madison, quite tall for her age, hit with uncommon power and won five of the six points. That result put Madison on everyone's tennis radar. People raved about her strong righthanded serve, which already set her apart from other girls, and her punishing forehand. Her two-fisted backhand also impressed, but her serve and forehand were the major weapons, the strokes likely to carry her into the sport's upper echelon. People also could not help but notice her attractive face, toothy smile, and café au lait skin. So, when reporters got close enough, the questions about race began.

"What are you, Madison?" "Are you black?" "Mixed?" What do you call yourself?"

Madison's reply to the race question at the 2015 Australian Open is consistent with what she had always said on the subject before putting the issue to rest: "It's something that's always there, obviously, but I'm very much right in the middle. I don't really identify myself as white or African American. I'm just me. I'm Madison."

Her stock response is good enough for some people, not enough for others. But, as someone who is asserting her right to self-identify, Madison has deemed it good enough for her.

At five feet ten, Keys is one of the biggest hitters in women's tennis. She has been ranked as high as No. 7 in the world, attaining that position in October 2016. She has reached a U.S. Open final, two U.S. Open semifinals, an Australian Open semifinal, a French Open semifinal, and a Wimbledon quarterfinal. Since she is only twenty-three, it would appear that a major title is on the horizon. But in tennis, there are no sure things. In her only major final, the 2017 U.S. Open against African American Sloane Stephens, Keys resembled a deer mesmerized by headlights in a 6–3, 6–0 defeat. Conquering her nerves in big matches has been a recurring problem for Keys.

"I was obviously nervous all morning," she said after the Open final, which began shortly after four o'clock in the afternoon in New York City. "Sloane's a tough opponent to play when, you know, you're not making a lot of balls. But, then, at the same time, she's not going to miss, either. So, it was kind of, I didn't totally know what to do once I got on court, which just intensifies those nerves even more."

In addition to her ongoing battle with nerves, Keys faces another challenge in her efforts to win a major title: health. Already she has undergone two surgeries on her right wrist, which is anathema for a power player who relies heavily on her serve. She has also been plagued by abdominal and rib injuries. In her final tournament of 2018, the WTA Elite Trophy Zhuhai in China, she withdrew from a semifinal match against Garbiñe Muguruza because of an ailing left knee.

For four years, Keys was coached by Lindsay Davenport, an ideal pairing because of the similarities in their games. Like Keys, Davenport had a powerful right-handed serve to which she could add spin, which makes the ball kick sharply and pulls the returner off the court. And like Keys, Davenport struck the ball hard and clean from the baseline and possessed a solid, two-fisted backhand and above-average volleys. Davenport was also not an exceptional mover on court; nor is Keys. Yet Davenport used her considerable assets to win the 1998 U.S. Open, Wimbledon 1999, and the 2000 Australian Open, holding the world No. 1 ranking in singles for ninety-eight weeks. She is one of only six players in the Open Era to be ranked world No. 1 in singles and doubles simultaneously. (Venus and Serena have also achieved that distinction.) Davenport won the 1996 Olympic gold medal in singles. She also captured three major doubles titles—1996 French Open, 1997 U.S. Open, and Wimbledon 1999. If ever a coach could say to an up-and-coming player, "Been there, done that," it is Davenport, a 2014 inductee in the International Tennis Hall of Fame.

"I started coaching Maddy as a favor to her agent [Max Eisenbud], who is a friend of mine, but it turned into a relationship with someone who is like a daughter to me," Davenport, who is white, said in an interview at the WTA Connecticut Open at Yale University, where she and James Blake participated in a mixed doubles exhibition. "There's not a day that goes by when I don't speak to her. We're incredibly close. We're like family now."

However, the forty-two-year-old Davenport has her own family—a husband and four school-age children—and a side gig as a commentator for Tennis Channel. Traveling the world with Keys took Davenport away from home too often. In June 2018, she gave herself a demotion and became Keys' advisor. In an arrangement that suggested a case of "too many cooks," Keys took advice at the Open from Davenport; Kathy Rinaldi, the Team USA Fed Cup captain; and Ola Malmqvist, a Swedish man in charge of the USTA's women's tennis program.

"I talk to Lindsay all the time, more for not-tennis reasons," Keys said before her first-round U.S. Open match. "I feel like we're just constantly texting back and forth. She's always there to help me with tennis or, really, anything."

But, Madison, what if Davenport wants you to do one thing, and Rinaldi wants you to do something else, and Malmqvist doesn't agree with either of them?

"I have to be the one to figure it out through the tough times," Keys said. "It's predominantly Lindsay and Ola, and they're very much on the same page. If one is giving me a message, the other one is usually there to hear what they're saying."

Keys, whose powerful strokes often elicit "oohs" from tennis fans, fed off the energy from crowds pulling for American players during a strong run at the 2018 U.S. Open. The right wrist pain that had caused her to withdraw from two tournaments earlier in the summer did not return. Her fourth-round victory over five-foot-three Dominika Cibulkova of Slovakia, 6–1, 6–3, looked like a heavyweight battering a lightweight. Keys led in winning shots, 15–3, and used a punishing serve and heavy groundstrokes to dominate the match. "I think the biggest thing was being able to push her back off the baseline, where she likes to hold her ground, and be able to dictate points like that," said Keys, who was seeded No. 14 at the Open (two spots ahead of Venus, three ahead of Serena).

In the quarterfinals, Keys overpowered Carla Suarez Navarro of Spain, a crafty player whose spins and slices often befuddle opponents. In a 6–4, 6–3 win, Keys played with patience during rallies, probing until she got the right ball to unleash her power. "It was more about staying calm and knowing that she was going to play well and just waiting for my opportunities," said Keys, who hit twenty-two winners to her opponent's ten. There were only two service breaks in the match—one in each set, both by Keys. She thrilled the partisan crowd when she abruptly ended a rally in the tenth game of the first set with a stinging forehand down the line on her second set point. In the sixth game of the second set, she deftly sliced a backhand to Suarez Navarro's backhand. The Spaniard had difficulty extending her arms, and her reply hit the net to give Keys an insurmountable 4–2 lead.

The victory set up a semifinal against another power hitter, Naomi Osaka. The last time Keys faced Osaka at the U.S. Open, in a third-round match in 2016, Keys trailed 1–5 in the final set before rallying to win the match in a tiebreak, thanks largely to Osaka's stage fright. But two years later, a more poised and mentally tougher Osaka turned the tables in an impressive 6–2, 6–4 triumph. Osaka, competing in her first major semifinal and first night match at Arthur Ashe Stadium, took control early and never relinquished it. On thirteen separate occasions, Keys had a break point that could have changed the complexion of the match—and Osaka saved each one. "I felt like if I could break, maybe I could get back into it," Keys said. "You're in the match and you're thinking, 'Okay, she's going to let up eventually.' She didn't." Rarely has the hard-hitting Keys been beaten at her own power game on a big stage. When Keys falls, it is usually to a junk-baller who assiduously avoids getting into baseline rallies. However, Osaka consistently outhit Keys in an impressive performance to advance to her first major final. Since Keys and Osaka were born just two years apart, theirs should be a rivalry for fans to savor.

Keys began 2019 with a new coach, Jim Madrigal, who used to coach Tennys Sandgren, a Tennessee native who made a surprising run to the 2017 Australian Open quarterfinals. However, Sandgren's run was overshadowed by a history of social-media posts that expressed homophobic and bigoted views. For example, one post in 2012 read, "Stumbled into a gay club last night. My eyes are still bleeding." He also referred to people in that club by the derogatory term "trannies."

Sandgren's online posts have been deleted but hardly forgotten. On at least two occasions, he posted insulting comments about Serena. In 2013, presumably after a Serena defeat, he wrote, "Always a good day when Serena goes down." In 2015 he wrote "Disgusting" above a photo of Serena with her fist clenched and in full roar during her U.S. Open semifinal match against Roberta Vinci. Sandgren has never made clear what he found "disgusting" about the twenty-three-time major champion. Serena called on Sandgren to apologize, but not to her. "I don't need or want one, but there is an entire group of people that deserves an apology," she wrote on Instagram. "I can't look at my daughter and tell her I sat back and was quiet. No! She will know how to stand up for herself and others, by my example." Sandgren has not apologized.

Keys figures to be a noncontroversial client for Madrigal. For Keys to reach her potential, it is imperative that she stay healthy. In 2017 she played at Wimbledon despite pain in her wrist and lost in the second round. Fortunately, she did not aggravate the injury. Wiser from that experience, she withdrew from the 2018 finale in China after feeling pain in her knee. She ended 2018 with $10,088,678 in career earnings, including $2,554,853 for the year.

Learning from past mistakes and tapping into inner strength are messages that Keys delivers to audiences as an ambassador for FearlesslyGIRL, an international organization that aims to build self-confidence in girls and encourage them to use their voices rather than be cowed by bullying.

Keys is a periodic consumer of social media. She has become more cautious about what she posts and when, because of the frequency of attacks against females online. "I go through phases when I'm willing to share things and when I'm not," said Keys, who went public recently about her romantic relationship with Bjorn Fratangelo, an ATP tour pro from Pittsburgh. "Sometimes, if I'm not in a good mental space, you'll notice that I don't post much and I'm not really active. Then, other times when I feel good and I know I can handle it, I'll share things and I'm willing to put my life out there. But the biggest thing is not thinking I have to do it all the time and knowing when I need to not do it just for my own mental well-being."

After a FearlesslyGIRL event in her hometown in the Quad Cities on November 16, 2018, that was live-streamed to more than four thousand girls across America, Keys said, "Sitting there and talking to the girls about your mistakes and how you fixed them and your struggles, they immediately relate to you. I think the biggest thing I've noticed has been how big a fan base I've created of people who don't watch tennis. There are all these girls who are saying, 'Gosh, I love *you*, not the tennis-playing you.'"

Another female player who has chosen not to self-identify by race is Alexandra Stevenson, who made a big splash two decades ago at Wimbledon only to be swept up in controversy regarding her parentage—a controversy which, contrary to popular belief, did not end her tennis career.

Stevenson, the daughter of African American basketball legend Julius "Dr. J" Erving and Samantha Stevenson, a white former sports journalist who used to cover Erving's games, grew up in San Diego, in an otherwise all-white environment. Alexandra's manner of speaking sounds so Southern Californian that the one-time tennis phenom acquired the nickname "Volley Girl."

In 1999 Alexandra caused a sensation at Wimbledon. Just out of high school, the eighteen-year-old served and volleyed her way into the semifinals, and charmed British fans and the international media in the process. After defeating Julie Halard-Decugis of France in the third round on Court 13, she gracefully curtsied to the cheering spectators. Her ebullient personality and commercial-ready smile compelled one British tabloid writer to call her a "sex symbol." During a rain delay in an era when none of Wimbledon's courts had roofs (both Centre Court and No. 1 Court now have roofs), Alexandra sang show tunes for viewers on the British Broadcasting Company. She had acted and sang in productions of *Grease, Bye Bye Birdie*, and *The Pajama Game* at La Jolla Country Day School, where classmates voted her best athlete and most likely to be famous.

Samantha Stevenson assumed the role of Alexandra's manager and essentially goaded journalists into uncovering the identity of Alexandra's father, whom she would only say was "famous." Samantha Stevenson made a tactical decision at Wimbledon that year: She would try to shift media and public attention toward a guessing game about the secret identity of Alexandra's father, hoping that it would take the pressure off her daughter, who was attempting to become a longshot winner of tennis's most sought-after title. The gambit failed. It did not take long for a Florida newspaper reporter to simply buy a copy of Alexandra's birth certificate. This sort of purchase could be done twelve years before the September 11, 2001, terrorist attacks in the United States made everyone more circumspect. The birth certificate showed that the father of Alexandra Winfield Stevenson was Julius Winfield Erving. The reporter was persuaded by his peers not to out Alexandra during her storybook run at Wimbledon. Instead, the information was temporarily withheld, but Alexandra knew it was coming. Since the age of four, she had known that her father was a six-foot, eight-inch basketball icon whose slam dunks seemed to defy gravity. She simply did not know him as a man, nor did she believe the public had any right to know about her connection to him. But by the time Alexandra, playing tentatively for the first time in the fortnight, had laid an egg in her semifinal and lost 6–1, 6–1 to the eventual champion Lindsay Davenport, the *Orlando Sentinel* had outed Dr. J—and published his initial denial. "I came into Wimbledon as Alexandra Stevenson, and I left as Dr. J's daughter," she said wistfully.

However well-meaning Samantha Stevenson's actions may have been, her public comments did not do her daughter any favors. Leaving aside for a moment her dare to journalists to find out who had fathered Alexandra, she also alienated her daughter from many women on the pro tour by saying that her presence was necessary to protect Alexandra from lesbians. "I want my daughter to marry a man and have babies," she told a group of reporters at Wimbledon.

Alexandra did become childhood friends of the Williams sisters in Southern California. She is six months younger than Venus and nine months older than Serena. Given her buzzworthy debut, Alexandra figured to develop into a challenger to the Williams sisters' supremacy on the pro tour. It was not to be.

Yet Stevenson's tennis career did not implode because of Wimbledon 1999. Three years later, she reached a career high of No. 18 in the world. She lost a pair of WTA title matches in Memphis, Tennessee, and Linz, Austria, in 2002, and she teamed with Serena to win a doubles title in Leipzig, Germany. But later that year, she began to feel pain in her right shoulder. After two years of trying unsuccessfully to play through the pain, she underwent surgery in 2004 on a torn labrum. She has yet to fully recover. The previous sentence is not in the past tense because Stevenson, at age thirty-eight, is still playing professionally, albeit on the outskirts of professional tennis. She plays on the Challengers circuit, where the total prize purses are small, usually $15,000, and the players have to make their own line calls (there is only a chair umpire) and retrieve their own balls.

"You have to pay $40 to get into the event, and if you lose in the first round, you get nothing," Stevenson said in a 2016 podcast hosted by journalist Jon Wertheim. "If anybody out there is a billionaire and wants to sponsor me, they should call me." Stevenson's famous father, although not a billionaire, is unlikely to become that sponsor. Father and daughter have met, including a sit-down for an ESPN feature, but the two no longer communicate, according to Stevenson. When father and daughter first met, Stevenson was seven. Erving came to San Diego for a promotional appearance, and she was just another kid waiting in line for an autograph. He signed her paper, not knowing who she was. She then replied, "I don't really want your autograph," and tossed the paper aside.

Even if a benefactor comes forward , an essential question to Stevenson would have to be, "Why are you still doing this?" She ended 2018 with more losses than wins in her career (427-448), and a world ranking of No. 1,037. Since her debut at Wimbledon 1999, she has received $1,472,403 in prize money. But since players are responsible for their own travel, lodging, and meals away from a tournament, she has undoubtedly spent more money than that to keep her dream alive. In all of 2018, she had $2,453 in tennis earnings. Either she loves the game or cannot get it out of her system. Or a combination of both.

No longer does she receive endorsement money from Nike or representation from International Management Group. No longer is she coached by Robert Lansdorp, whose list of former pupils also includes Hall of Famers Lindsay Davenport, Tracy Austin, and Pete Sampras, and five-time major champion Maria Sharapova. Now, Stevenson is coached solely by her mother, and the duo drive a Volvo to minor-league tournaments in outposts such as Latham, Alabama, or they fly to Manchester, England, so Stevenson can try to advance past the qualifying rounds and into the main draw of a WTA tour event.

So, why does she still play? Ambition. With her shoulder healthy again, she wants to get back into the world top fifty and win a major tournament. "My age doesn't mean anything to me," she has said. "It's a hard sport. It's not forgiving. But one of my goals is to be at Grand Slams. I want to win one. I think I have that in me." It cannot be easy for her to hang up her racket, not when she remains the only woman ever to win eight matches in one year at Wimbledon—three in the qualifying tournament and five in the main draw. But that happened in the previous century. Many tennis fans have forgotten it. Wimbledon, at least, never will. Her magical run to the semifinals made her a lifetime member of Wimbledon's exclusive society for players who have reached the quarterfinals or better, the Last 8 Club.

Fortunately, it has not been all tennis, all the time for Stevenson. In 2007 she earned a bachelor's degree in sociology from the University of Colorado. In 2002 she gave a speech to the South Carolina legislature to advocate for the removal of the state's confederate flag (which finally came down after a mass shooting by a white supremacist at a black church in Charleston in 2015). While in her twenties, Stevenson hoped to apply for admission to the Yale University School of Drama, but, as she put it, "tennis got in the way." Someone with her looks, way with words, personality, and willingness to express strong opinions could do well on television. Perhaps Tennis Channel or ESPN could be her future home, if she ever puts down the racket. But for now, trips to Pelham and Lathan in Alabama to play Challengers matches still hold a certain appeal for her. Such trips may also be a good source of material for the book she says she wants to write. For instance, there was a day in Pelham in 2016 when nineteen-year-old Taylor Townsend, once the world's No. 1 junior, played a professional match against a sixty-nine-year-old lady.

Let the record show that on April 11, 2016, nineteen-year-old Taylor Townsend defeated sixty-nine-year-old Gail Falkenberg, 6–0, 6–0, in a second-round match at an ITF Futures event in Pelham. For Falkenberg, who first played on the pro circuit in the 1980s, achieving a career-high ranking of No. 360 in 1987, the future is now. For Townsend, who lost only six points against Falkenberg, the future seems to be entirely up to her. Her primary goal is to accumulate enough ranking points to avoid all-comers tournaments in outposts such as Pelham. The surest way to avoid the Challengers circuit and the win-or-go-home qualifying rounds at the major events is to become a solid, consistent top fifty player.

Townsend appeared headed in that direction a few years ago. At that time, she drew raves as part of a new wave of African American talent, inspired by Serena and Venus, destined to compete for major titles. Townsend, a Chicago native, may still get there. She is only twenty-two. But the road to stardom has been far rockier than expected.

"It's tough when you perform well as a junior and everybody has high expectations for you," she said in a private interview room with faux grass on the walls at the 2018 Australian Open in Melbourne, her first appearance ever in the main draw at that event. "When I turned pro at sixteen, I had some big wins and I thought I would get to the top fifty like my peers, Sloane Stephens and Madison Keys. But I haven't yet. Some players burst onto the scene. For others, it's a gradual journey. My career has been up and down. But it's made me really appreciate where I am now and how I got to where I am."

Townsend ended 2018 ranked No. 90 in the world, a sign of progress because she had fallen out of the top hundred. She began the 2019 season with $1,408,759 in career prize money, including $418,834 in the previous year. She is a lefthander with a very good serve, good groundstrokes, and crisp volleys. In March 2018, she won her first WTA tour doubles title at Indian Wells with partner Yanina Wickmayer of Belgium. But in singles matches, Townsend has had a tendency to start slowly. That led to a first-round defeat against No. 19 seed Magdalena Rybarikova of Slovakia at the 2018 Australian Open, 6–0, 7–5. Townsend fared better at the 2018 U.S. Open, winning her opening-round match and then losing a grueling three-setter to Jelena Ostapenko of Latvia, 4–6, 6–3, 6–4. Playing so well against Ostapenko, the 2017 French Open champion, on a stiflingly humid afternoon left Townsend encouraged. "I'm proud of the way I battled under very tough conditions and against a great player," said Townsend, who patterns her game after that of legendary lefty Martina Navratilova. "Even though it's a loss, it's the kind that gives you confidence."

A negative experience with the USTA could have shattered Townsend's confidence. She is five foot seven and a fuller-figured woman, somewhat like Serena, but not nearly as athletically gifted. No one is. Some people, including those in the USTA player development program, may have focused too much on Townsend's weight and not enough on developing her overall game. In 2012 Patrick McEnroe, then the USTA director of player development, told Townsend not to play in the U.S. Open, but to stay in Florida and work on her conditioning. He said this even though Townsend was the world's No. 1 junior at the time. "While everybody else was in New York, I was in Florida hitting balls twice a day while wearing a heart monitor," Townsend said, shaking her head. Her coach at the time, Kamau Murray, organized a fundraiser in Chicago to get Townsend to New York. She arrived too late to use a wild card that could have placed her in the U.S. Open main draw. "But I ended up winning the junior doubles title with my friend Gabby Andrews, which was really satisfying," she said with a smile of vindication.

Townsend achieved a unique distinction in 2012 by winning three of the four major junior doubles titles—the U.S. Open and Australian Open with Andrews, an African American player from Pomona, California, who stars at UCLA, and Wimbledon with Eugenie Bouchard of Canada. Townsend severed ties with the USTA player development program after the 2012 U.S. Open and worked with Murray and Zina Garrison.

"Taylor is one of the most talented players on the tour," Murray said. "If she's able to put a few good weeks together, she'll become one of the best players in the world." Townsend put together a good 2018 in World Team Tennis, earning Female Player of the Year honors in the summer league as a member of the Washington Kastles.

After working with a number of coaches, Townsend has returned to the one whom she said knows her game best, Donald Young Sr., the father of ATP tour pro Donald Young. "I've known the Young family since before I was born," she joked. "Donald Young Jr. was the ring bearer at my parents' wedding. Donald Young Sr. literally taught me to play tennis. My parents [high school administrators Sheila and Gary Townsend] brought me to him when I was about three. I played righthanded then, and I was having balance problems on the court. But once Mr. Young put the racket in my left hand and I started hitting, the balance problems went away."

Townsend moved from Chicago to Atlanta to be closer to Donald Sr., who coaches two other pros: his son, and Chris Eubanks, a promising six-foot, seven-inch player who traded basketball for tennis.

Townsend and Donald Jr. compete as a mixed doubles team at virtually every major tournament. "In mixed doubles, sometimes the guy will get frustrated with the girl, but Donald and I get along very well," Townsend said. "We're both very competitive and self-motivated."

The tennis world has been waiting for a while for Townsend to emerge. She remains a player of considerable potential. Whenever she seeks motivation, she looks to two African American sisters who have revolutionized the sport she loves.

"It was so inspiring to see Venus and Serena winning titles on TV when I was growing up; otherwise, it would have been tough to see myself winning in a sport where there aren't many people who look like you," said Townsend, whose older sister, Symone, played tennis at Florida A&M. "It's great to have role models, people who look like you and are achieving the things that you want to achieve. That's how I look at Venus and Serena. They give me hope. Both of them have been where I want to go. Certain bumps and bruises that they've taken along the way have made it so the younger black players like myself and Sloane don't have to experience that. Or not to the same extent as they did. I totally commend Venus and Serena for everything they're doing, as individuals and together."

Townsend is not the only female player of color to look at the Williams sisters and see unlimited possibilities for herself. A young woman of Japanese and Haitian ancestry used to often dream about standing across the net from Serena and defeating her in a major tournament. On one Saturday afternoon in September 2018, in the most turbulent atmosphere ever for a championship match, that young woman summoned the inner strength to make her dream real.

14 | Serena vs. Naomi Osaka

You owe me an apology.

SERENA WILLIAMS

Had there been a survey among the twenty-three thousand spectators who filled Arthur Ashe Stadium for the U.S. Open women's championship match on September 8, 2018, an overwhelming majority surely would have admitted they had come to see a coronation. Serena Williams needed one more victory to earn her twenty-fourth major title and equal the all-time record held by Margaret Court. But the tie with Court would have favored Serena, since she has won all of her major titles in *professional* tennis, during the Open Era of publicly declared prize money and more legitimate competition that began in 1968. Unlike Court, whose career began in the era of amateur tennis, Serena has not faced opponents who played tennis part time. She has faced other pros in a career that has spanned three decades, and she has reigned supreme.

A thunderous ovation greeted Serena when she took the court after a full-throated, boxing-style introduction that is now common in major tennis. A victory on this day would give her a seventh U.S. Open crown, breaking the record that she shares with Chris Evert. A victory would also mark Serena's first major championship as a mother; she missed the 2017 Open because of the birth of Alexis Olympia. Serena also vied to become the first woman to win a major title in a tutu, owing to her fashion-forward decision to wear a ballet-inspired, silhouetted outfit in each of her matches. Considering the superb form Serena displayed in her first six matches, she likely would have stormed through to the final in a burlap sack. She dropped only one set in her first six matches—the middle set to power-hitting Kaia Kanepi of Estonia, who had ousted No. 1 seed Simona Halep in the first round—and she dropped only three games against her semifinal opponent, Anastasija Sevastova of Serbia, who had upset 2017 U.S. Open champion Sloane Stephens in the quarterfinals.

Serena would face an opponent in the final for whom she had respect, an opponent she publicly called "very dangerous." But Serena usually did not falter with a championship at stake. If the outcome had been decided by popular vote, Serena would have been a landslide winner. But such is the beauty of competitive sports: There is no script. The athletes write the story.

Naomi Osaka had spent many of her first twenty years dreaming of a day like this. She would trade powerful forehands and backhands with her tennis idol, Serena, on the biggest stage in American tennis. The first time Osaka saw Serena in the locker room at a professional tournament, the youngster was too nervous to speak. Osaka is quite shy unless she is whacking a tennis ball with serious intentions. Her style of play is more like Serena's than any other player on the women's tour, Venus included. Osaka's childlike voice belies her solidly built, five-foot, eleven-inch frame. After she outslugged American Madison Keys in straight sets in the semifinals, Osaka expressed unabashed glee about her final-round matchup. Most players don't relish a match against Serena. Osaka is not like most players.

"I really want to play Serena," she said with a wide grin.

"Why?" a reporter asked.

"Because she's Serena."

As a third-grader, Osaka wrote a report for school on the person she most wanted to be like: Serena. In 2018 Osaka wore her hair big and frizzy on the court because Serena often does. Osaka favors the color black in her tennis wardrobe because Serena also does. Osaka, who used to be church mouse-quiet during matches, began in 2018 to yell "come on!" after winning an important point. That's what Serena does. The two had faced each other on court once before, six months earlier, but that match deserved an asterisk. Osaka routed her idol, 6–3, 6–2, in the first round of the Miami Open. It was only Serena's second tournament and third match after the birth of her child. That match also occurred three days after Osaka established herself as a new force in women's tennis by winning the BNP Paribas Open in Indian Wells, California, defeating former world No. 1 players Maria Sharapova, Karolina Pliskova, and Simona Halep in the process.

No one doubted Osaka's talent coming into the U.S. Open final. But many wondered if she was ready to defeat Serena at a Grand Slam event. Was Osaka ready to make history as the first player of Japanese and Haitian origin to win a major championship? The Japanese side of her ancestry garners the most media attention; Japan is a powerhouse in the global marketplace while Haiti is an impoverished Caribbean island still reeling from the effects of an earthquake in 2010. Osaka was born, coincidentally, in Osaka, Japan. Her Haitian-born father, Leonard Francois, and her mother, Tamaki Osaka, were college students when they met in Sapporo, Japan, in the early 1990s. When they married, her father said the union had brought "disgrace" to his family. The marriage has produced two daughters, Mari, the elder by eighteen months, and Naomi. The family used the mother's surname because they thought it would make things easier when seeking an apartment or registering the girls for school. However, ongoing tension with Tamaki's parents compelled the family to leave Japan. They moved to Elmont, a suburb of New York City, to live with Francois's parents. At the time, Naomi was three.

After Francois watched Venus and Serena win the 1999 French Open doubles championship on television, he studied the Williams sisters' backstory and decided to try to recreate it with his own daughters. "The blueprint was already there," he said. "I just had to follow it." Just as Richard Williams had bought a mound of tennis books and

VHS tapes to teach himself the game, Francois did likewise with tennis books and DVDs. Soon, Francois had his girls hitting hundreds of tennis balls every day and playing sets against each other. Mari won consistently until Naomi's growth spurt gave her a physical advantage over her now-shorter sister. Just as the Williams family had relocated to Florida so Serena and Venus could play tennis in optimal weather conditions and be home-schooled by their mother, so did the Osaka family. Like the Williams sisters, the Osaka girls largely avoided junior tennis tournaments, opting to play pro matches as teenagers on the smaller satellite circuit to gain experience. Because the Osaka girls lacked impressive junior tennis credentials, the USTA did not invest much time in their development. Francois then decided that his daughters would represent Japan, partly because of the USTA's lack of interest and partly because of the realization that if one or both of his daughters made it big, they would find far greater endorsement opportunities as Japanese sports stars. Mari Osaka, slowed by injuries, has yet to make a mark as a professional. In 2018 her picture did not even appear on the WTA tour website, as if she were just a rumor instead of an actual player. She ended the year ranked No. 337 in the world. But Naomi Osaka, seeded No. 20 at the U.S. Open, would certify herself as a global superstar if she defeated Serena in the final.

If Osaka had an ace up her sleeve heading into the championship match, it was her coach, Sascha Bajin, a German of Serbian ancestry. For eight years, Bajin was Serena's hitting partner and de facto assistant coach. After the two amicably parted in 2015, Bajin worked as a hitting partner for three other major champions—Sloane Stephens; Victoria Azarenka, the 2012 and 2013 Australian Open winner; and Caroline Wozniacki, the 2018 Australian Open titlist. Bajin, who is thirty-four, knows Serena's on-court tendencies, her greatest strengths (the serve, her competitive fire), and her most vulnerable stroke (the backhand), and he imparted that information to Osaka. Bajin also was acutely aware of the ball-striking similarities between Serena and Osaka. "I hit with Serena almost every day for eight years, and Naomi's weapons are just as big," he said. "She's not afraid of center

stage either, and that's why I believe she has greatness within her."
Osaka came into the U.S. Open in the best physical condition of her
life thanks to trainer Abdul Sillah, whose list of clients also includes
New York Yankees center fielder Aaron Hicks. A stronger and fitter
Osaka now has a quicker first step to get to balls earlier and produce
winning shots.

Osaka had already endeared herself to the international media and
rabid tennis watchers with her quirky responses during interviews at
the 2018 U.S. Open. Even if she lost to Serena, she could probably count
on attracting additional corporate sponsors and higher appearance
fees for events because of comments like these:

> OSAKA: My name is Osaka because I was born in Osaka. Every-
> body from Osaka is named Osaka.
>
> REPORTER: Is that true?
>
> OSAKA [laughing]: No!
>
> REPORTER: Since you love New York City so much and you're
> familiar with the city, what have you been doing to enjoy your
> time on off days?
>
> OSAKA: I just like walking in the city. It's just that there is a lot of
> energy. And then, you come back to the hotel very angry because
> everyone just makes you very angry [she smiles]. You're, like,
> why are these people walking so slow?

Before play began, Serena and Osaka—both dressed in black—were
brought onto the court for a photo opportunity with twelve-time major
champion Billie Jean King, as well as last-minute instructions from the
umpire, Carlos Ramos of Portugal, a forty-seven-year-old known as a
stickler for tennis rules and decorum. Ramos holds a gold badge, the
highest level in officiating, which qualifies him to serve as an umpire at
any tournament in the world including matches at the Davis Cup, Fed
Cup, and the Olympics. His resume includes what umpires call a Golden
Slam: He has officiated a singles final at all four Grand Slam events
plus the Olympics. He umpired the Olympic men's gold-medal match
in 2012, when Scotland's Andy Murray defeated Swiss maestro Roger

Federer. "Carlos is an outstanding umpire who will always enforce the rules," said Cecil Hollins, a black retired umpire who once held a gold badge. "He's not someone who will tolerate any misbehavior or inappropriate comments from players."

The final would be Serena's seventh match on Ashe Stadium court during the fortnight. Understandably, the USTA always put her on the biggest stage. Osaka did not get to play at Ashe until the semifinals. But her straight-set win over Keys proved her readiness for the spotlight. As is Osaka's custom before every match, she bowed first to her opponent and then to the umpire. Now, with all the formalities out of the way, the most contentious championship match in tennis history could begin.

Serena, in her thirty-first major final, began play by serving to Osaka, appearing in her first major final. However, the experience gap proved irrelevant in the opening set. Osaka outhit Serena from the baseline to win the first two points, and then Serena unleashed her vaunted serve for two aces followed by a volley winner to take the opening game. Crowd noise amplified every point Serena won. Osaka needed to stay mentally tough while playing before a crowd that did not dislike her, but adored her opponent. Like Serena, Osaka lost the first two points of her initial service game before recovering to even the set. Afterward, Osaka served notice that she had come to the title match not just for the experience, but to win. She hit forehands and backhands harder and cleaner than Serena, and she pushed her idol from one corner of the baseline to the other in a stunning display. After Serena double-faulted on break point to trail, 2–1, Osaka consolidated the break with a blistering ace to Serena's backhand on game point to take a 3–1 lead. Already a pattern had developed. Osaka was winning points by serving or hitting hard to Serena's backhand. There is no weak shot in Serena's repertoire, but the backhand is more attackable than the forehand. Bajin, a first-time coach who had worked closely with Serena for eight years, clearly made that tactic an essential part of Osaka's plan.

Osaka won a lengthy baseline rally to earn another break point, and then elicited another backhand error from Serena to take a commanding 4–1 lead in the set. Murmurs from the crowd followed both players to their seats after which an impromptu rhythmic chant of "Se-re-na! Se-re-na!" broke out and filled the stadium, the roof of which was closed because of a threat of rain. But the crowd's pro-Serena display affected Osaka not one bit. At love-15, Osaka drew gasps with a Serena-like crosscourt passing shot, and then she punctuated her fifth straight winning game with a service winner to Serena's backhand. At 5–1 Osaka, Serena rallied from down love–30 to hold serve, but she shook her head while walking to her chair. Perhaps only Osaka, during fantasy matches against her idol, ever thought she would be leading 5–2 with the first set now firmly on her racket. The only nerves that Osaka showed in the eighth game were steely. She fired three more service winners and wrapped up the set, 6–2.

If not for the preplanned music pumping through the Ashe Stadium sound system during the changeover, the atmosphere would have resembled that of a wake. The crowd seemed somewhat shocked. Osaka had outhit, outserved, and thoroughly outplayed Serena in the opening set of the U.S. Open final. Yes, Serena had rallied from a set down to win many important matches in her career. But this match seemed completely different. Perhaps Serena sensed that as well. Osaka played with a determination that essentially said to her idol, "You're going to have to beat me today. I am not going to collapse." Perhaps the high level of Osaka's play contributed to the on-court histrionics from Serena that followed.

Serena held serve to open the second set, briefly allaying the concerns of her supporters, which included Venus in a courtside seat near Serena's coach, Patrick Mouratoglou of France. While awaiting serve in the second game of the set, Serena stood on the baseline, to the right of Ramos, the umpire. As Osaka prepared to serve, Ramos saw Mouratoglou move his hands forward twice as if they were shark fins—a clear signal that he wanted Serena to work her way to the net, to play more aggressively. It is highly doubtful that a player of Serena's stature needed such advice. Nor was it clear that Serena even saw her coach's hand signals. But those points are moot. This point is irrefutable: hand signals from a coach are illegal in tennis. When it occurs, the umpire is supposed to call a penalty, or, as it is known in tennis, a code violation. And the code violation is issued to the player, not the player's coach.

"I don't cheat!" Serena told Ramos angrily. "I have never cheated in my life! [My coach and I] don't even have hand signals! I don't need hand signals! You owe me an apology!" The crowd rallied to Serena's defense and booed lustily, even though Ramos had accused her coach of cheating, not her. Besides, the code violation was essentially a warning. Serena did not lose a point because of her coach's hand signals. But if Serena, or her coach, were to commit a second code violation, then she would lose a point.

A different umpire may have chosen to ignore the hand signals, or may have given Serena a soft warning. ("Serena, your coach is using hand signals. If he does it again, I'm calling a code violation.") But Ramos is a no-nonsense umpire, one who enforces the rules. Under the penalty system in tennis, the first code violation is a warning (unless it is for something egregious, like throwing a ball at someone; then the penalty would be harsher). A second code violation results in a one-point penalty. A third code violation results in a one-game penalty. Any subsequent code violation could result in disqualification.

Ramos had essentially put Serena on notice: Another violation will cost you a point, and a third one will cost you a game. Tennis players usually exercise enough self-control to avoid being hit with three code violations in a match. Serena, however, played as if she did not realize Ramos had issued a code violation. He had announced it to the crowd. Still, Serena seemed to believe that he had issued a soft warning, not an actual code violation.

"I think if Carlos had it to do over again, he might have been a bit clearer with what he was doing and how he was sanctioning her," said Tony Nimmons, a black former umpire who has officiated at twenty U.S. Opens. "Clearly, Carlos saw the coaching. That's not allowed at the Grand Slams."

Mouratoglou erased any doubt that he had used illegal hand signals in an interview during the match with ESPN courtside reporter Pam Shriver. "I'm honest; I was coaching," he told a national television audience. "But I didn't think Serena saw me. Everybody coaches." ESPN also showed its audience video footage of Mouratoglou giving the hand signals.

Whether or not Serena saw the signals is irrelevant. Whether or not Mouratoglou thinks all coaches get away with using illegal signals is irrelevant. What matters was that Serena was not able to put Ramos's ruling behind her, despite breaking serve for the first time in the match to take a 3–1 lead.

The crowd roared its approval after Serena's service break, hoping to spur her to a dramatic comeback. While noise filled the stadium, Osaka walked toward the wall behind the baseline. With her back to her opponent, she faced the wall and stood silently for a few seconds, an apparent moment of zen to compose herself. Serena now had the lead, but she was still seething about the code violation. A moment of zen would have benefited her.

"If Serena had taken the position that she was just going to ignore the umpire, to basically say to him, 'You're invisible to me,' she would have been so much better off," said MaliVai Washington, a 1996 Wimbledon finalist. "She became fixated on the umpire and it's very tough to win that way. Naomi Osaka as an opponent was tough enough."

In a pivotal fifth game, Serena double-faulted twice to give Osaka a break point and then lost a baseline rally, which reduced her lead to 3–2. So frustrated was Serena by her inability to expand her lead that she slammed her racket to the ground, the frame irreparably mangled. Ramos issued a second code violation for racket abuse, which resulted in a one-point penalty. The second violation allowed Osaka to begin the sixth game with a 15–love advantage.

Any umpire in the sport would have docked Serena for racket abuse. Had it been her first and only offense of the match, it would have resulted in a relatively small fine of $3,000 and been quickly forgotten. But this was Serena's second code violation, and she firmly believed she had not deserved the first one.

"You stole a point from me! You're a thief! I don't cheat!" she said vehemently. "I'm a mother and I'm trying to teach my daughter right from wrong. I don't cheat!"

With a boom microphone at courtside, the crowd heard much of what Serena said to Ramos but very little of what he said in response. The umpire had enough experience to turn off his microphone before responding to Serena. Not satisfied with what she had heard from Ramos, Serena summoned tournament referee Brian Earley and WTA supervisor Donna Kelso onto the court during the changeover to talk about the raw deal she believed she was getting. The conversation did not diminish Serena's feeling of being cheated by an overly officious umpire. Her every finger wag toward Ramos underscored her fury. Had Serena, still leading 3–2, been able to channel that fury into positive energy, she still could have won the set. But she had become so convinced that she had been wronged that she could not regain her poise.

Osaka held serve to even the set, as Serena glared at Ramos several times. Then, Osaka won several baseline rallies in the seventh game, finally whipping a forehand past Serena on break point to take the lead, 4–3. During the changeover, Serena continued to rebuke Ramos, gesticulating with each comment as the boos from the crowd intensified.

"You owe me an apology! Are you going to apologize? I have never cheated in my life! You stole a point from me! . . . You are the liar! You're a thief, too! . . . Don't even look at me!"

According to the tennis rule book, verbal abuse is a comment toward an official that "implies dishonesty or is derogatory, insulting, or otherwise abusive." The crowd's torrent of boos drowned out much of the back-and-forth between Serena and Ramos, even for many seated at courtside. So when Ramos leaned forward and spoke into his microphone, "Code violation. Verbal abuse. Game penalty, Mrs. Williams," many spectators were unaware of the decision. But Serena knew.

"Are you kidding me? Are you kidding me?" Serena yelled while waving her right index finger at Ramos. "Because I said you're a thief? Because you stole a point from me? But I'm not a cheater! I told you to apologize to me! Excuse me, I need a referee."

Because Serena resembled a baseball manager chewing out an umpire—but without the dirt-kicking—the crowd roared its approval. But as soon as they noticed the scoreboard change to 5–3 in favor of Osaka, the boos were deafening.

Earley and Kelso walked briskly back onto the court, trying to restore order. Serena, her voice cracking, told them, "This is not fair. This is not fair. Men do much worse. Because I'm a woman, you're going to take a game away from me? This happens to me every single year when I'm trying to play here—it's not fair."

There were three specific U.S. Open matches which Serena was referencing:

In a 2004 quarterfinal loss to Jennifer Capriati, Serena received at least a half-dozen bad calls, including one on a backhand winner that umpire Mariana Alves overruled and called out. Alves also lost track of the score during the match. The next day, the USTA issued a rare public apology to Serena for the poor officiating. That match played a significant role in the introduction of video replay for line calls in 2006.

Facing match point against Kim Clijsters of Belgium in the 2009 semifinals, Serena was called for a foot fault by lineswoman Shino Tsurubuchi. (A foot fault occurs when the server's foot touches the baseline before the ball has been struck.) It is believed to be the only time in major tennis history that a foot fault was called when a server faced match point. An irate Serena walked toward the lineswoman and snapped, "I swear to God, I'm fucking going to take this fucking ball and shove it down your fucking throat! You hear that? I swear to God." A CBS courtside microphone allowed the obscenities to be heard on national television. After umpire Louise Engzall asked the lineswoman what Serena had said, Engzall penalized Serena one point for verbal abuse. Since the one-point penalty was her second code violation, Serena lost the match. She was also fined $10,000 by the USTA and another $82,500 by the Grand Slam committee.

In the first set of the 2011 final against Samantha Stosur of Australia, Serena hit an apparent winning shot, which she punctuated by yelling, "Come on!" Chair umpire Eva Asderaki ruled that Serena's yell distracted Stosur's effort to retrieve the shot. Hence, the point was disallowed. Serena then received a code violation for harsh language toward Asderaki, including, "You're a hater," and, "You're unattractive inside." Serena lost the match in straight sets.

When play finally resumed in the 2018 final, Osaka stood one game from a major championship—without having had to hit a ball in the eighth game of the second set. For the remainder of the match, many of Serena's fans filled what are usually moments of silence between points with expressions of anger or support: "They're robbing you, Serena!" "We love you, Serena!" "You're still the greatest!"

After Serena held serve to cut the deficit to 5-4, fans stood and cheered, hoping to will her toward a comeback for the ages. The atmosphere during the changeover certainly tested Osaka's resolve. She had played brilliantly. But for it to truly be the match of her life, one that would forever list her as a major champion, she needed to control her nerves and hold serve one more time. If Serena were to break serve and square the set at 5-5, the tide could turn irreversibly. As someone who idolized Serena, who patterned her tennis game after Serena's, who proudly wore her hair full and frizzy like Serena's, Osaka needed to prove herself here and now. She could not allow to happen to her what befell Victoria Azarenka when she served for the 2012 U.S. Open title at 5-4 against Serena. The occasion got to Azarenka. She failed to hold serve. Serena won the last three games and the championship. There are no guarantees that Azarenka will ever play in another U.S. Open final. There are no guarantees for Osaka. She needed to close the deal now.

Osaka understood the importance of getting her first serves in play. If she missed the first serve, her body could tense, causing her to miss the second serve. But on this day, Osaka served like a champion throughout. She won the first point with a forehand passing shot. Serena answered with a backhand volley winner for 15-all. Osaka hit a service winner to Serena's backhand. Osaka had so much success hitting to that side all day. She led 30-15. Osaka then struck an ace to Serena's backhand, giving her two championship points. She would need only one. She pounded a serve to Serena's backhand—again— that could not be returned.

Game, set, match, championship.

As both players walked to the net for the traditional handshake, the crowd booed vociferously. They booed the work of Ramos, and what they considered the shafting of Serena. Osaka, still new to all this, could not be sure of why they were booing. She began to cry. And Serena, like the tennis-playing parent she is, wrapped Osaka in a tight motherly hug.

"Serena showed her true character right there," MaliVai Washington said. "She didn't let the end of the match be about the controversy during the match. She knew how great Osaka had played, and she wanted Osaka to know that she knew."

As boos continued to fill the stadium, Serena wanted to convey something else to everyone before the trophy presentation. Rather than shake hands with Ramos in his high chair, she pointed up at him and snapped, "You owe me an apology!"

It is customary for the umpire to be introduced to the crowd during the trophy ceremony, as Eva Asderaki had been after the 2017 U.S. Open women's final. But this time, Ramos was hustled off the court. He was unavailable for comment. If he received a commemorative watch or lapel pin from the USTA, then the gifting took place in a corridor somewhere. Even without Ramos, the booing continued. Osaka was still unsure about whether she was being booed. In a scene that broke hearts, the newly crowned champion covered her eyes with her visor and cried. Serena wrapped a protective arm around her again, and showed class in her remarks to the crowd.

"Stop booing," Serena told the audience. Her words finally reduced the volume and the temperature inside Ashe Stadium. "She played an amazing match. She deserves the credit and deserved to win."

Osaka had truly earned it. A straight-set victory over her idol. Just the way she had dreamt it—but without all the yelling, finger-pointing, and racket-smashing. As superbly as Osaka had played, her ability to block out the cacophony inside the stadium had been equally impressive. "I think I was able to do that because it was my first Grand Slam final," she said in a jam-packed interview room. "I felt like I shouldn't let myself be overcome by nerves or anything. I should just focus on playing because that's what's gotten me to this point."

No matter how loud and crazy things became inside the stadium, Osaka kept her primary goal in mind. Her emotional maturity was as instrumental to her first major title as her serve, returns, forehands, two-fisted backhands, and execution of a game plan built on attacking the Serena backhand early and often. Proud of her achievement on one hand and cognizant of how disappointed Serena was on the other, Osaka gave voice to her conflicting emotions in the interview room. "I know that, like, she really wanted to have the twenty-fourth Grand Slam [title], right? Everyone knows this. It's on the commercials. It's everywhere. But when I step onto the court, I feel like a different person. I'm not a Serena fan. I'm just a tennis player. But when I hugged her at the net, I felt like a little kid again."

Many postmatch narratives argued that Serena had spoiled the occasion for Osaka, that everyone should have been talking about how beautifully Osaka played instead of the controversial officiating or the contentiousness between Serena and Ramos, as if people could not talk about all three. Serena certainly commandeered the headlines. As a truly iconic athlete, she always does. Certainly, the headlines would have been markedly different had Serena not lost her poise because of officiating that many in the tennis community deemed unfair to her. But Serena has always hated to lose more than she loves to win. She has that in common with her fellow athletic icons. That has always been part of the package that comes with the most celebrated champion in professional tennis history. As a girl, Osaka was so drawn to that package that she wanted to replicate it. Yes, the 2018 U.S. Open champion did not get to celebrate on court the way champions traditionally do. However, she took that in stride.

"I'm always going to remember the Serena I love," Osaka said. "It doesn't change anything for me. She was really nice to me, like at the net and at the podium. I don't really see what would change."

So much has changed for Naomi Osaka since her U.S. Open triumph. She ended 2018 as the No. 5 player in the world. Her $3.8 million paycheck in New York City helped boost her earnings to $6,394,289 for the year, and $7,629,197 in a career that is just getting started. She will forever be remembered as the first player of Haitian or Japanese descent to win a Grand Slam singles title. She is now cashing in on the Japanese side of her ancestry. The week after the Open, she signed a multiyear extension of her clothing endorsement deal with Adidas that the company called the richest contract it had ever offered to a female athlete. Yet the contract likely paled in comparison to deals Adidas has given to male athletes. Retired soccer star David Beckham, for instance, has a lifetime deal with Adidas worth $160 million. Osaka also signed a three-year deal as a brand ambassador for Nissan automobiles. A creatively written statement from Nissan has Osaka saying, "I'm so honored to represent Japan and Nissan on the world stage. I was drawn to partner with Nissan because of its strong Japanese DNA and global competitive spirit." Osaka's U.S. Open title also triggered bonus clauses in her existing endorsement contracts with Yonex rackets, Citizen watches, Nissin Foods, All Nippon Airways, and Wowow, the Japanese network that televises tennis. Osaka may soon rival her countryman Kei Nishikori in sponsorship money. Nishikori makes a reported $33 million a year in endorsements, even though he has yet to win a major title. Nishikori may always have more appeal in Japan because each of his parents is Japanese, but Osaka may have more global appeal. Stuart Duguid, her agent at International Management Group, said he hopes Osaka can change the way multicultural Japanese citizens are perceived there. "I hope she's opened the door for other people to follow," he said. "Not just in tennis or sports, but for all of society. She can be an ambassador for change."

Change has been almost constant for Osaka since her U.S. Open triumph, which she followed by winning the Australian Open title in January 2019—a victory that not only made her a two-time major champion but also the first player of Haitian or Japanese descent to be ranked world No. 1. Osaka has added significantly to her endorsement portfolio as well, ditching her sportswear deal with Adidas to sign a multiyear contract with Nike worth $8.5 million annually plus bonuses for winning major titles, according to the *Times of London*. She also signed a multiyear deal with MasterCard. However, her biggest change stunned the sport: in February 2019 she parted ways with coach Sascha Bajin. Neither has publicly explained why. But Osaka said the split had nothing to do with money. She has since hired Jermaine Jenkins—Venus's former hitting partner—to be her coach. Bajin signed on to coach Kristina Mladenovic of France.

Osaka, now twenty-one, answered questions from Japanese reporters in English during the U.S. Open. Her older sister, Mari, is fluent in Japanese. In time, Naomi should be as well. She will be one of the faces of the 2020 Summer Olympics in Tokyo, and one of the faces of tennis for a long time. Her ascension is proof that the Williams family blueprint for creating a global tennis champion works—as long as the girl has game.

A sight we will never see again is a Serena match officiated by Carlos Ramos. Every player and chair umpire in professional tennis has a "no list." On the list, players and umpires tell the International Tennis Federation who they don't want to work with anymore because of a past conflict. That is why Serena made it clear in her comments after the U.S. Open final that Ramos would never officiate another of her matches.

Perhaps all the controversy could have been avoided if the USTA had assigned Ramos to work the next day's men's final between Novak Djokovic and Juan Martin del Potro. The USTA chose Alison Hughes, a British woman, to officiate the men's final. Had Hughes worked Serena's match against Osaka, there may not have been any contentiousness—not because of the gender of the respective umpires, but because of their approaches. In the first set of the men's final, Hughes gave Djokovic a soft warning for taking longer than the allotted twenty seconds to serve. Several times after that, Djokovic took more than twenty seconds before serving. He had already been given a soft warning. But Hughes chose not to penalize him. Although Djokovic had gone a few seconds over the limit, something he has done in other matches, Hughes did not consider it to be an unfair advantage for him. She chose not to inject herself into the match by taking a point from a player in a major final for something inconsequential. She let the players decide the match.

There is no way of knowing if Hughes would have let Serena's coach get away with illegal hand signals, or given Serena a soft warning. But her approach suggests that she would have let Serena and Osaka decide the match instead of letting things escalate to where a one-game penalty was issued.

"Carlos could have done a better job of communicating to Serena after the first violation and before he issued the one-game penalty," said Cecil Hollins, the former umpire. "If things get out of hand, an umpire always has to be thinking, 'How can I defuse this situation?' That did not happen in Serena's match."

From Serena's second-place check for $1,850,000, she was docked $17,000 for the three code violations: $10,000 for verbal abuse; $4,000 for her coach's hand signals; and $3,000 for racket abuse. "I've seen men call umpires several things," Serena said after the match. "For me to say 'thief' and for him to take a game [away], it made me feel like it was a sexist remark."

Serena could take solace from the support she received from the USTA, WTA, and many players and fans.

Novak Djokovic said, "Maybe the chair umpire should not have pushed Serena to the limit, especially in a Grand Slam final. He did change the course of the match, maybe unnecessarily."

Former ATP tour pro Jesse Levine tweeted, "I have called an umpire a lot worse than a thief and never got a warning . . . that was just awful."

Hall of Famer Pam Shriver said, "Ramos helped derail a championship match by being rigid beyond normal protocol by not giving a soft warning for coaching, by not communicating effectively to defuse an emotional player, and by not allowing a player to let off more steam before giving the third code violation that gave a game at a crucial time in a final."

Katrina Adams said, "We watch guys do this all the time—they badger the chair umpire on the changeover. Nothing happens."

Billie Jean King tweeted after the match, "When a woman is emotional, she's 'hysterical' and she's penalized for it. When a man does the same, he's 'outspoken' and there are no repercussions. Thank you,

@serenawilliams, for calling out this double standard. More voices are needed to do the same."

Unfortunately, in a patriarchal society, people often react more harshly when a woman expresses anger. Negative reaction toward an angry *black* woman is even more pronounced. Serena is aware of the double standard. "There's literally [research] papers about it, how black women are treated if they're angry, as opposed to white women, white men, black men," she said.

As previously noted, Serena called Ramos's reaction toward her "sexist." Her word choice underscored the perception that a black female tennis player had been held to a higher standard to control her emotions than, say, a white man nominated for the United States Supreme Court. Brett Kavanaugh is now Justice Kavanaugh despite an emotional rant in his opening statement and unusually combative responses to questions during his 2018 Senate confirmation hearing. "Kavanaugh's a white man; I'm a black woman," Serena said. "His limit is higher; my limit is way lower. And that's where we stand right now in the world. It's a fact. It is literally a fact."

The day after the women's final, WTA chief executive Steve Simon said, "The WTA believes there should be no difference in the standards of tolerance provided to the emotions expressed by men versus women and is committed to working with the sport to ensure that all players are treated the same. We do not believe that was done last night."

Taking a somewhat opposing view was Martina Navratilova, the eighteen-time major champion. In a *New York Times* column, she took Serena to task for having a somewhat twisted take on feminism. Navratilova wrote, "I don't believe it's a good idea to apply a standard of, 'If men can get away with it, women should be able to, too." On Tennis Channel, Navratilova said that if she had behaved as Serena did in the final, then she would have deserved to be penalized as Serena was.

Without question, the harshest criticism of Serena came from Mark Knight, an editorial cartoonist for the *Herald Sun* newspaper in Melbourne, Australia. His September 10, 2018 cartoon depicted

Serena as an obese mammy figure about to stomp her racket, her mouth wide open in rage, while her slim, blonde-haired opponent asks the umpire, "Can you just let her win?" With his caricature of Serena, Knight attained a triple crown of bigotry—racism, sexism, and body shaming—while also erasing the identity of the brown-skinned Osaka.

Serena decided after the U.S. Open to spend the rest of the year away from tennis. That meant more quality time with her husband and daughter, and more time for emotions to cool down. A week after the Open, umpires threatened to boycott Serena's matches in 2019 because of what they perceived as the vilification of Ramos and a lack of support for umpires from the USTA and WTA. However, when Serena made her 2019 debut in January at the Hopman Cup tournament in Australia, the umpires did not boycott her matches.

Time away from tennis also allowed Serena to bask in the afterglow of being named the Associated Press Female Athlete of the Year for the fifth time. (She also received the honor in 2002, 2009, 2013, and 2015.) Additionally, she was named the Woman of the Year by *Gentlemen's Quarterly* magazine. On the cover, next to the words "of the year," GQ playfully crossed out "Man" and "Men" to write "Woman." Serena's stature as a cultural icon continues to grow. Yet it is tennis for which she is best known, and in 2019 she returned to the sport in pursuit of her twenty-fourth and twenty-fifth major singles titles, which would allow her to own the record and cement her legacy as the greatest champion ever. An intriguing question is whether 2020 will be the final year in tennis for one or both of the Williams sisters. Venus, soldiering on despite Sjögren's syndrome, played in three significant finals in 2017. Yet she entered 2019 having not won a title since an event in Kaohsiung, Taiwan, in 2016. She turned thirty-nine on June 17, 2019. Serena turned thirty-eight on September 26, 2019. Really, neither has anything left to prove. Since the 1990s, they have inspired so many people of color to take interest in—or grab a racket and play—a sport once reserved for whites at the highest level. Years ago, Richard Williams predicted that Venus and Serena would retire together so they could enter the International Tennis Hall of Fame together. That comment does not sound so farfetched anymore. Nor does the idea of Richard Williams and Oracene Price being enshrined in the Hall of Fame as contributors. Would it not make sense for tennis to pay homage to four members of a black family who rose from humble backgrounds to change the sport forever?

BIBLIOGRAPHY

Agenor, Ronald, and Mark D. Alleyne. *Tilted Courts: The Power Politics of International Tennis*. Los Angeles, 2007.

Akersten, Teresa. "Caught in a Tennis Net: Rosemary Darben Faced Gibson, Ashe and Racism." *Montclair Times*, November 5, 2003.

"Althea Gibson Quits as N.J. Sports Chief." *New York Post*, January 19, 1977.

"Althea Gibson Signs Pro Contract for Nearly $100,000." *New York Times*, October 20, 1959.

"Althea Trying Court Comeback." *New York Daily News*, December 24, 1968.

Alvarez, Anya. "At the Height of Her Tennis Career, Althea Gibson Turned to Golf." WBUR Radio, Boston, December 23, 2017. https://www.wbur.org/onlyagame/2017/12/22/althea-gibson-golf.

Amdur, Neil. "Althea Gibson Feature." *New York Times*, August 26, 2002.

———. "Tennis Weathers One Eligibility Crisis over U.S. Open but Another Is Brewing; No Ban on Team Pros; Black Player in Limbo." *New York Times*, August 28, 1973.

American Masters. Season 29, episode 6, "Althea." Aired September 4, 2015. https://www.pbs.org/video/american-masters-althea/.

Araton, Harvey. "Addressing an Attitude Problem." *New York Times*, July 6, 1999.

———. "50 Years Later, Ashe's Shadow Looms Large." *New York Times*, September 9, 2018.

———. "Sisters Rise Above, and Emerge on Top." *New York Times*, September 9, 1997.

Arsenault, Raymond. *Arthur Ashe: A Life*. New York: Simon & Schuster, 2018.

Asbury, Edith Evans. "City Pays Tribute to Althea Gibson." *New York Times*, July 12, 1957.

———. "'Queen' Althea Hailed by Harlem Neighbors." *New York Times*, July 10, 1957.

Ashe, Arthur. *A Hard Road to Glory, Vols. 1–3*, abridged edition. New York: Amistad, 1991.

Ashe, Arthur, and Arnold Rampersad. *Days of Grace: A Memoir*. New York: Ballantine, 1993.

Ashe, Arthur, and Neil Amdur. *Off the Court*. New York: New American Library, 1991.

Association of Tennis Professionals. ATP *World Tour Media Guide*. Quebec, Canada, 2018.

Badenhausen, Kurt. "Inside Serena Williams's Plan to Ace Venture Investing." *Forbes*, June 3, 2019.

Barner, George. "Ticker Tape Parade for Althea." *New York Amsterdam News*, July 13, 1957.

Bell, Taylor. "Serena Williams' Net Worth: Tennis, Business Deals and 'Being Serena.'" AOL, June 29, 2018. https://www.aol.com/article/finance/2018 /06/29/serena-williams-net-worth-tennis-business-deals-being-serena /23471320/.

Bembry, Jerry. "James Blake Is Now an Author, an Activist and Back in Tennis—as a Tournament Director." *The Undefeated*, November 9, 2018. https:// theundefeated.com/features/james-blake-is-now-an-author-an-activist -and-back-in-tennis-as-a-tournament-director/.

Bieler, Des. "Serena Williams Was Out of Line, Say Martina Navratilova and Mary Carillo." *Washington Post*, September 10, 2018.

Bissinger, Buzz. "Serena's Love Match." *Vanity Fair*, August 2017.

Blake, James. *Breaking Back: How I Lost Everything and Won Back My Life*. New York: HarperCollins, 2007.

Blake, James, and Carol Taylor. *Ways of Grace: Stories of Activism, Adversity, and How Sports Can Bring Us Together*. New York: Amistad, 2017.

"Blake's Confidence Grows with Ranking." *USA Today*, March 24, 2006.

Blankenbaker, Betsy, and Rachel Viollet, dirs. *Althea and Angela: A Perfect Match*. Figaro Films, 2012.

Bondy, Filip. "Just Turn It On? Sister, You Got Another Thing Coming." *New York Daily News*, September 5, 2006.

Boren, Cindy. "After Serena Williams Incident, the USTA Head Says There's a Double Standard in Tennis." *Washington Post*, September 11, 2018.

Bowden, Ebony. "Williams Calls on Sandgren to Apologize for 'Disgusting' Tweet." *Sydney Morning Herald*, January 25, 2018.

Bricker, Charles. "Arthur Ashe Inspired a Generation of Black Americans." *Fort Lauderdale Sun-Sentinel*, June 22, 2006.

British Broadcasting Company. "Ashe vs. Connors: 1975 Wimbledon Gentlemen's Final." July 5, 1975.

Burchard, James A. "This Could Be Althea's Year for Net Heights." *New York World Telegram*, July 20, 1955.

"Challenger Q&A: Mmoh Cracks Top 100 with Tiburon Title." ATP Tour (website), October 1, 2018. https://www.atptour.com/en/news/challenger-qa-2018-tiburon-mmoh.

Clarey, Christopher. "Are Women Penalized More Than Men in Tennis? Data on Fines Says No." *New York Times*, September 14, 2018.

———. "Williams Is Trying to Recover the Magic." *New York Times*, July 1, 2006.

Clay, Bobby. "American Tennis Association." *Black Enterprise*, September 1996.

Coffey, Wayne. "Young Ideas." *New York Daily News*, September 9, 2006.

Collins, Bud. *The Bud Collins History of Tennis, Third Edition*. Chicago: New Chapter Press, 2016.

———. *Bud Collins's Total Tennis*. New York: SportClassic Books, 2003.

———. "Racial Barriers No Match for Pioneer Gibson." *Boston Globe*, October 1, 2003.

———. "Venus in for Paris Near Miss." MSNBC, June 5, 2006.

Collins, Marion. "Arthur Ashe Quietly Ascends to Hall of Fame." *New York Daily News*, July 28, 1985.

Constantinesco, Kim. "U.S. Open Highlights Tennis Pro Vicky Duval's Artwork for Good Reason." *Purpose 2 Play*, September 4, 2018. https://purpose2play.com/2018/09/03/u-s-open-highlights-vicky-duvals-artwork-for-good-reason/.

Couch, Greg. "For Staying Power, Hingis Has Serena Beat." *Chicago Sun-Times*, May 28, 2006.

Danzig, Allison. "Off the Court There Were Victories Too." *New York Times*, December 7, 1958.

Davidson, Sue. *Changing the Game: The Stories of Tennis Champions Alice Marble and Althea Gibson*. Emeryville CA: Seal Press, 1997.

Dawson, Alan. "Naomi Osaka Is Reportedly Set to Sign Adidas' Biggest Deal with a Female Athlete." *Business Insider*, September 12, 2018.

de Jonge, Peter. "Two Boys Dreamed of Playing Tennis." *New York Magazine*, June 2016.

Dell, Donald. "Arthur Ashe." *Washington Post*, February 6, 2003.

DeSimone, Bonnie. "Young Not Concerned Despite Winless Record." ESPN, March 23, 2006. http://www.espn.com/sports/tennis/news/story?id= 2381413.

Dickstein, Corey. "Marine's Second Vietnam Tour Helped His Brother, Arthur Ashe, Win U.S. Open 50 Years Ago." *Stars and Stripes*, August 31, 2018.

Dillman, Lisa. "Davenport Rips Stevenson, and Then Her Mother." *Los Angeles Times*, July 4, 1999.

Djata, Sundiata. *Blacks at the Net: Black Achievement in the History of Tennis.* Syracuse NY: Syracuse University Press, 2006.

Dosh, Kristi. "Venus Williams Partners with NBC's 'Shop with Golf' to Bring Clothing Line EleVen to Golfers." *Forbes*, June 17, 2019.

Duffy, Bob. "Hidden Treasure Althea Gibson Made History but Not Money in Tennis and Has Become a Virtual Recluse." *Boston Globe*, June 24, 2001.

"Editorial: Wimbledon Winner." *New York Times*, July 8, 1957.

Ellen: The Ellen DeGeneres Show. Season 16, episode 7, "LeBron James/Channing Tatum/Naomi Osaka/Dave Matthews Band." Aired September 12, 2018.

ESPN. "'Venus Vs.,' a Documentary on Women's Tennis' Battle for Equal Prize Money at Wimbledon." July 2, 2013.

Feldman, Kate. "Venus Williams Reportedly Settles with Family in Fatal Florida Car Crash." *New York Daily News*, November 20, 2018.

Fendrich, Howard. "Venus, Serena Williams Join Billie Jean King Equal Pay Push." Associated Press (website), April 10, 2018. https://apnews.com /75febb8c3cef42a3a5940b191ef82d23.

Finn, Robin. "Hingis Dominates, and Then Reconciles." *New York Times*, September 12, 1999.

———. "Stevenson's Big Shot Pays Off." *New York Times*, July 1, 1999.

Fraser, Stuart. "Umpires May Boycott Serena Williams Matches After Outburst at U.S. Open Final." *Times of London*, September 11, 2018.

Friedman, Roger. "Tennis Anyone? U.S. Open CEO Was Paid $1.3 Mil Last Year." *Showbiz 411*, September 15, 2015. https://www.showbiz411.com/2015 /09/15/tennis-anyone-us-open-ceo-was-paid-1-3-mil-last-year-usta-calls -itself-non-profit-organization.

Fucillo, David. "Here Is a List of Every Organization to Which Colin Kaepernick Donated Money." *SB Nation, Niners Nation*, January 31, 2018. https://www .ninersnation.com/2018/1/31/16956016/colin-kaepernick-donations-full -list-of-organizations-one-million-dollars.

Gannon, Louise. "Tennis Ace Heather Watson: 'You Have to Be Prepared to Sacrifice Everything.'" *London Daily Mail*, June 10, 2017.

Garrison, Zina. "Remembering Althea Gibson." 2004 U.S. Open Program, August 2004.

Garrison, Zina, and Doug Smith. *Zina: My Life in Women's Tennis*. Berkeley CA: Frog Ltd., 2001.

Geoffreys, Clayton. *Serena Williams: The Inspiring Story of One of Tennis's Greatest Legends*. Winter Park FL: Calvintir Books, 2017.

Gibson, Althea. *I Always Wanted to Be Somebody*. New York: Harper and Brothers, 1958.

———. "Transcript of Althea Gibson Interview at International Tennis Hall of Fame." July 14, 1979.

Gilman, Kay. "Althea Gibson: Still Every Inch a Queen." *New York Daily News*, June 30, 1974.

Good Morning America. "Interview with Venus Williams." Aired September 1, 2011.

Gray, Frances Clayton, and Yanick Rice Lamb. *Born to Win: The Authorized Biography of Althea Gibson*. Hoboken NJ: John Wiley and Sons, 2004.

Gregory, Sean. "Serena's Heir." *Time*, June 3, 2013.

Gross, Jane. "Noah Captures French Crown." *New York Times*, June 6, 1983.

Harris, Cecil, and Larryette Kyle-DeBose. *Charging the Net: A History of Blacks in Tennis from Althea Gibson and Arthur Ashe to the Williams Sisters*. Chicago: Ivan Dee, 2007.

Harrison, Emma. "Althea, Pride of One West Side, Becomes the Queen of Another." *New York Times*, September 7, 1957.

Harwitt, Sandra. "Williams a 'Lone Flag Waving Gently in the Wind.'" Associated Press, June 4, 2006.

Horner, Peter. "ATA: The Best Kept Secret in Tennis?" *Tennis USTA*, July 1981.

"James Blake." *ATP Tennis Weekly*, March 20, 2006.

Jensen, Mike. "Joakim Noah Making His Own Racket." *Philadelphia Inquirer*, March 31, 2006.

Johnson, Julian. "A Whirlwind Event." Black Athlete Sports Network, June 22, 2006. http://blackathlete.net/2006/06/a-whirlwind-event/.

Kadison, Dan. "Line Judges Spur 'Bias' Probe of USTA." *New York Post*, April 10, 2006.

Kai, Maiysha. "Serena Williams Is the First Athlete to Make *Forbes'* List of the World's Richest Self-Made Women." *The Root*, June 4, 2019. https://

theglowup.theroot.com/serena-williams-is-the-1st-athlete-to-make-forbes
-list-1835225476?utm_medium=sharefromsite&utm_source=theroot_copy
&utm_campaign=top.

Kane, David. "Stephens on Shaking 'One-Hit Wonder' Label, Channeling
Criticism in Singapore." WTA (website), October 27, 2018. https://www
.wtatennis.com/news/stephens-shaking-one-hit-wonder-label-channeling
-criticism-singapore.

Kaplan, Daniel. "Stephens Builds Global Endorsement Lineup." *Sports Business
Journal*, March 19, 2018.

King, Michelle. "How Powerful Women Experience Extreme Online Sexual
Harassment, and What You Can Do to Stop It." *Forbes*, November 14, 2017.

Lamorte, Chris. "Venus Williams Shares Her Love of Fashion and Interior
Design." *Chicago Tribune*, October 2, 2018.

Lapchick, Richard. *Smashing Barriers: Race and Sport in the New Millennium*.
New York: Madison Books, 2001.

Larmer, Brook. "Naomi Osaka's Breakthrough Game." *New York Times*, August
23, 2018.

Laskas, Jeanne Marie. "Serena Williams Is the Champion of the Year." *Gentlemen's Quarterly*, November 15, 2018.

Lerner, Noah, dir. *Being Serena*. HBO Sports, May 2018.

Lichtenstein, Grace. "Where Is the Next Althea Gibson?" *Ms. Magazine*,
December 1973.

MacPherson, Alex. "The 100 Club: How Sachia Vickery Stepped Up." WTA
(website), July 20, 2018. https://www.wtatennis.com/news/100-club-how
-sachia-vickery-stepped.

Maher, Erin. "Drop Shots and Doodles: Tennis Player and Artist Vicky Duval."
U.S. Open (website), August 30, 2018. https://test.usopen.org/en_US/news
/articles/2018-08-30/2018-08-30_drop_shots_and_doodles_tennis_player
_and_artist_vicky_duval.html?promo=nextArticle.

McCarvel, Nicholas. "Initial Wimbledon Run Still Drives a Former Semifinal-
ist." *New York Times*, July 3, 2014.

McEnroe, John, with James Kaplan. *You Cannot Be Serious*. New York: Berkley
Publishing, 2002.

McKinley, James. "Tennis Cinderella's Father Has a Name: Julius Erving."
New York Times, July 3, 1999.

Mendell, David. "He Coached Sloane Stephens to a U.S. Open Title, but Kamau
Murray's Big Goal Is a Youth Tennis Center in Chicago." *The Undefeated*,

February 23, 2018. https://theundefeated.com/features/sloane-stephens
-coach-kamau-murray-youth-tennis-center-in-chicago/.

"Miss Gibson Keeps Wimbledon Title." *New York Times*, July 6, 1958.

Moscatello, Caitlin. "Cannes Shoe Controversy: Film Festival Requires Women to Wear Heels, Not Flats." *Glamour*, May 19, 2015.

Navratilova, Martina. "What Serena Got Wrong." *New York Times*, September 10, 2018.

Nguyen, Courtney. "Sloane Stephens Blasts Serena Williams." *Sports Illustrated*, May 4, 2013. https://www.si.com/tennis/beyond-baseline/2013/05/05/sloane-stephens-serena-williams-2.

Niebuhr, Keith. "Ashe's Wimbledon Win Is Tops in Black History." *St. Petersburg Times*, February 15, 2005.

Oddo, Chris. "Madison Keys Hires Jim Madrigal as New Coach." *Tennis Now*, December 2, 2018.

Ozanian, Mike. "Lew Sherr on the Economics of the U.S. Open and the USTA Billie Jean King National Tennis Center." *Forbes*, September 7, 2018.

Panja, Tarik, and Andrew Keh. "Umpire in Serena Williams Dispute Was a Stickler from the Start." *New York Times*, October 3, 2018.

Parascandola, Rocco. "NYPD Cop Accused of Using Excessive Force on James Blake Wants to Stand Trial After City Fails to Prove the Tennis Star Won't Sue." *New York Daily News*, April 20, 2017.

Poston, Ted. "The Story of Althea Gibson." *New York Post*, September 1, 1957.

Pucin, Diane. "Parents Say the Dumbest Things." *Los Angeles Times*, July 1, 1999.

Rhoden, William C. "The Father Really Did Know Best." *New York Times*, September 8, 2001.

———. "For Sisters, Ambivalence Overshadows Performance." *New York Times*, September 7, 2002.

Rineberg, Dave. *Venus and Serena: My Seven Years as Hitting Coach for the Williams Sisters*. Hollywood FL: Frederick Fell Publishers, 2003.

Rodney, Lester. "Gibson Leads Brough, Rain Stops Play." *Daily Worker*, August 10, 1950.

Roswell, Gene. "Althea Hasn't a Thing to Gain in Tennis Now." *New York Post*, September 8, 1958.

Rothenberg, Ben. "Flurry of Coaching Changes Adds to Upheaval in Women's Tennis." *New York Times*, December 11, 2018.

———. "Was That Serena Williams in the Hotel Room Next to Mine?" *New York Times*, September 2, 2018.

Rovell, Darren. "Are Venus and Serena Bad for Tennis?" *ESPN Sports Business*, February 3, 2003. https://www.espn.com/sportsbusiness/s/2003/0202 /1503084.html.

Rust, Edna, and Art Rust Jr. *Art Rust's Illustrated History of the Black Athlete*. New York: Doubleday, 1985.

Schoenfeld, Bruce. *The Match: Althea Gibson and Angela Buxton: How Two Outsiders—One Black, One Jewish—Forged a Friendship and Made Sports History*. New York: Amistad, 2004.

Scott, Bill. "Controversial French Federation President Bernard Giudicelli Quits ITF Board." *Grand Slam Tennis Online*, October 22, 2018. https:// grandslamtennis.online/news-in-brief/controversial-french-federation-president-bernard-giudicelli-quits-itf-board/.

Sharapova, Maria, and Rich Cohen. *Unstoppable: My Life So Far*. New York: Sarah Crichton Books, 2017.

Smith, Doug. "Color Blind: Fair or Not, Gael Monfils Plays for More Than Himself." *Tennis Week*, June 2006.

——. *Whirlwind: The Godfather of Black Tennis*. Washington DC: Blue Eagle Publishing, 2004.

Stevens, Matt. "Venus Williams Lawfully Entered Intersection Before Crash, Police Say." *New York Times*, July 7, 2017.

Strunsky, Steve. "Wimbledon Champion Gibson Remembered as Pioneer." Associated Press, October 2, 2003.

The Sunday Project. "Serena Williams Interview with Lisa Wilkinson." Aired September 23, 2018.

Tandon, Kamakshi. "U.S. Open Ratings Increase with Big Numbers During Chaotic Women's Final." Tennis Channel (website), September 11, 2018. http://www.tennis.com/pro-game/2018/09/ratings-increase-tv-numbers -us-open-final-djokovic-serena-osaka/76898/.

Tennis Australia. *2018 Australian Open Media Guide*. Melbourne, Australia, 2018.

"That Gibson Girl." *Time*, August 26, 1957.

Thomas, Robert McG, Jr. "Althea Gibson, the First Black Player to Win Wimbledon and U.S. Titles, Dies at 76." *New York Times*, September 29, 2003.

Tillet, Salamishah. "Serena Williams's Gift to Naomi Osaka, and Women, at the U.S. Open." *New York Times*, September 10, 2018.

Tupper, Fred. "Ashe Topples Connors for Crown at Wimbledon." *New York Times*, July 6, 1975.

——. "Miss Hard Routed: Althea Gibson Becomes First Negro to Take Wimbledon Tennis." *New York Times*, July 6, 1957.

United States Tennis Association. *2018 Media Guide and Record Book*. New York, 2018.

"USTA Agrees to Use More Women, Minorities as Chair Umpires." CBS Sportsline, September 14, 2006.

Vecsey, George. "Where Are Next Gibsons and Ashes?" *New York Times*, August 29, 1957.

"Venus: How Business Interests Have Helped My Tennis." WTA (website), November 29, 2018. https://www.wtatennis.com/news/venus-how-business -interests-have-helped-my-tennis.

"Venus Williams Signs $40 Million Reebok Deal." Associated Press, December 22, 2000.

Wade, Stephen, and Mari Yamaguchi. "Osaka Charms Japan with Her Manners, and Broken Japanese." Associated Press, September 10, 2018.

———. "Osaka's U.S. Open Win Re-opens Identity Discussion in Japan." Associated Press, September 13, 2018.

Wagner, Laura. "Black Chair Umpire Tony Nimmons Sues U.S. Tennis Association for Racial Discrimination." *Deadspin*, May 1, 2018. https://deadspin.com /black-chair-umpire-tony-nimmons-sues-u-s-tennis-associ-1825658979.

Waterman, Frederick. "Ashe to Enter Hall of Fame." UPI, July 13, 1985.

Waxman, Sharon. "Blood, Nurture and Victory: Suddenly Volley Girl Alexandra Stevenson Is Forced to Examine What She's Made Of." *Washington Post*, August 28, 1999.

Wertheim, Jon. "Alexandra Stevenson." *Beyond the Baseline with Jon Wertheim*, April 14, 2016. Podcast, 48:45.

Williams, Richard, and Bart Davis. *Black and White: The Way I See It*. Atria, New York, 2017.

Williams, Venus, Serena Williams, and Hilary Beard. *Venus and Serena: Serving from the Hip*. Boston: Houghton Mifflin, 2005.

"Williams' Parents Finish Divorce." Associated Press, October 30, 2002.

"Wimbledon Winner Proves Value of Tenacity." *New York Times*, July 7, 1957.

Women's Tennis Association. WTA *Media Guide*. Quebec, Canada, 2018.

Zimmerman, Jonathan. "Stop Defending Serena Williams: Claims of Sexist Double Standards Are No Excuse for Her Rude, Ugly American Behavior." *New York Daily News*, September 10, 2018.

PERSONAL INTERVIEWS

Adams, Katrina. May 31, 2006; August 29, September 1, 2018.

Agenor, Ronald. September 29, November 21, 2006.

Azarenka, Victoria. August 31, 2018.

Bajin, Sascha. September 5, 2018.

Bangoura, Sekou, Jr. August 27, 2017.

Blackman, Martin. August 27, 2018.

Blake, James. March 23, March 25, March 27, June 30, August 26, August 30, 2006; August 23, 2018.

Buxton, Angela. September 3, 2006.

Caldwell, Dale. November 2, 2018.

Collins, Bud. March 27, 2006.

Cornet, Alize. August 29, 2018.

Davenport, Lindsay. August 21, 2018.

Davis, Bob. November 3, 2018.

Djokovic, Novak. September 9, 2018.

Doller, Ben. September 1, 2018.

Drysdale, Cliff. September 27, 2006.

Federer, Roger. August 24, September 4, 2018.

Goulder, Eric. September 1, 2018.

Haas, Tommy. August 23, 2018.

Halep, Simona. August 24, August 27, 2018.

Higueras, Jose. August 27, 2018.

Hollins, Alvin. October 22, 2018.

Hollins, Cecil. August 8, August 9, 2006; October 25, 2018.

Ireland, Gary. October 5, 2018.

Isner, John. September 4, 2018.

Jenkins, Scoville D. August 30, August 31, 2006; October 21, 2018.

Keys, Madison. January 16, August 24; August 29, September 1, September 3, September 6, 2018.

King, Billie Jean. August 28, 2006.

Malmqvist, Ola. August 27, 2018.

Monfils, Gael. August 1, 2017.

Morton, Skylar. August 28, 2017.

Murray, Andy. August 24, 2018.

Murray, Kamau. November 28, December 1, 2018.

Nadal, Rafael. August 24, September 7, 2018.

Nimmons, Tony. October 5, 2018.

Osaka, Naomi. January 16, January 20, August 28, August 30, September 1, September 8, 2018.

Osuigwe, Desmond. August 18, 2018.

Osuigwe, Whitney. August 17, August 27, 2018.

Rinaldi, Kathy. August 27, 2018.

Ryland, Bob. January 17, 2006.

Sands, Kim. July 22, August 8, November 6, 2006.

Smith, Roger. November 6, 2006.

Stephens, Sloane. September 9, 2017; January 15, August 24, August 27, August 29, August 31, September 2, September 4, 2018.

Stosur, Samantha. August 17, 2018.

Terry, Roger. October 26, 2006.

Tiafoe, Frances. August 28, 2018.

Townsend, Taylor. January 15, 2018.

Tsonga, Jo-Wilfried. January 15, 2018.

Vickery, Sachia. August 17, August 21, 2018.

Wade, Virginia. August 24, 2018.

Washington, MaliVai. September 2, 2006; October 18, 2018.

Watson, Heather. January 16, August 22, August 27, 2018.

Williams, Serena. August 26, August 30, September 3, September 4, 2006; August 25, August 27, August 31, September 2, September 4, September 6, September 8, 2018.

Williams, Venus. June 25, June 28, June 29, July 1, 2006; January 15, August 27, August 31, 2018.

Young, Donald, Jr. March 22, August 28, 2006; January 16, 2018.

Young, Donald, Sr. January 16, 2018.

INDEX

Williams, Richard: accusations and racist remarks against, 6–7; on Irina Spirlea, 33; Sachia Vickery and, 96–97; as Serena and Venus's coach, 27, 29, 30–31, 160–61

Williams, Serena: activism by, 138; championship titles of, 1–2, 7, 15, 16, 43–44, 147, 185; coaching of, 27, 29, 30–31, 160–61; conflict of, with Carlos Ramos, 202–8, 211–14; cover features on, 4–5, 20; drug testing of, 10; endorsements of, 5; family of, 3, 10, 13, 20, 127, 197; fashion and, 6, 8, 20–23, 197; financial gains of, 5; health of, 14, 17, 18; honorary awards for, 214; influence of, on other black players, 2–4, 9–12, 25, 28–29, 43, 96–97, 159, 169; matches of, 1, 2, 3, 4, 7, 10, 12–14, 15, 24–27, 36–38, 40, 105, 125–26, 147, 201–9; philanthropic work of, 8; playing style of, 19–20; pregnancy and childbirth of, 3, 4, 14, 17–18, 122; racism and sexism against, 4, 6–7, 15, 213–14; rankings of, 3; Sloane Stephens and, 125–27; social media and bartering of, 102; Taylor Townsend on, 195; Tennys Sandgren and, 187; training of, 11–12, 31–32, 160–61; on Venus Williams, 24, 29–30

Williams, Venus: automobile accident and, 34–35; championship titles of, 1–2, 5, 6, 15, 43–44, 185; coaching of, 27, 29, 30–31, 160–61; endorsements of, 5; fashion and, 5, 6, 8, 23–24; financial gains of, 5, 19, 30; health of, 5–6, 18, 214; influence of, on other black players, 2–4, 9–12, 25, 28–29, 43, 96–97, 159, 169; on legacy, 28–29; matches of, 1, 2, 3, 6, 7, 12–14, 15, 18–19, 23–27, 32–33, 40–41, 105, 113, 121, 147, 214; on pay equity, 39–42, 138; philanthropic work of, 8, 175; playing style of, 32; racism against, 4, 6–7, 15, 32–33; Serena Williams's comments about, 24, 29–30; Taylor Townsend on, 195; training of, 11–12, 31–32, 160–61

Wills Moody, Helen, 46

Wilson, Russell, 170

Wimbledon, 2; (1956), 53; (1957), 10, 87; (1958), 10, 88; (1971), 71; (1975), 10, 64–65; (1990), 115; (1996), 73, 141, 173; (1999), 184, 185, 189; (2000), 147; (2002), 15, 16; (2004), 10; (2005), 39–41; (2008), 6; (2013), 125, 126; (2015), 16; (2017), 18–19; (2018), 3, 37, 181; invitation to black players at, 9; Last 8 Club, 192; prize money of, 39–42, 138

Witt, David, 29

Woman of the Year, 214

women's tennis: dominance of, 1, 8; dress codes in, 21–23; list of black players in, 9; pay equity and, 38–42, 138, 143, 210. See also men's tennis; sexism in tennis; tennis industry

Women's Tennis Association (WTA), 19; on dress code, 22;